Presidential Frontiers

PRESIDENTIAL FRONTIERS

Underexplored Issues in White House Politics

Edited by
Ryan J. Barilleaux

Praeger Series in Presidential Studies

PRAEGER

Westport, Connecticut
London

Library of Congress Cataloging-in-Publication Data

Presidential frontiers : underexplored issues in White House politics
/ edited by Ryan J. Barilleaux.
    p.   cm.—(Praeger series in presidential studies, ISSN
1062–0931)
   Includes bibliographical references and index.
   ISBN 0–275–96107–9 (alk. paper)
   1. Presidents—United States.   I. Barilleaux, Ryan J.
II. Series.
JK516.P68   1998
324.6'3'0973—dc21   97–43955

British Library Cataloguing in Publication Data is available.

Library of Congress Catalog Card Number: 97–43955
ISBN: 0–275–96107–9
ISSN: 1062–0931

First published in 1998

Praeger Publishers, 88 Post Road West, Westport, CT 06881
An imprint of Greenwood Publishing Group, Inc.

Printed in the United States of America

∞™

The paper used in this book complies with the
Permanent Paper Standard issued by the National
Information Standards Organization (Z39.48–1984).

10 9 8 7 6 5 4 3 2 1

Contents

Acknowledgments   ix
Introduction   xi

I. The First Frontier: The Nature of the Office

1. The Normative Study of the Presidency   3
   Scott E. Yenor, Travis S. Cook, and Raymond Tatalovich

2. The President as Representative   23
   Gary L. Gregg II

3. Washington and/or Versailles: The White House as a Court
   Society   37
   Daniel P. Franklin

4. Electing Presidents and Other Potentates   53
   Jody Baumgartner

II. New Insights on Power and Policy

5. The Overlooked Relevance of the Pardon Power   79
   Mark Morris

6. The Presidency and Social Policy   99
   Byron W. Daynes and Glen Sussman

7. The Other Side of War: Presidential Peace Powers   119
   Ryan J. Barilleaux and Christopher Kelley

8. The President and Federal Reserve Nominations   135
   Russell Lightfoot and Scott Huffmon

III. New Political and Cultural Frontiers

9. The Presidency as a Cultural Pulpit   151
   Kevan M. Yenerall

10. The Other Side of Power: Who Is Left Out of Presidential
    Rhetoric?   179
    Mary E. Stuckey and Richard Morris

11. First Partner: First Ladies and Their Roles   195
    Pamela J. Van Zwaluwenburg

Afterword   227

Index   231
About the Contributors   235

Acknowledgments

In more than one way, this volume marks the twentieth anniversary of my career as a professional student of political science. In the fall of 1976, I was an eager sophomore at the University of Southwestern Louisiana, a political science major on an academic scholarship who wanted to make a splash in the world but was unsure of how to proceed. That semester changed my life, for I came under the benevolent influence of Professor Herbert M. Levine.

I entered Herb Levine's course on International Politics without quite knowing what I was getting into. He was a legend on campus, although I did not yet know the legend. He was famous as a demanding teacher, a prolific author, and a man of sharp wit. He dreamed big dreams for his students and sent them off into the wide world. For a student body composed mostly of young people from Louisiana, he was a New Yorker who had (and frequently brought to campus) friends and acquaintances in Britain, New York, Washington, and who knew where else. He usually taught at 8:00 in the morning, so he could devote much of the rest of the day to writing. I often dragged myself out of bed early to visit him during his 7:00 A.M. office hours. His class involved *lots* of reading, a daily quiz on the reading, extensive note-taking, a "killer" research paper, and several exams. It was the hardest course I had in four years of college and the most rewarding.

Herb Levine possessed a quality that I think is essential to a great teacher: he inspired in me—and in a number of students over the years—the desire to please and impress him. In order to win his admiration, I reorganized my life around his class. I spent hours in the library researching my paper topic; I pulled the only all-night study sessions of my college career in preparation for his exams; I wrote and rewrote everything he would see; and I read every word he assigned or recommended. He taught me how to be a scholar, how to be a better writer, how to find an outlet for publishing my work. His highest praise was to describe something as of "professional quality." He encouraged me to do a number of things I had never considered before as within the grasp of a twenty-year-old Cajun kid—write for academic publication, work on Capitol Hill, apply for prestigious scholarships, reach for higher accomplishments. I responded eagerly, and whatever I have been able to accomplish in my academic career flows from those days spent in his classroom or in his office.

When Herb decided to retire a few years ago, I knew that he was not slowing down. He merely decided to shift gears. He had decided to become a writer full time, and I knew that he would be a successful one. He has done well since then, writing and editing many books and articles, sometimes even asking me to contribute a piece here or there to a project of his. But his real contribution to my life, and to the lives of many others I know, was in his daily work in his overcrowded faculty office and in the spartan classrooms of a midsized public university campus in south Louisiana. I dedicate this volume to Herb Levine with affection and admiration. I hope that he will think it worthy of his association with it.

A number of people deserve thanks for their role in helping to produce or support this work. Susan Kay, my department chair, has continually supported and encouraged the project from its inception, offering detailed assistance to some of its graduate student contributors and moral support as well. She also kept silent when work on this project took time away from my administrative duties as her assistant chairman. Robert Denton, editor of Praeger's Series on Presidential Studies, encouraged the project from the time that he first learned of it. The staff of Praeger Publishers has been most helpful. John Donohue of Rainsford Type saved the book from a plethora of errors and ambiguities. The contributors to this volume have put up with my deadlines, demands, and requests for revisions.

My family, especially my wife, Marilyn, has endured with good humor that "elaborate hobby" that I call my research. They also remind me that there is much more to life than political science.

As editor, I share with the contributors responsibility for everything in this book. I do not necessarily agree with everything that the authors have to say, but I think that in each case the contributors have produced a work of professional quality that deserves serious attention.

Introduction

The field of presidency studies is a fairly young subdivision of the discipline of political science. Of course, academic interest in the presidency is not new. Woodrow Wilson and William Howard Taft—both professors at one point in their respective careers—wrote and lectured on the office. James Bryce's magisterial *The American Commonwealth* also included his famous observations on the chief executive. Later in the twentieth century, Edward S. Corwin wrote an important treatise on the power of the president that served as a standard text for decades. Clinton Rossiter also produced an influential volume—so influential that most students of the office are unaware that it was Rossiter who first described in a systematic way the various roles or "hats" of the president: chief of state, chief executive, party leader, leader of public opinion, and so on.

Nevertheless, the field of presidency studies is a fairly young corner of the discipline. The book that many scholars regard as the beginning of the "modern" era of presidential scholarship—Richard Neustadt's *Presidential Power*—appeared in 1960. As late as 1979, Hugh Heclo reported to the Ford Foundation that most of the literature on the office was didactic in nature. The Presidency Research Group, an organized section of the American Political Science Association, was founded only in 1981.

The relative youth of presidency studies makes it possible for young scholars to meet those considered to be the "founders" of the field. Indeed, in 1996 a conference on the thirty-fifth anniversary of the publication of *Presidential Power* brought together many young scholars with Richard Neustadt and other senior luminaries in the area.

Despite this youth, presidency studies has become a well-established, active, and multifaceted part of the discipline. Papers, articles, and books on the presidency are fixtures of academic political science, and dissertations on the office are common.

As a result of this boom, one might think that nearly every topic related to the chief executive has been explored. Certainly, many subjects—including the organizational evolution of the presidency, presidential communications, and decision making—have received sustained and fruitful scholarly attention. Although clearly more work needs to be done, these aspects of the presidency are well-traveled roads.

There are, however, a number of underexplored issues in presidency studies. This book is an attempt to look at some of these topics and illuminate why they deserve more attention from scholars. In the best traditions of the field, it brings together established scholars and younger researchers to examine some of the frontiers of the field.

In the chapters that follow, these frontiers are divided into three broad categories. Part I focuses on "The First Frontier: The Nature of the Office." As readers will see, we are still hard at work trying to understand the nature of the presidency itself. In Chapter 1, Scott E. Yenor, Travis S. Cook, and Raymond Tatalovich survey the changing normative interpretations of the office that have influenced presidential scholarship in the twentieth century. Their chapter provides a useful guide to the shifting fashions in the field. In Chapter 2, Gary L. Gregg II draws attention to the role of the president as representative, a role that chief executives since Andrew Jackson have claimed but that has received little attention from scholars. Daniel P. Franklin provides another perspective on the office in Chapter 3, wherein he examines the White House as a royal court. Most scholars are familiar with George Reedy's observation that the life of the White House is that of a royal court, but Reedy never really examined other courts in order to explore the implications of his observation. Franklin compares the White House to court life at Louis XIV's Versailles, a court society *par excellence*. Finally, in Chapter 4, Jody Baumgartner examines the personalized nature of presidential selection—both in the United States and abroad—in order to help round out our understanding of the office. While the field of presidential studies contains a large body of electoral research, Baumgartner offers a fresh perspective: he links the increasing personalization of American presidential politics to larger trends, suggesting that the relationship between presidents and their parties is changing in more places than Washington.

Part II turns our attention to "New Insights on Power and Policy." In Chapter 5, Mark Morris demonstrates the overlooked relevance of the president's pardon power. Long overlooked by scholars, this power has gained special political importance in the age of independent counsels. Byron W. Daynes and Glen Sussman explore the presidency and social policy in Chapter 6, moving scholarship beyond the traditional areas of concern (economic policy, foreign policy, education, and civil rights policy). In Chapter 7, Ryan J. Barilleaux and Christopher Kelley examine the subject of presidential peace powers, a topic largely overlooked in the mainstream literature on the presidency and on foreign affairs.

Finally, in Chapter 8, Russell Lightfoot and Scott Huffmon bring to light the importance of presidential nominations beyond those to the Supreme Court and cabinet. Specifically, Lightfoot and Huffmon examine nominations to the Federal Reserve Board, an institution that has tremendous power over the lives and fortunes of Americans but that has been generally overlooked by students of presidential power.

In Part III, the contributors turn to "New Political and Cultural Frontiers." In Chapter 9, Kevan M. Yenerall looks at the intensive attention given to cultural issues in the Clinton presidency. His chapter breaks new ground by systematically studying the presidency as a "cultural pulpit" from which chief executives expound on issues such as school uniforms, the family, and social relations among Americans. In Chapter 10, Mary E. Stuckey and Richard Morris argue that we can understand presidential rhetoric and power differently if we apply insights drawn from new perspectives. Specifically, they call upon Native American sources to provide an alternative conception of leadership than is usually found in political science. Finally, in Chapter 11, Pamela J. Van Zwaluwenburg applies techniques of systematic data analysis to the First Ladies of the United States, attempting to move beyond anecdotal and biographical treatments. Her research looks for evidence of factors affecting how individual First Ladies fulfill the various roles inherent in the status of being the president's spouse.

Each chapter contains recommendations for future research in the areas examined by these scholars. In the Afterword, I try to sketch out a research agenda for pushing farther out into the frontiers of the presidency. I make no claim that this volume is exhaustive. It takes on some issues that need more attention; certainly, others remain to be explored. To those readers who wonder why one topic or another has not been included, I respond simply, "Thanks for pointing that out. Now get to work."

When I began my career as a professional student of the presidency in 1980, I was attracted not only by the subject itself but also by the fact that there was plenty of work to be done in the field. As those of us studying the presidency compared ourselves to aspiring scholars of voting behavior or British politics, for example, we saw that we were getting in on the ground floor. There were ample opportunities to carve out significant niches for ourselves in the scholarly community. Today, nearly two decades later, those opportunities still exist. As I hope this volume demonstrates, the frontier is not yet closed.

Part I

The First Frontier: The Nature of the Office

Chapter 1

The Normative Study of the Presidency

SCOTT E. YENOR, TRAVIS S. COOK, AND RAYMOND TATALOVICH

Shifts in the methods of political science have often affected research on the presidency differently than other fields. Progressive critics of American Constitutionalism, for example, were wont to claim that scientific students of politics must seek their subject in the "rough practice" of political life rather than in the descriptions offered by mere "literary theory" (Wilson 1885: 10). The "literary theory" of all governmental institutions—legislative, executive, and judicial alike—was reexamined in light of the greater Progressive realism. Later, behavioral critics of the institutional approach accepted the Progressive criticism of American Constitutionalism but did not think that their predecessors had been radical enough in seeking the "rough practice" of politics. Realism demanded application of the scientific method as developed in the "rising science of political psychology" to political life (Merriam and Barns 1924: 18; also see Ceaser 1990: 70–87 and Crick 1959: 95–117).

Behavioral research has made less progress in the study of the presidency, perhaps, than in other parts of the American political system. In the words of Edwards and Wayne, "research on the presidency . . . has often failed to meet the standards of contemporary political science, including the careful definition and measurement of concepts, the rigorous specification and testing of propositions, and the use of empirical theory to develop hypotheses and explain findings" (1997: 481). Behavioral political scientists have found the executive branch more difficult to penetrate because of the relatively small number of cases and the problem of securing reliable information about successive administrations. The paucity of significant, quantifiable phenomena could be taken as both a blessing and a curse to the study of the presidency. It has been a blessing insofar as scholars have been encouraged to raise important normative questions about the adequacy of presidential government and the sort of leadership req-

uisite to a modern democracy. It has been a curse, however, insofar as scholars
have approached their questions without appreciating the nature of American
Constitutionalism. Errors fall into two broad categories. Some presidential scholars underestimate the importance of the Constitution in shaping presidential action. Richard Neustadt (1960: 51), for example, claims that *"the probabilities
of power do not derive from the literary theory of the Constitution"*; yet, few
would deny that the Constitution establishes the broad contours of political conflict in the American polity. Others overestimate the importance of the Constitution when they impute to it a certain model of policy-making.[1] Generally
speaking, these scholars take what might be understood as temporary features
of American political life (for example, gridlock or congressional government)
to be part of the Founding Fathers' essential intention. This confusion could be
corrected by an appreciation for how the Constitution combines popular government with what James Madison calls the "valuable ingredients" of good
government (37: 227).[2]

In this chapter we will first try to show how the presidency contributes to
good government within the Constitution. The Constitution tries to secure capable leaders through the presidential selection process and encourages presidential initiative on policy matters. The precise form of the policy-making
process, however, is not determined by the Constitution; in fact, we will argue
that the Constitution can accommodate (and has accommodated) several forms
of policy-making. Second, we will examine how various schools of constitutional criticism reflect degrees of dissatisfaction with the constitutional order.
Initial dissatisfaction with the "imperiled presidency" of the separation of powers system led some to recommend wholesale constitutional changes. Later, others suggested that "heroic" presidential leadership could overcome the
structural impediments of constitutional government. Since scholarly opinion has
fluctuated between fears of a hopelessly weak "imperiled" president on the one
hand and an out-of-control "imperial" presidency on the other, a reassessment
of how political scientists approach the presidency may be in order. Finally, we
will suggest that an exploration of presidential frontiers within the Constitution
provides the best hope for future research into the presidency.

IN THE BEGINNING: THE INTENDED PRESIDENCY

Alexander Hamilton reports of the Constitution that "there [was] hardly any
part of the system which could have been attended with greater difficulty" than
the establishment of the executive department (67: 436). In *Federalist* 1 he
anticipates that "an enlightened zeal for the energy and efficiency of government
will be stigmatized as the offspring of a temper fond of despotic power and
hostile to the principles of liberty" (1: 5). Opponents of the Constitution feared
that a "vigorous executive" was incompatible with republican liberty. Edmund
Randolph, for example, thought that a strong executive would prove to be "the
foetus of monarchy" (Farrand 1937: I 66). The authors of *The Federalist Papers*

concede that the requisites of energy seem to be in tension with those of liberty. "The genius of republican liberty seems to demand on the one side, not only that all power should be derived from the people, but that those intrusted with it should be kept in dependence on the people, by a short duration of their appointments; and that even during this short period the trust should be placed not in a few, but in a number of hands." On the other side, energy in government "requires not only a certain duration of power, but the execution of it by a single hand" (37: 228).

Needed: Energy in the Executive

Hamilton states quite candidly that well-wishers of republican government had better hope that energy is not incompatible with republican liberty, for "energy in the executive is a leading characteristic of good government" (70: 454). The founding generation had only to reflect on the experience of the state and national governments under the Articles of Confederation to see the power of this claim. The states tried to secure liberty by distributing the legislative, executive, and judicial powers into separate departments, but state governments were by and large dominated by their legislatures. State magistrates were typically characterized "by short terms, strict limitations on eligibility, and election by the legislature" (Thatch 1969: 28). Many magistrates could not act without the advice of an executive council, which was also chosen by the legislature. As a result, the legislative branch exerted "an imperious control over the other departments" that threatened "the balance of the constitution" (71: 466). The national government under the Articles lacked an executive department altogether. Congress itself tried to administer its resolutions first through standing committees and later through departments established by statute (Thatch 1969: 68). As a result, the state and national legislatures were forced to waste time on the minutiae of administration instead of devoting time and energy deliberating public issues, and the laws lacked thorough and consistent administration.[3] Government under the Articles was, in the words of the *Federalist*, "destitute of energy" (15: 89).

According to James Madison, the "mutability," "multiplicity," and "injustice" of state laws represented as serious a problem as the want of consistent executive authority. The great number of laws passed and the rapidity with which they were "repealed or superseded" caused confusion and "instability" in the states (Meyers 1973: 88). John Marshall wrote that "in the state governments generally no principle had been introduced which could resist the wild projects of the moment" (cited in Thatch 1969: 51).[4] Most state executives lacked the independent will or power to stabilize the legislative process. According to the *Federalist*, however, stability is essential "to that repose and confidence in the minds of the people, which are among the chief blessings of civil society" (37: 227). In short, the Founders' difficulty lay "in combining the requisite stability and energy in government, with the inviolable attention due to liberty and to the republican Form'' (37: 226–28).

The states had tried to secure republican liberty through a strict understanding of the separation of powers doctrine. Madison offers an alternative interpretation, which, interestingly enough, is superior on republican grounds. Precisely because the legislature is naturally dominant under a republican constitution, it is the most likely department to extend "the sphere of its activity . . . drawing all power into its impetuous vortex" (48: 322). Madison argues that if liberty is to be preserved, the departments must be sufficiently "connected and blended" as to give to each a security against the encroachment of the others. The Founders intended to provide "constitutional means and personal motives" for each department to resist the others (51: 337). Besides the familiar system of balances and checks, the Constitution provides the occupants of the departments with the necessary personal motives for protecting their powers. "Ambition must be made to counteract ambition," writes Madison. "The interest of the man must be connected with the constitutional rights of the place" (51: 336). As president, an individual's prestige is intimately connected with the powers of the presidency.

While the separation of powers clearly aims at securing liberty, it also serves energy and stability by establishing a truly independent executive. The president is chosen by the people and their electors rather than by the Congress. The Founders thought that if the president were appointed by the legislature, he would become little more than a servant to its will (Farrand 1937: I 68). Separation of powers requires that each branch develop a will of its own. The independence of the executive enables each branch to perform particular functions well. By focusing the Congress's attention on legislative matters, the separation permits careful deliberation on matters of public policy. By freeing the executive from Congress, separation promotes steady administration of the laws. While the balance of power within Congress can influence a president, the Constitution gives him an independent responsibility for the execution of the law.

Executive power under the Constitution is vested in a single person rather than in several. This is essential if the office is to be energetic—that is, characterized by the appropriate "decision, activity, secrecy and despatch" (70: 455). A unified executive is also safer to liberty because it provides "a single object for the jealousy and watchfulness of the people" (70: 460). An executive council or advisory cabinet along the British model of executive was rejected for the same reason (Farrand 1937: II 542; Thatch 1969: 125). Splitting the executive would diminish both energy and accountability.

The Presidency and the Public Interest

Duration in office is also essential to energy and stability in government. The Constitution encourages duration in the administration of government through its longish and renewable presidential term. The Founders proposed a term long enough "to give to the officer himself the inclination and the resolution to act his part well, and to the community time and leisure to observe the tendency of his measures" (72: 469). If the community is pleased with a president's policies, it can "continue him in his station." The president would be able to "act his own opinion with vigor and safety," confident that he had the time "to make the community sensible of the propriety of the measures he might incline to pursue" (71: 467). A continuous administration also provides stability to policy. According to the *Federalist*, republican rulers should be guided by the "deliberate sense of the community" rather than "every sudden breeze of passion" that blows through the community (71: 464). A long tenure encourages the president to consider the likely long-term effects of legislation. The "impressions of the moment may sometimes hurry [the legislature] into measures which itself, on maturer reflection, would condemn" (73: 477). Armed with the veto, the president will "furnish an additional security against the enaction of improper laws" by forcing the legislature to reconsider its measures (73: 477). Finally, duration contributes to stability by diminishing the likelihood of policy reversal. New presidents are likely to assume that the dismissal of their predecessor "proceeded from a dislike to his measures" and will want to mark the office as their own by new measures (72: 469).

While the limited veto can clearly check hasty congressional action, the Founders seemed to expect more from the presidency than a stabilizing role in legislation. The president also has considerable energy to pursue "his measures." As the nation's chief administrator, the president commands considerable expertise and information because the principal officers of the various executive departments report directly to him (Article II, section 2). The president is well poised to bring new measures to the attention of Congress, and the Constitution invites the president to play a positive role in legislation: "He shall from time to time give to Congress information of the state of the Union, and recommend to their consideration such measures as he shall judge necessary" (Article II, section 3; cf. Corwin 1948: 321). While some presidents of the nineteenth century preferred that Congress shape policy for the nation, others took an active hand in crafting new measures (see, e.g., McDonald 1994: 209–74; White 1948). It may not be too strong to say that the energetic character of the presidency made the "modern" model of presidential policy-making a possibility from the beginning (Nichols 1994). At the very least, however, the Constitution permits both ends of the separated system to initiate policy. As James Ceaser remarks, "in the modern policy arena, we have not only ambition counteracting and thwarting ambition but ambition prodding ambition" (1990: 200).

According to James Madison, "the aim of every political constitution is or ought to be, first to obtain for rulers men who possess most wisdom to discern, and most virtue to pursue, the common good of society; and in the next place, to take the most effectual precautions for keeping them virtuous whilst they continue to hold their public trust" (51: 370). The Founders thought that the system of election they established for the president would almost certainly produce excellent leaders. In order to be elected, the president would have to be a character of national reputation, "preeminent for ability and virtue" (68: 444). Moreover, the Founders expected the "highest office" to attract individuals ambitious for power and preeminence. While the ambitious individual would entertain the hopes of meriting a long duration as president, the most noble characters would strive for an enduring reputation. Hamilton writes that the love of fame would "prompt a man to plan and undertake extensive and arduous enterprises for the public benefit" (72: 470). Since the president is dependent on the people for continuation in office, the Constitution ameliorates the threat executive energy poses to liberty; a further precaution is provided by the threat of impeachment. The presidency is thus a clear example of the concern the Founders had for finding rulers with good character and the care they took to obtain them.

THE IMPERILED PRESIDENCY: WILSON'S CRITIQUE

Soon after the Civil War, political observers such as Woodrow Wilson, James Bryce, and Walter Bagehot voiced dissatisfaction with the American separation of powers system. Since Wilson is considered the most influential American critic of the separation of powers, we rely primarily on his works to develop their shared objections.[5] In his early work *Congressional Government*, Wilson claims that "the Constitution in operation is manifestly a very different thing from the Constitution of the books" (1885: 9–10). The establishment of extra-constitutional institutions—political parties and the congressional committee system—transformed the Constitution; only research into the "Constitution in operation" would yield an accurate portrait of the American system of governance. Wilson also maintained that the seeds of the expanded constitutional system were sown in the Constitution itself. In asserting that the contingent features of the "Constitution in operation" are the inevitable outcome of the Constitution as such, Wilson effaces the distinction between the "Constitution in operation" and the Constitution as such on which he appears to found his political science. Either way, Wilson's approach amounts to an attack on the Constitutionalism of the Federalists.

As the title of his 1897 essay suggests, Wilson believes that the Constitution leads to "Leaderless Government." Under the Constitution "there is no one supreme, ultimate hand—whether magistrate or representative body—which can decide at once and with exclusive authority what shall be done at those times when some decision there must be, and that immediately." The lack of authoritative leadership, though most acute in times of crisis, "is of course felt at all times" (1885: 283). By separating the executive from the legislative authority, the Constitution deprives the legislature "of the opportunity and means for making its authority complete and convenient" (1885: 312). The separation of powers is, on this account, merely a means to avoid the dangers of majority tyranny. Although Wilson may recognize the possible dangers of the concentration of power (1885: 92), he maintains that power in a separated system becomes too fragmented and irresponsible for effective policy-making. As Bryce says of the American Constitution, "power is so much subdivided that it is hard at a given moment to concentrate it for prompt and effective action" (1995: 268).

Wilson takes the declining prestige of the presidential office only as a symptom of greater disease in the American system. He acknowledges that past presidents have greatly affected the substance of public policy. Changes in the original constitutional system of checks and balances, however, made statesmanlike policy leadership within the separation of powers impossible. The presidential office "has fallen from its first estate of dignity because its power has waned; and its powers have waned because the power of Congress has become predominant" (1885: 43). In Wilson's estimation, the separation of powers contributed to the erosion of executive power rather than to its security. Congress "has virtually taken into its own hands all the substantial powers of government" through efficient internal organization and vigorous use of oversight powers (1885: 45).[6] The problems associated with the accumulation of power in Congress would be relieved if the exercise of that power were made "complete and convenient."

According to Wilson, the rise of committee government paralyzed national government during much of the late nineteenth century.[7] Under the committee system, the functions of Congress were divided and "parceled out" to forty-seven independent committees (1885: 67). This dispersion of power and responsibility resulted in "slipshod, haphazard, unskilled and hasty legislation" (1889: 163). Moreover, "the absence of any concert of action amongst the Committees leaves legislation with scarcely any trace of determinate party course" (1885: 325). Whereas the clumsy approach to legislation may have sufficed in simpler times, Wilson asserts that the "tasks set the government now differ both in magnitude and in kind from those set it in days gone by" (1897: 353). In Wilson's view, the industrial revolution, the "new sectionalism," and a more assertive American foreign policy demanded more positive efforts than the Constitution would permit.

Yet Wilson did not consider legislative paralysis of committee government under the separation of powers its greatest failure. Even worse was the inability of Congress to perform its "informing function." He writes that "legislation which is not thoroughly discussed by the legislating body is practically done in a corner" (1885: 303, 78). Wilson endorses a domestic version of "open covenants, openly arrived at" not only to prevent the nefarious influence of special interests, but also to promote the education and elevation of public opinion: "The chief, and unquestionably the most essential, object of all discussion of public business is the enlightenment of public opinion" (1885: 83). Under the committee system, public policy issues are divided into small pieces and then analyzed minutely in closed-door committee meetings. The insignificant subject matter of most committee hearings fails to engage the attention of most people. Such hearings:

have about them none of the searching, critical, illuminating character of the high order
of parliamentary debate, in which men are pitted against each other as equals, and urged
to sharp contest and masterful strife by the inspiration of political principle and personal
ambition, through the rivalry of parties and the competition of policies. . . . They could
scarcely either inform or elevate public opinion, even if they were to obtain its heed.
(1885: 84–85)

According to Wilson, such elevation of public opinion requires statesmanship,
but committee government does little to cultivate statesmen.

The American system appears to be inconsistent with the demands of good
government. "As at present constituted," Wilson writes, "the federal government lacks strength because its powers are divided, lacks promptness because
its authorities are multiplied, lacks wieldiness because its processes are round-
about, lacks efficiency because its responsibility is indistinct and its action without competent direction" (1885: 318). Since the Founders thought the executive
would be characterized by strength, promptness, energy, and efficiency, Wilson's indictment of the federal government is first and foremost an indictment
of the intended presidency.

On the basis of his evaluation of the "Constitution in operation" Wilson
recommends wholesale constitutional changes. He contends that "simple
method, single, unstinted power, and clear responsibility" can be accomplished
only by replacing the separation of powers with what Jeffrey Tulis aptly calls
"institutionally structured cooperation" (Tulius 1987: 123; Wilson 1885: 333).
The separation of powers inhibits such cooperation because the president does
not and cannot depend on a majority in Congress for support. Under such an
arrangement, the United States cannot enjoy "real party government such as we
desire, and such as it is unquestionably desirable to set up in every system like
ours." Such government "can exist only when the absolute control of administration, the appointment of its officers as well as the direction of its means and
policy, is given immediately into the hands of that branch of the government
whose power is paramount, the representative body" (1885: 267–68; also 118).
Unlike the Founders, who sought to resist legislative excesses through the creation and fortification of an independent executive, Wilson and his late nineteenth-century colleagues believed that legislative power cannot and should not
be resisted. Instead, they proposed making legislative control over the executive
complete in the name of greater simplicity, energy, and accountability.

According to Wilson, "*power and strict accountability for its use* are the
essential constituents of good government" (1885: 284; emphasis added). Party
or cabinet government, he suggests, best secures these goods. First, it concen-
trates all policy-making authority in one institution of the political system. Energy in the executive is thought to be enhanced under this arrangement because
the party in power has "complete and convenient" control of the formulation,
passage, and administration of public policy. Second, cabinet government is
thought to promote accountability because the executive cabinet is chosen by

the democratically selected legislature and is held continuously responsible to the parliament for conduct in office.[8] Moreover, since the executive can count on partisan support for policy proposals, there is a clear sense that the governing party alone is accountable for any consequences (1885: 98). The concern for stability under constitutional government must, in this view, give way to rapidly adaptable policy programs for a rapidly changing world.

More importantly, the concentration of power and accountability will "foster practical, energetic, and trustworthy statesmanship" (1885: 284). Power and accountability will attract great men to the debate of political principles and the public good. The Founders constructed offices in order to attract individuals of ability and virtue to government, but they seemed to expect that society itself would produce such individuals (35: 213–16; 80: 516). Wilson, on the other hand, thought parliamentary parties were necessary for the training of statesmen. Not only would the "high order of parliamentary debate" educate public opinion, but also it would guarantee the regular production of great individuals for office.

SEARCHING FOR SUPERMAN: THE HEROIC PRESIDENCY PARADIGM

Like the late nineteenth-century critics of the Constitution, adherents to the heroic presidency believed that the executive office under the separation of powers was in itself inadequate for the demands of good government. According to these scholars, adherence to the separation of powers leads to "dull government" (Laski 1940: 270) or "the deadlock of democracy" (Burns 1963: 20–22; also Commager 1943: 7). Like the advocates of cabinet government, these later students of the presidency thought the separation of powers system often led to "incoherency and irresponsibility" (Laski 1940: 116). Unlike the previous school of thought, however, these scholars, to differing degrees, believed that the president can be, in the words of Clinton Rossiter, "a kind of magnificent lion who can roam widely and do great deeds so long as he does not try to break loose from his broad reservation" (1960: 73). The heroic presidency sought statesmanship from the president rather than from a parliamentary leader. In its *ideal* form, advocates of the heroic presidency saw a way to overcome the reputed defects of the separation of powers. This ideal, however, may be corrupted in two directions: an incumbent who ignores democratic norms will be thought *imperial*, while a weak administration under the heroic model will be called *impotent*.

The Idealized Presidency

The roots of this view are found in Woodrow Wilson's reassessment of presidential leadership in *Constitutional Government of the United States* (1908). Wilson was reconciled to the possibilities of the executive office by the experience of powerful incumbents such as Grover Cleveland and Theodore Roosevelt.[9] The larger intellectual community did not embrace this understanding until they witnessed Franklin D. Roosevelt's performance as president. Roosevelt's policy-making success convinced many that the president possesses "an authority over public opinion sufficient to make his purposes compete successfully with all other elements in the national life" (Laski 1940: 269). Such leadership is especially successful during crises. In times of crisis, "public opinion compels the abrogation of the separation of powers" in favor of executive-directed, positive government (Laski 1940: 154–55; also Rossiter 1948: 289). As "America has now entered the epoch where the requirements of the positive state can no longer be denied," there will be a perpetual need for crisis leadership from the president (Laski 1940: 241).[10] Harold Laski sums up the policy and institutional objectives of the advocates of the idealized presidency: "America needs strong government; it needs strong leadership to attain strong government; only the president, granted its characteristics, can provide it with the leadership it requires" (1940: 271–72).

Generally, these scholars recommend that presidents accumulate as much personal power as possible to compensate for the lack of institutional power. In the formulation of Neustadt, the most prominent advocate of the heroic presidency, following the Constitution makes the president merely a "clerk"; a president must transcend the office to become a "leader" (1960: 3–9). Presidents must transcend the constitutional office to pursue the kind of personal power necessary for leadership. Advocates of the idealized presidency generally agree on the means by which a president obtains power. Disagreement centers around the utility of what might be called the subsidiary tools of personal power.

Public support. A president should attempt to rally public opinion behind himself and his policy agenda. Neustadt provides the classic statement of the experienced politician gaining popular support: "Any President who valued personal power would start his term with vivid demonstrations of tenacity and skill in every sphere. . . . This is no more than Franklin Roosevelt did in his first term. It is the ideal formula for others" (1960: 54). Personal power can best be secured through divining and articulating the "Voice of the People" (Rossiter 1960: 32–34). A president must be both "of" the people and "above" the people. Laski captures the ambivalent nature of popular leadership: "He must have 'common opinion.' But it is equally imperative that he be an 'uncommon man.' The public must see themselves in him, but they must, at the same time, be confident that he is something bigger than themselves" (1940: 38). The scholarly advocates of the idealized presidency, then, hope that the Constitution permits the elevating debate centered on "the rhetorical presidency," which an earlier generation of scholars thought to be the exclusive domain of parliamentary government (Tulis 1987).

The power to persuade. A president armed with popular support should actively bargain and persuade Congress to adopt the president's agenda. Neustadt has been especially influential in propagating what Thomas Cronin (1980) has called the "textbook presidency." Presidential power is for Neustadt the power to persuade, and persuasion can best be accomplished through effective bargaining. The president must become, as Rossiter suggests, the "Chief Legislator": "His tasks as leader of Congress are difficult and delicate, yet he must bend to them steadily or be judged a failure" (1960: 30). Louis Koenig summarizes the hopes of the heroic presidency scholars: "By adroit and moving appeal, he aims to stir the masses into a state of such general and intense approval that the opposition will crumble and his measures will prevail" (1964: 202).

Neustadt seems to believe that a president can exert influence on decision makers absent the party loyalty that often facilitates the interactive process. A president following Neustadt's advice will rely on the heroic leadership of persuasion and reputation (Sperlich 1975). Other adherents of this school of thought embrace party as a necessary supplement to heroic presidential leadership. Advocates of strong presidential leadership of parties try to meld what they see as the virtues of parliamentary government (responsible parties) with the potential virtues of the separation of powers system (checks and balances). Presidential leadership, however, must place parties on what Laski calls a "rational basis." "For where the choice between policies that has to be made is real, effective party discipline will follow . . . ; and a president who is anxious to lead his party will then find that he has a party anxious to follow his lead" (1940: 271–72).[11] James MacGregor Burns (1963) carried Laski's hopes into the modern era of political science. Burns believed that the stalemated politics of America's deadlocked democracy could be overcome by a combination of presidential leadership and responsible party behavior. This transformation, which Burns saw afoot in the 1964 Johnson landslide, would make the presidency into "the crucible of leadership" (1965: 315).

Executive vigor. After success in Congress, a president should vigorously administer policies. There are generally two approaches to successful heroic administration. On the one hand, Neustadt argues that a president should concentrate as much responsibility for policy implementation as possible into his person. Neustadt's model was Franklin Roosevelt: "Competitive personalities mixed with competing jurisdictions was Roosevelt's formula for putting pressure on himself, for making his subordinates push up to him the choices they could not make for themselves" (1960: 132; also Burns 1965: 314–15). The cabinet, according to Neustadt, is a possible source of presidential headache. Cabinet members must serve many masters besides the president, and "the men who have to serve so many masters cannot help but be somewhat the 'enemy' of any one of them" (1960: 34). Other scholarly advocates of the heroic presidency favored an elevation of the cabinet as a format for collective decision making and responsible administration. They feared that the concentration of personal power for all facets of policy-making would overburden the chief executive. Herman Finer argued that "the gravest problem of America's government is . . . that no one man alone can handle the job with efficiency and democratic responsibility'' (1960: 21, viii; also Laski 1940: 90 and Rossiter 1960: 246). Finer recommends an amendment to the Constitution which would make ''a President and (say) eleven Vice-Presidents, elected on the same ticket for four years'' responsible for the discharge of executive duties (1960: viii). Not all of these scholars recommend Finer's changes to the Constitution, but many endorse Dwight Eisenhower's use of the cabinet for the delegation of duties, tasks, and initiatives (Laski 1940: 84–89; and Rossiter 1960: 243–46).

The vital center, but not Caesar. Just as the Founders intended, the idealized president is a vital center of energy. The executive will be involved in formulating, passing, and administering laws. Unlike the Founders, however, these scholars seem to concentrate governmental accountability and energy only in the executive. This ''heroic'' understanding of policy-making under the Constitution appears to assume that Congress cannot produce creative and intelligent legislation in the absence of presidential leadership or even despite presidential resistance. It turns the policy-making flexibility of the Constitution into a one-size-fits-all system for producing progressive change. Furthermore, unlike the Founders, advocates of the idealized presidency regard Congress as the primary agent of stability and the president as the embodiment of the country's demands for change.

The accumulation of personal power in the presidency did not worry these scholarly advocates overmuch.[12] Neustadt, for instance, writes that ''if one wants effective policy in the American system, danger does not lie in our dependence on a man; it lies in our capacity to make ourselves depend upon a man who is inexpert'' (1960: 181). We must not fear the accumulation of presidential power because the checks and balance system will continue to prevent the abuse of power. The checks and balances provided by Congress and the judiciary will not rein in a truly ambitious president:

In the end . . . the checks that hold the President in line are internal rather than external. His conscience and training, his sense of history and desire to be judged well by it, his awareness of the need to pace himself lest he collapse under the burden—all join to halt him far short of the kind of deed that destroys a President's ''fame and power.'' . . . If he knows anything of history or politics or administration, he knows that he can do great things only within ''the common range of expectation,'' that is to say, in ways that honor or at least do not outrage the accepted dictates of constitutionalism, democracy, personal liberty, and Christian morality. (Rossiter 1960: 70)

''If angels were to govern men,'' Madison wrote in *Federalist* 51, ''neither external nor internal controls on government would be necessary.'' The institutional arrangements of checks and balances were designed as ''auxiliary precautions'' to supply for ''the defect of better motives'' (51: 337). Advocates of the heroic presidency, in contrast, appear to presume that there is no need to supply for the ''defect of better motives'' because angels will be elected to govern men.

The Imperial Presidency

Scholars and advocates grasped the naivete of their earlier hopes after the devilish Johnson and Nixon administrations. Many disillusioned commentators on the presidency, such as Edwin C. Hargrove, James David Barber, George Reedy and Louis Koenig, wanted to preserve the increased power of the heroic presidency in the name of progressive change. They began to fear, however, that "something inherent in the office and its powers leads" to the abuse of power by the occupant (Hargrove 1974: 3; also Reedy 1970: 14; Schlesinger 1973: viii). Unlike Woodrow Wilson, who feared that the Constitution produced "leaderless government," wary advocates of the heroic presidency feared the concentration of personal power in what came to be called the "imperial presidency." Unwilling to sacrifice the heroic leadership provided by the president, which they regarded as the linchpin of progressive change, these scholars emphasized the need to find the right kind of man or personality type for the presidential office.

The importance of presidential personality presumes the withering of the checks and balances which were once thought to be the defining characteristic of the Constitution. President Johnson's press secretary George Reedy asserts that "in the White House, character and personality are extremely important because there are *no other limitations* which govern a man's conduct." Instead of Madison's notion that ambition counters ambition, Reedy suggests that "restraint must come from within the presidential soul and prudence from within the presidential mind" (1970: 20, emphasis added). Others may not go as far as Reedy in this respect,[13] but these revisionist scholars generally tend to emphasize the paramountcy of psychological characteristics rather than the constitutional office or a president's political horizons.[14] James David Barber argues that an understanding of "character makes possible a realistic estimate of what will endure into a man's White House years" (1972: 145–46).

The "democratic personality" presumed by the earlier advocates of the heroic presidency could no longer be taken for granted. These revisionist scholars attempt to outline sufficiently ambitious yet healthy psychological profiles to assist the population in choosing the correct presidential personality. Barber (1972) hoped that the "active-positive" president would combine the "active" energy necessary for the exigencies of modern government with the "positive" respect for democratic politics. Johnson and Nixon were "active" according to Barber, but their "negative" impulses eroded respect for the "accepted dictates" of American Constitutionalism which Rossiter had hoped would rein in the ambitious.[15] Similarly, Hargrove believed that presidents "must be democratic personalities, with a feel for politics and a high degree of self-respect" (1974: 307).[16] Louis Koenig added a section on presidential personality to the third edition of his *The Chief Executive* in which he also distinguishes "high-democracy" presidents like Franklin Roosevelt from "low-democracy" presidents like Nixon (1975: 336ff.). The qualities sought by Barber, Hargrove, and

Koenig do not derive from a reexamination of the nature of American Constitutionalism. Such a reexamination would lead them ultimately to recommend solutions to the problem of character in light of the enduring principles of the separation of powers system, with particular emphasis on laws affecting the selection process and the conduct of the presidential office. Instead, they devise personality profiles wherein presidential ambition is somehow checked internally by a regulating respect for democracy.

Both aspects of desirable presidential character are revealing. Presidents must be "active" or possess a "feel for politics" because governmental energy is concentrated in the executive. "Positive" or "democratic personalities" are attached somehow to the wishes of the populace. Presidents are for the most part held accountable by this unexplained inner attachment to the public's opinions. Congress and the courts are valued as institutions of restraint after the failure of this unexplained attachment. As Arthur Schlesinger writes, "when Presidents begin to succumb to delusions of grandeur, when the checks and balances inside themselves stop operating, external checks and balances may well become necessary" (1973: 409). Revisionist scholars who emphasize character as a solution to the imperial presidency endorse the goals of personalized power put forth by an earlier generation. Sobered by what they regarded as the abuse of personal power, however, they hope to reconcile the strong executive with democracy. They hoped Rossiter's heroic "magnificent lion" would arrive on the scene tamed.

The Impotent Presidency

The perceived failure of the Ford and Carter administrations showed that reports of an imperial presidency were greatly exaggerated. Major works during these years bemoaned "the tethered presidency" and the "illusion of presidential government."[17] Crabb and Mulcahy argue that Carter "came to exemplify the 'impotent presidency'—a chief executive who apparently lacked the power or the will (or both) to respond to events decisively" (1993: 276). Carter's impotence was found wanting in light of Franklin Roosevelt's idealized presidency. These scholars and advocates did not call into question the underlying assumptions of the heroic presidency—namely, that the concentration of personal power in the president was the model for producing political change. Instead, they held Carter's "passionless presidency" in contempt. His character, it would seem, was sufficiently "positive" but not sufficiently "active."

THE INFLATED PRESIDENCY: A PARADIGM RECONSIDERED

Gradually, political scientists have come to question the underlying tenet of the heroic presidency. Much recent empirical work has examined "the president's ability to influence Congress or the public" (Edwards and Wayne 1997: 482). The ability of the president to persuade the legislature appears to work only, in Edwards' (1989) phrase, "at the margins" (also Bond and Fleisher 1990). Stephen Skowronek (1993) also finds that modern presidents are increasingly encumbered by legislative and administrative machinery. Earlier "presidency-centered" explanations of policy-making underestimated the effects of the legislature's independence from the executive and have thus generated expectations that the office cannot satisfy (Lowi 1985: 151). David Mayhew (1991) and Charles O. Jones (1994) show that the separated system nevertheless continues to produce legislation. The separation of powers system constructs obstacles to presidential leadership, yet meets the exigencies of government through a flexible and competitive policy-making structure. This recent research shows, to use Wilson's formulation, that the "rough practice" of political life can be understood in light of the "literary theory" of the Constitution. Attempts to understand the "rough practice" without moorings in the Constitution's "literary theory," however, have led to "inflated" and false expectations from the presidential office.

There appear to be limits to what contemporary political science can accomplish in the study of the presidency on its own terms. Normative questions will probably continue to constitute a considerable part of the literature on the presidency. It is important, therefore, that political scientists appreciate the Founders' various reasons for separating the executive from the legislature. As long as political scientists see the separation of powers system merely as a means of thwarting policy despotism, the theoretical framework of their scientific inquiry will distort their findings. The separated constitutional structures hope to promote "energy" in the executive for the purposes of securing regular administration of the laws and circumspect presidential leadership. They seek to promote "stability" by providing the necessary conditions for deliberating on public policy matters. The separation of powers equips each branch to perform its appropriate functions effectively. Developments in the American polity may have changed how energetic, stable governance is secured by the separated system. Much recent political science literature points to the fertility of the marriage between normative and empirical work, but also suggests that a proper appreciation for the constitutional basis of the normative issues is the *sine qua non* of inquiry into the presidency.

NOTES

1. Ceaser (1990: 193, 195) contends that the Constitution was not "intended to define fully the exact character of the policy-making process or to establish any one particular form of it." But critics of the Constitution nevertheless "attribute to the Founders and the Constitution a specific model of the policy-making process, which has usually been the model in existence at the time. Dissatisfied with the status quo, they have held the Founders responsible for it."

2. References to *The Federalist* begin with the number of the paper and end with page reference to the Earle (1937) edition.

3. See Thatch (1969: 63–73); McDonald (1994: 125–53).

4. There has been some debate on the historical accuracy of this view, but most scholars accept the Federalist view of the so-called Critical Period; see McLaughlin (1905), Thatch (1969: 25–54), and McDonald (1994: 125–53); cf. Jensen (1950).

5. See Tulis (1987) and Ceaser (1979) for accounts of Wilson's paramount importance as a critic of American Constitutionalism. The kinship between Wilson, Bryce, and Bagehot has not been adequately established in current scholarship. Let it suffice to say that both Wilson (1885: 9–10, 243, 309–10) and Bryce (1995: 83, 254) claim to be indebted to Bagehot (1966) for many of their insights. Moreover, Wilson wrote a very sympathetic review of Bryce's classic *The American Commonwealth* (1889).

6. Historians of the post–Civil War era generally share Wilson's description of Congress usurping power from a defenseless executive through exacting congressional control over what is properly considered executive business. Leonard D. White, for example, writes that "Congress reached into the executive branch and dealt with the individual case" (1958: 78; see also White 1958: 20–44). Historians have not agreed with Wilson's contention that executive weakness is endemic to the institutional arrangements established by the Constitution. Instead of forwarding purely institutional explanations for the supine executive, with the benefit of hindsight historians generally contend that the legislative forays into administrative business were part of the evolution of regularized official procedures. In other words, unlike Wilson, historians see no permanent barriers to the economical efficient administration of the law (Skowronek 1982: 35; White 1958: 92).

7. White (1958: 45, 48–67) generally agrees with Wilson's assessment of the decline of congressional competence due to the dispersion of leadership, although White points out that such centrifugal pressures are not a necessary feature of the Constitution.

8. Accountabilty under the cabinet government does not mean that majority control for a cabinet can be chosen by a legislative party that does not enjoy majority support. Margaret Thatcher, for instance, received 42 percent of the vote in the British parliamentary elections of 1983, but her Conservative Party possessed 61 percent of the seats in the House of Commons.

9. For useful discussions of the changes in Wilson's on the adequacy of the presidential office, see Wann (1958) and Burns (1965: 90–97).

10. Many proponents of the idealized presidency thus advocate the routinization of Franklin Roosevelt's achievement. Louis Koenig, for example, believes that "the United States's world responsibilities and domestic urgencies require a Presidency that is continuously strong" (1964: 15; see also Burns 1965: 351; Neustadt 1960: 54–55; and (Rossiter 1960: 238).

11. The Committee on Political Parties of the American Political Science Association also hoped that party government could be engrafted onto the Constitution. "The President in office at any given time can probably be more influential than any other single individual in attaining a better organized majority party, and thus also prompting the minority party to follow suit" (1950: 89).

12. Advocates of the idealized presidency often expressed reservations about potential abuses of power. Clinton Rossiter writes that the strengthened presidential office means that a "President is in a position to do serious damage, if not irreparable injury, to the ideals and methods of American democracy" (1960: 47, also 257). On the other hand, these scholars state that such concerns are on the whole quite far-fetched. Again, Rossiter, argues that "whatever grotesque shapes the Presidency may have assumed in Latin Amer-

ica, it has not been a matrix for dictatorship here in the United States; and I hardly think it an act of bravery, even an act of faith, to predict that it will not become one for a very long time, if ever'' (1960: 46).

13. James David Barber echoes Reedy's sentiments: "If you can't really control the President effectively by law, if you can't really control him effectively during his term of office by a skeptical attitude of public opinion, then basically what you're left with is the thought that you'd better control him at the time you're picking him'' (quoted in Tulis 1981: 285).

14. Before the escalation of the Vietnam War, Louis Koenig (1964) expressed no interest in presidential character. Similarly, Edwin C. Hargrove (1966) presents a happy picture of personality profiles producing skilled presidential leadership for the future. After the war escalated and the Nixon administration further undermined public confidence in the office, both Koenig (1975) and Hargrove (1974) placed emphasis on reconciling skillful and ambitious leadership with democratic principles. Hargrove explicitly acknowledges his previous errors: "This earlier formulation reflected the liberal optimism of the time that power would be used for the right purpose'' (1974: 34).

15. Barber's distinction between "active-positive" and "active-negative" presidents closely resembles Harold Lasswell's (1948) distinction between "democratic character" and the "political man." See Hargrove (1974) Mansfield (1989: 11–12), and Tulis (1981: 284), for Barber's debt to Lasswell.

16. Hargrove (1973; 1974: 50–51) more or less endorses Barber's psychological categories, although he disputes the application of Barber's scheme in a number of instances.

17. See Franck (1981) and Heclo and Salamon (1981).

REFERENCES

APSA. 1950. *Toward a More Responsible Two-Party System.* Washington, DC: American Political Science Association.

Bagehot, Walter. 1966. *The English Constitution.* Ithaca, NY: Cornell University Press.

Barber, James David. 1972. *The Presidential Character.* Englewood Cliffs, NJ: Prentice-Hall.

Bond, Jon R. and Richard Fleisher. 1990. *The President in the Legislative Arena.* Chicago: University of Chicago Press.

Bryce, James. 1995. *The American Commonwealth.* Indianapolis, IN: Liberty Fund.

Burns, James MacGregor. 1963. *The Deadlock of Democracy: Four Party Politics in America.* Englewood Cliffs, NJ: Prentice-Hall.

———. 1965. *Presidential Government.* Boston: Houghton Mifflin.

Ceaser, James. 1979. *Presidential Selection: Theory and Development.* Princeton: Princeton University Press.

———. 1990. *Liberal Democracy and Political Science.* Baltimore, MD: Johns Hopkins University Press.

Commager, Henry Steele. 1943. *Majority Rule and Minority Rights.* London: Oxford University Press.

Corwin, Edwin S. 1948. *The President: Office and Powers*, 3rd ed. New York: New York University Press.

Crabb, Cecil V. and Kevin V. Mulcahy. 1993. "The Elitist Presidency: George Bush and the Management of Operation Desert Storm." In *The Presidency Reconsidered*, ed. Richard W. Waterman. Itasca, IL: Peacock Publishers.

Cronin, Thomas E. 1980. *The State of the Presidency*, 2nd ed. Boston: Little, Brown.

Crick, Bernard. 1959. *The American Science of Politics: Its Origins and Conditions.* London: Routledge & Kegan Paul.

Earle, Edward Meade, ed. 1937. *The Federalist Papers*. New York: Modern Library.

Edwards, George C. 1989. *At the Margins: Presidential Leadership of Congress*. New Haven: Yale University Press.

Edwards, George C. and Stephen J. Wayne. 1997. *Presidential Leadership: Politics and Policy Making*, 4th ed. New York: St. Martin's Press.

Farrand, Max. 1937. *The Record of the Federal Convention of 1787*. 3 vols. New Haven: Yale University Press.

Finer, Herman. 1960. *The Presidency: Crisis and Regeneration*. Chicago: University of Chicago Press.

Franck, Thomas M., ed. 1981. *The Tethered Presidency*. New York: New York University Press.

Hargrove, Erwin C. 1966. *Presidential Leadership: Personality and Political Style*. New York: Macmillan.

————. 1973. "Presidential Personality and Revisionist Views of the Presidency." *American Journal of Political Science* 17: 819–35.

————. 1974. *The Power of the Modern Presidency*. Philadelphia: Temple University Press.

Heclo, Hugh and Lester M. Salamon, eds. 1981. *The Illusion of Presidential Government*. Boulder, CO: Westview Press.

Jensen, Merrill. 1950. *The New Nation: A History of the United States during the Confederation*. New York: Alfred A. Knopf.

Jones, Charles O. 1994. *The Presidency in a Separated System*. Washington, DC: Brookings Institution.

Koenig, Louis W. 1964. *The Chief Executive*. New York: Harcourt, Brace & World.

————. 1975. *The Chief Executive*, 3rd ed. New York: Harcourt, Brace & World.

Laski, Harold J. 1940. *The American Presidency*. New York: Grosset & Dunlap.

Lasswell, Harold. 1948. *Power and Personality*. New York: Viking Press.

Loni, Theodore. 1985. *The Personal President*. Ithaca, NY: Cornell University Press.

Mansfield, Harvey C. 1989. *Taming the Prince: The Ambivalence of Modern Executive Power*. Baltimore, MD: Johns Hopkins University Press.

Mayhew, David R. 1991. *Divided We Govern*. New Haven: Yale University Press.

McDonald, Forrest. 1994. *The American Presidency: An Intellectual History*. Lawrence: Kansas University Press.

McLaughlin, Andrew Cunningham. 1905. *The Confederation and the Constitution, 1783–1789*. New York: Harper & Brothers.

Merriam, Charles E. and Harry Elmer Barns, eds. 1924. *A History of Political Theories of Recent Times*. New York: Russell & Russell.

Meyers, Marvin, ed. 1973. *The Mind of the Founder: Sources of the Political Thought of James Madison*. Indianapolis, IN: Bobbs-Merrill.

Neustadt, Richard. 1960. *Presidential Power*. New York: New American Library.

Nichols, David K. 1994. *The Myth of the Modern Presidency*. University Park: Pennsylvania State University Press.

Reedy, George E. 1970. *The Twilight of the Presidency*. New York: World Publishing Co.

Rossiter, Clinton L. 1948. *Constitutional Dictatorship: Crisis Government in the Modern Democracies*. Princeton: Princeton University Press.

———. 1960 [1956]. *The American Presidency*. New York: Harcourt, Brace & World.

Schlesinger, Arthur M. 1973. *The Imperial Presidency*. Boston: Houghton Mifflin.

Skowronek, Stephen. 1982. *Building a New American State: The Expansion of National Administrative Capacities, 1877–1920*. Cambridge: Cambridge University Press.

———. 1993. *The Politics Presidents Make*. Cambridge, MA: Belknap Press of Harvard University Press.

Sperlich, Peter W. 1975. ''Bargaining and Overload: An Essay on Presidential Power.'' In *Perspectives on the Presidency*, ed. Aaron Wildavsky. Boston: Little, Brown.

Thatch, Charles C. 1969. *The Creation of the Presidency 1775–1789*. Princeton: Princeton University Press.

Tulis, Jeffrey K. 1981. ''On Presidential Character.'' In *The Presidency in the Constitutional Order*, ed. Joseph M. Bessette and Jeffrey Tulis. Baton Rouge: Lousianna State University Press.

———. 1987. *The Rhetorical Presidency*. Princeton: Princeton University Press.

Wann, A. J. 1958. ''The Development of Woodrow Wilson's Theory of the Presidency: Continuity and Change.'' In *The Philosophy and Policies of Woodrow Wilson*, ed. Earl Latham. Chicago: University of Chicago Press.

White, Leonard D. 1948. *The Federalists: A Study of Administrative History*. New York: Macmillan.

———. 1958. *The Republican Era: 1969–1901*. New York: Macmillan.

Wilson, Woodrow. 1885 (1994). *Congressional Government*. Boston: Houghton Mifflin.

———. 1889. ''Bryce's *American Commonwealth*.'' In *College and State*, 2 vols., ed. Ray Stannard Baker and William E. Dodd. New York: Harper & Brothers (1925).

———. 1897. ''Leaderless Government.'' in *College and State*. New York: Harper & Brothers.

———. 1908. *Constitutional Government in the United States*. New York: Columbia University Press.

Chapter 2

The President as Representative

GARY L. GREGG II

The presidency has come to occupy center ground in the American political system. Over the last century we have invested a considerable amount of power and prestige in the office in the hopes of placing it where it could do the most good. Students of the institution have also informed us that we can and should equate the health of the office with the general health of the nation. As the presidency goes, so goes the United States, or, as Richard Neustadt has put it, "what is good for the country is good for the president and vice versa" (Neustadt 1990: 156). Presidents themselves have also not been shy about encouraging us to see the office as one providing "moral leadership" for the nation, as well as being the primary judge of the national interest. Though some observers have counseled us to beware of investing too much in "Caesar" and becoming too reliant on executive benevolence, the general trend over the last century has been in the opposite direction—toward a more empowered executive at the center of a more powerful federal government.

At the same time, the United States has widely been considered the world's model democracy. We are part of a government "of the people, by the people, and for the people," according to our political heritage. Our fundamental law sounds the same theme in its opening line that begins "We the people" and continues with a list of the goals of that compacting people. The modern presidency, with its central position within the expanded American government, begs a number of important questions for our democratic political tradition.

THE PRESIDENCY AND THE DEMOCRATIC TRADITION

Fundamentally, we might ask if the two strains of a strong presidency and democratic self-rule can be reconciled. If so, on what basis? Can a democracy long exist when the people have invested in one man, or in one office, the expectations and centrality of position like that now occupied by America's chief executive? A degree of tension may exist in our political culture. We tend to value, revere, and respect a powerful presidency as we equally value our democratic traditions and our cultural dedication to freedom and self-governance. It has not always been assumed that these two elements are consistent.

As a nation and a people, we historically have stabilized and maintained this tension between executive power and democratic legitimacy through the system of institutional representation established by the Constitution of 1787. For the founding generation direct democracy was never an option for national governance. Most saw representation as necessary both for logistical purposes to govern a scattered and growing nation and to encourage the development of proper laws. Even the anti-Federalists argued for an improved system of representation and not for any type of direct democracy or popular participation in actual governance.

But what of the American presidency? Can a single executive elected over a diverse and extended nation be a representative? It seems clear that our answer to this question must be that in some fashion such an office must offer representation. Otherwise we will be forced to admit that we have elevated an office to the heart of our political life as a nation that is alien to our roots in self-governance and liberal democracy. We are loath to make such a conclusion.

A more scholarly answer to the question necessitates a serious exploration of the very concept of representation and of representative government itself. It would involve consideration of the idea of representation in political theory and in the American public philosophy, the various ideas of the possibility of executive representation and the forms it might take, as well as the intended and actual place of the presidency in the American regime and the operation of the office itself.[1] Presidential scholars have vastly underexplored this element of the American presidency.

Presidential Views

Presidents themselves have been among the most fervent supporters of the idea that the president occupies a role as a representative in American democracy. That presidents should make such an assertion should not be surprising. Especially since the start of the democratization of American politics that has continued by fits and starts since the early days of the Republic, presidents have understandably wanted to be considered "representatives of the American people." With democratization comes the legitimation of political institutions based on their perceived popular character. If presidents were not to assert their role as representatives, they would run the risk of holding an office of questioned legitimacy. In an era when "democracy has become so much the primary recognized ground of political legitimacy, the occupant of an institution that was not considered to somehow wield governmental power in a "democratic" or representative'' way would occupy a considerably weakened office with a narrowed scope of legitimate behavior.

In his famous ''Farewell Address,'' President Washington recognized the Constitution as having divided political power into different depositories, including the presidency, and thereby made *''each* the Guardian of the Public Weal''* (Allen 1988: 521). And at least since Thomas Jefferson presidents have claimed to represent a distinctly national constituency or national interest—usually in contradistinction to members of the legislature whose representative positions, in Jefferson's words, do not ''command a view of the whole ground,'' and who might, ''condemn what they would not if seen in all its parts'' (Peterson 1977: 294).

The idea of the president as the direct representative of the American people, however, is most closely associated with the presidency of Andrew Jackson. In 1828 Jackson became the first president since George Washington to be chosen without the involvement of Congress either through nomination of the candidate or through outright election in the House of Representatives, as was the case with Jefferson in 1801 and with John Quincy Adams after the electoral deadlock of 1824. For this reason it has been said that Jackson may have been the first popularly elected president in U.S. history (Binkley 1962: 83). As president, Jackson convulsed the congressional whigs by asserting that ''The President is the direct representative of the American people,'' and he is ''elected by the people and responsible to them'' (*Register of Debates in Congress*, 1st Session of 23rd Congress, 1833–1834: 1334).

The presidency of Andrew Jackson marked a significant revolution in the American system of free government. Following Jackson's presidency and his espousal of his doctrine concerning the direct link between the people and their president, subsequent presidents continued to adhere to Jackson's view of the office (see Binkley 1962: 105–32). In his fourth Annual Message, James K. Polk, for example, wrote of the president representing ''in the executive department the whole people of the United States, as each member of the legislative department represents portions of them'' (Richardson 1903: 665).

Theodore Roosevelt also advocated a representational function for the presidency. In his autobiography, Roosevelt asserted that ''the executive is or ought to be peculiarly representative of the people as a whole.'' He went on, ''As often as not the action of the executive offers the only means by which the people can get the legislation they demand and ought to have'' (306). Roosevelt's ''stewardship theory'' of executive power was also based on an understanding of the president as the embodiment of all the people. He wrote, ''My view was that every executive officer, and above all every executive officer in high position, was a steward of the people bound actively and affirmatively to do all he could for the people, and not to content himself with the negative merit of keeping his talents undamaged in a napkin'' (quoted in Herschfield 1973: 82). Woodrow Wilson put it this way, ''No one else represents the people as a whole, exercising a national choice . . . the nation as a whole has chosen him, and is conscious that it has no other political spokesman. His is the national voice in affairs" (Link 1974: 113–14). In a campaign speech in 1960, then senator John F. Kennedy claimed "only the president represents the national interest. And upon him alone converges all the needs and aspirations of all parts of the country, all departments of government, all nations of the world" (Cronin 1980: 75).

The Views of Others

Moving beyond individual presidents, Barbara Hinckley has recently shown how presidential rhetoric has become institutionalized around certain elements of symbolic politics. Among her findings is that each modern president tends to emphasize in his public speeches the president's centrality in the political process and life of the nation. Presidents tend to identify themselves with the American people and with the nation—to use "we" to create a "symbolic equivalence" among the three. The president thereby not only represents the nation and the people, but also *becomes* them. Presidents also rhetorically paint a picture of government that ignores or diminishes the other branches of government as almost "nonactors." Such institutionalized rhetorical symbolism by presidents shows clearly the place they feel they occupy as *the* representatives of the people (Hinckley 1990: 38–64).

Presidents and presidential candidates have not been the only public officials to assert the representational role of the presidency. The Supreme Court, the so-called final arbiter of the Constitution, has also asserted this position of the executive. For example, in *U.S. v. Curtiss-Wright Export Corporation*, the Court declared that at least in regard to the international arena, "with its important, complicated, delicate and manifold problems, the president alone has the power to speak as a representative of the nation" (81L.Ed., 299, 1936). Twentieth-century presidents have ridden such assumptions to levels of presidential power in foreign affairs unparalleled in American history.

THE STATE OF SCHOLARSHIP

Despite these public assertions and their consequences for the American political system, the scholarly community has virtually ignored this important concern. In the literature that does mention a representational conception of the office, the tendency has been simply to assert the role. Such declarations usually come with little or no supporting evidence and generally take the form of self-evident and undisputed dogma.

Writing of the limitations that he found placed on the presidency toward the close of the last century, James Bryce nonetheless added that "his office retains a measure of solid independence in the fact that the nation regards him as a direct representative and embodiment of its majesty" (Bryce 1891: 278). Clinton Rossiter recognized the president as "the leading formulator and expounder of public opinion in the United States'' (Rossiter 1960: 29) and ''the American people's one authentic trumpet,'' possessing ''no higher duty than to give a clear and certain sound'' (Rossiter 1960: 31). Similarly, Edward S. Corwin called the presidency the ''sole representative of the nation as a whole,'' and said that it is ''the natural and responsible, because the sole, representative of that citizenship'' which is, ''independent in its affiliation of either labor or capital'' (Corwin 1957: xi–xiii). Here we see numerous assertions of a representative role of the president as a representative, but no serious engagement of the question.

Not only is the literature on the presidency lacking in a serious and prolonged scholarly discussion, but the important literature coming at the question from the other end—from the political theory concern for the idea of representation—is similarly disappointing. For example, two of perhaps the most widely cited pieces on the theory of political representation produced in this century dealt with the idea of presidential representation only to the extent of noting that it might be an issue (Fairlie 1940; Pitkin 1967). On that score, the extent of John Fairlie's discussion of presidential representation amounts to one line noting that some find the presidency to be a more representative institution than Congress (Fairlie 1940: 238). This does not satisfy the important need for scholarship on this basic question that cuts to the very core of modern American democracy.

When asserting the representative nature of the office of chief executive, most recent scholars have done so by contrasting its characteristics with those they find in Congress. This comparison has almost universally taken the form of a contrast between the so-called parochialism that characterizes legislative representation and the more unified and national focus of presidential representation. Grant McConnell has written that ''the president represents the nation as a whole, while the Congress represents it as a collection of states and congressional districts (McConnell 1976: 42). Where Richard Rose has found the job of a member of Congress to be ''to represent his or her district in Washington,'' he adds that ''the job of the President is to represent the whole of the nation in an uncertain and sometimes hostile world'' (Rose 1991: 5). Similarly, Ruth Morgan writes that ''the President, as well as Congress represents the nation. . . . Each has its own constituency—the President a national one and Congress a state and local one'' (Morgan 1970: 84). Such assertions are fairly common in the literature on the presidency and Congress, which makes the lack of rigorous study of the issue of presidential representation all the more curious (see also Curtis 1981; Moe 1991).

We might also mention the considerable literature that seems to make certain presumptions about the role of the president as a representative in the American regime. For instance, the presidocentric conceptions of the system that puts the office of the presidency at the center of the governmental process contain an implicit assumption about presidential representation. To wit, those like Richard Neustadt who have come to interpret the health of the regime in terms of the president getting his way with Congress and the bureaucracy assume a view of representation, though implicit, that holds the president to be the proper representative of the nation as a whole (Neustadt 1990). In this view, congressional representation is assumed to be inadequately energetic, overly parochial, or democratically less legitimate than the representation of one man elected by the country as a whole.

The opposite, yet still largely implicit, assumption is found in the work of those who have resisted what some have referred to as the "hero worship" of the presidency and maintained a congressionally centered view of the proper operation of the political system. Underlying such a view is the assumption that political representation is properly exercised through an assembly containing numerous locally elected men and women. This also seems to be the assumption of most scholars who have taken political representation under consideration as they have routinely applied the concept to elected legislators while virtually ignoring elected executives.

Though most literature that touches on the role of the president as representative would fall into the above categories, a few scholars have at least attempted to deal with the issue in a more explicit, though still incomplete, manner. In 1951 Alfred DeGrazia published *Public and Republic*, his classic tour of representative government in America. Here he traces the idea of executive representation to what he calls "enlightened individualism" and finds that the roots of the modern executive office stem from Puritan leaders in New England. DeGrazia's study (1951), however, is limited to a brief but useful historical narrative. Willmoore Kendall discovered the existence of two majorities in American politics—one majority represented by Congress and the other by the presidency—and warned against the modern tendency to view the presidency as representing a higher majority will, a will more worthy of finding its expression in government (Kendall 1985).

Facing a general dilemma similar to that which concerned Kendall, David Vogler and Sidney Waldman have also examined the perceived differences in congressional and presidential representation (Vogler and Waldman 1985). Particularly concerned with the intersection between the two primary institutions of representation in the American political system, they found the existing literature to be incomplete for it was almost all based on an "adversarial" approach to democracy where "presidents are said to win approval of economic programs or defense systems by assembling majority coalitions of diverse interests" (Vogler and Waldman 1985: 39). They propose the need to understand the interactions between Congress and the presidency through an alternative "unitary" model of democracy that puts a greater emphasis on consensus building through genuine deliberations animated by an understanding of the common good. Vogler and Waldman raise important questions related to issues of presidential representation, however, and it was not their intention to deal with many of the central concerns that arise when conceiving of the chief executive in the role of representative.

One of the few scholars who has explicitly attempted a serious analysis of the specific role of the president as representative has been Kathy B. Smith (1981). Smith's article does not provide a complete exploration of executive representation, but it does focus on one important aspect of the issue. Her main concern is to explore the various ways in which presidents have conceived of their office as being a place of representation. What place did the presidents see their office occupying, and how did these executives view their representational role as being independent "trustees" or as dependent "delegates" meant to follow the will of an electorate? This is the guiding question of Smith's study. Although each of these studies adds to our understanding of the place of the presidency as an institution of representation in the American republic, they do not stand either on their own or collectively as a complete treatment of the topic at hand. The scholarly community still needs to do more work to fill this important void.[2]

UNDERSTANDING THE PRESIDENT AS REPRESENTATIVE

The American system of government is a representative democracy, and as such questions of representation must always be of utmost concern for political scientists dealing with the institutional and procedural elements of that system of government. The remaining pages of this chapter present a brief outline of what the concept of executive representation would provide the scholarly community in terms of organizing the existing literature as well as general questions for future scholarship generated by such a concern.

The Interrelatedness of Normative and Empirical Questions

For decades a considerable tension has existed between political scientists whose concern has been mainly normative and those more interested in empirical questions about the actual operation of politics. Indeed, this tension has often bordered on outright intolerance and dismissal of members of the rival camp of contemporary social scientists. One important advantage of using the concept of representation as a guidepost for discussing and exploring issues of presidential power is that it uniquely demands the attention of both camps. Political representation at its core is a normative question: How ought people to be represented in government? Normative judgments so rendered demand that empirical methods be brought to bear to measure the degree to which actual political institutions are living up to the standards set for properly representative agents. Taking the president to be a representative, then, provides us a framework within which both major elements of political science can be accommodated and can communicate with each other.

Symbolic and Active Politics

An agenda for scholarship on the presidency that is built around the concept of representative government affords us an almost unique opportunity to unite two other parts of the literature that are central to the presidency and yet often do not consult one another. Here we mean the traditional dichotomy between symbolic and active politics, both of which are uniquely part of the executive office in the United States. Both have also been long considered the two basic types of representation in politics—active in the sense of someone "acting for" another and symbolic as a person or other entity would "stand for" another.

No other public official in America is considered to be a symbol of the nation or an embodiment of its core values. The president occupies the role of chief of state and acts as figurehead for the nation, no less than he is the active executive and leader of the government. As Rossiter remarked, "The President . . . is the one-man distillation of the American people just as surely as the Queen is of the British people," or, in President Taft's words, the president is "the personal embodiment and representative of their dignity and majesty" (Rossiter 1960: 16).

Barbara Hinckley, for one, has noted the need to unite the literature on symbolic politics with that of the presidency since the former is also important to the office (Hinckley 1990). Although most of the concern with symbolic politics in relation to the office of the presidency has centered on presidential rhetoric, chief executives also carry out symbolic politics in a myriad of other ways that should be of concern to scholars. Because the officeholder has become the central cast member in our drama of democratic politics, scholars should shine a more clear and discerning light on presidential activities, personalities, and elements of the office that might be found to hold greater meaning than has heretofore been realized. Similarly, the scholarly community should be more aware of the importance of symbols to achieving, maintaining, and exercising power. As many historians and political scientists have demonstrated, the fact that the Constitution or statutes may delineate specific powers within institutions does not necessarily translate into political reality. Presidential scholars should strive to understand how symbols have been and are important to the office and to the place of the office within the regime.

Of course, presidents are more than symbols. As the bulk of the literature on the presidency tells us, the president is also an executive, an agenda setter for the political system, and a constitutional officer. That is to say, the president also provides active representation in the American political system as well as symbolic representation. Although the traditional literature on political representation has tended to separate symbolic and active representation, no such distinction can properly be made with regard to the presidency. Whereas in a parliamentary system such as that found in Great Britain, the roles of symbolic and active representation are divided between the monarch or other officer and the parliament and its leadership, the American Founders established an office that united both. In such a situation, we cannot come to an adequate understanding of the office without considering both symbolic and active representation as well as the intersection between the two.

More Specific Areas for Scholarly Attention

Besides the overarching normative and empirical questions dealing with symbolic and active presidential representation, concern for representation also raises a number of more specific areas for scholarly attention. Any such research agenda must surely deal with the relationship between those represented and the representative. When considering representation, scholars are also concerned with personal aspects of the individuals holding office and how the office itself impacts the representative in that office. Numerous scholars have demonstrated the institutionalization of the office, and any such changes in the institution would surely impact on the potential of representation. Presidential scholars considering the presidency as a place of representation will also be drawn to consider the president's relationship to the federal bureaucracy and the rest of the government. Each more specific level of scholarly concern is now addressed.

The president and the public. In any consideration of political representation, a concern with the relationship between the represented and their representative must be of prime importance, and the study of the presidency is no different. What serves as the primary representational "link" between the people and the president? Traditionally, elections have served this purpose, and so campaigns and elections will be of interest to scholars concerned with presidential representation. Have other elements arisen in history to augment the electoral link? Presidential rhetoric has certainly emerged as an important and central connection between the people and their representative in the Oval Office, and it too will be an important area for scholarly exploration.

What about the widely discussed but still not well understood concept of a president getting a "mandate" from the people? Does such a thing really exist? If so, how does its existence affect the representative responsibilities of members of the legislature? Is it possible that more than one mandate could exist at a given time—one held by the president and the other by members of the legislature? Is divided government just such a phenomenon? What is the nature of the presidential constituency? How have presidents responded to those constituencies in the past, and how has each president's constituency differed from that of his fellow presidents in the past?

Are there institutions or actors that function as "filters" in this relationship between the president and the public? The mass media, especially television, certainly provides the American people's primary method of gaining knowledge of, and hearing from, the president. The media also has an undoubted influence on the president's agenda and decisions, and so these relationships need to be explored as they influence the representational relationship between officeholder and public. Political parties and interest groups would also be important to study for similar reasons. A concern with representation finds the recent explosion of public opinion polling to hold great import for the representative nature of the office. To what extent do the institutionalization and proliferation of public opinion polling affect the public itself, and to what extent, and to what effect, do polls influence the way incumbent presidents carry out their duties?

In this same vein, we should not ignore the symbolic dimensions of the office and its place within the mind of the people as well as the individual occupant's actions, character, and style and how they may affect the representational relationship. As a representative of the public, the presidency's relationship with that public should be of utmost concern, and these are but a sampling of important avenues for the concern of presidential scholars.

The idiosyncratic presidency. Scholarship on executive politics that centers on the president as an individual human actor and the human factors of the office is also of concern to students of the representative presidency. What type of representative do the people wish to have occupy the office, and which have been the most effective in the past?

What type of personality would best fit the needs of a representative executive within the constitutional order? How much room do presidents have to make their own decisions within the institutional and political context of the office? What particular talents or skills might be necessary to represent the people from the Oval Office that might be similar or different from those that are useful in representing from a legislative body? Scholars enjoy playing the game of ranking presidents; accordingly, the concept of a representative executive could provide us with a more coherent and useful "representational" or "democratic" yardstick with which to measure our presidents.

How have presidents viewed their office, and how should they act in it? Have they regularly responded to "mandates" from the public? Have they refused to do the popular thing in an effort to do what they felt was in the best interest of the country? These questions go to the heart of the major normative concern of representation that has preoccupied political theorists at least since Edmund Burke so eloquently declared his independence from his constituency's will in 1777. With the proliferation of public opinion polling and its use within the White House, one would think there is much to understand about contemporary executive politics by posing these questions about our presidents.

Institutional organization and operations. Scholarship guided by a concern for representation will also be concerned with how the institution of the presidency has become institutionalized and how presidents have variously organized their administrations. If the presidency is an institution of representation, then the broader institutional dynamics of the office that both encourage and restrain presidential activity as well as the discretionary organizational environment of a given president should be of interest. Decision making in the White House should also be considered in light of the needs and values of representation as it so directly determines the nature of the representative relationship.

Scholars may also want to explore the representational dynamics of the presidential bureaucracy itself. Presidential candidate Bill Clinton's promise during the 1992 campaign to have "a cabinet that looks more like America," and the lengths to which his White House went to hire minorities and women to staff the executive bureaucracy beg important questions about what qualities presidents should look for in staffers and their impact on the representation the office offers. Behind Clinton's promise is a particular understanding of representation—that representatives should in some way "mirror" those they represent and that a white male president can best represent through a hiring process that is centered around diversity. A number of questions may be raised here, including what such an assumption would mean for the ideal of merit-based hiring and even the civil service system itself.

The president and the bureaucracy. As a result of the huge expansion in the size and scope of the federal government over the past century, students of democratic politics must devote continuing attention to the federal bureaucracy. Is the power of unelected, and in some cases nearly life-tenured, bureaucrats a problem for free government in the United States?

Scholars have shown how Congress as an institution as well as individual members of the legislative branch have come to serve as important links between the people and executive agencies (see Fiorina 1989). Congress, particularly in its capacity to investigate and control the allocation of funds, serves as a democratically elected check on the bureaucracy. Individual members of Congress in their role as ombudsmen for their constituencies also influence the bureaucracy as they intervene with their decisions and processes to benefit those they represent. Though themselves not elected, we might also see the media as serving an intermediate function between the public and the bureaucracy as they report, influence the national agenda, and investigate bureaucratic indiscretions and malfeasance. The president appoints and staffs the top positions of the agencies, the president is held responsible for the acts of his subordinates in a manner unmatched by Congress, and it is only through presidential elections that the public can have a wholesale effect on incumbent bureaucrats. For these reasons, studies of the bureaucracy and its relation to the presidency have important implications for understanding the president as a representative.

The president and the regime. Finally, and in some ways perhaps most important of all, considering the president to be a representative requires that scholars seriously consider the broader political and constitutional environment within which presidents operate. Studies on the presidency have historically been plagued by treatments of the office colored by institutional partisanship which have encouraged us to look at the American polity from the perspective of the presidency (see Andrews 1975).

Approaching the presidency as a representative institution forces us to consider the other institutions of the federal government where political representation takes place. Here we have Congress foremost in mind as the traditional representative body. Such a perspective might encourage us to view the office and the Republic from a regime level where the president is but one of a number of essential players.[3]

Under the regime level can be organized the many studies that have been produced dealing with the relationship between the presidency and Congress.

As the two most popularly elected organs of the national government and the ones through which the people's views are most directly represented, the inter-relation of the two is of utmost importance to the student of representative government. Studies concerning presidential leadership and power, the presidency in the public policy process, and the foreign policy presidency all are important at this level. So is a concern with the president's relationship with the federal courts, both in the appointment process and in the courtroom itself.

CONCLUSION

Presidents have long considered themselves to be the representatives of the American people. Political scientists, historians and other public thinkers, and even the Supreme Court have made similar assumptions about the office and its occupants. Although any regularly occurring thoughts about the office should occasion scholarly concern, conceiving of the president as a representative cuts so close to the heart of America's tradition of representative democracy as to demand special scholarly and public attention. And yet, puzzling as it is, the topic has gotten very little serious attention from students of the office.

Conceiving of the president as a representative in the American political system inevitably invites us to raise anew the central questions that have arisen about executive power throughout the history of free government in Europe and America. How much power should we invest in our chief executive? How is that one man to be held properly accountable for his actions? What is the proper relationship between the single executive and those other representatives assembled in the legislature? What should be the relationship between the people's will and the president's actions? What does the way we choose our executive say about the possibilities of the president being properly representative?

At the end of the twentieth century with the responsibilities of the federal government no longer growing, with the end of the Cold War, and with a variety of commentators urging us to make fundamental changes in our democratic processes, this is the proper time for scholars to rethink the presidency by thinking about its role as a representative in the political system. Such a concern is not only good for the field of presidential studies but will be a service to representative democracy as well.

NOTES

1. I have elsewhere attempted a preliminary exploration of these important questions dealing with the president as representative. See *The Presidential Republic: Executive Representation and Deliberative Democracy* (Lanham, MD: Rowman & Littlefield, 1997) on which part of the present chapter has been based.

2. I particularly exclude from this analysis my own study *The Presidential Republic*. It will be for others to determine the importance of that work.

3. For a fine example of a study that takes a systematic perspective on the office, see

Jeffrey K. Tulis, *The Rhetorical Presidency* (Princeton: Princeton University Press, 1987).

REFERENCES

Allen, William B., ed. 1988. *George Washington: A Collection*. Indianapolis, IN: Liberty Fund.

Andrews, William G. 1975. "The Presidency, Congress, and Constitutional Theory." In *Perspectives on the Presidency*, ed. Aaron Wildavsky. Boston: Little, Brown, pp. 24–45.

Binkley, Wilfred E. 1962. *President and Congress*, 3rd ed. New York: Vintage Books.

Bryce, James. 1891. *The American Commonwealth*, 2nd ed. New York: Macmillan.

Corwin, Edward S. 1957. *The President: Office and Powers*, 4th ed. New York: New York University Press.

Cronin, Thomas. 1980. *The State of the Presidency*, 2nd ed. Boston: Little, Brown.

Curtis, Kenneth M. 1981. "Presidency—An Imperfect Mirror." *Presidential Studies Quarterly* (Winter): 28–31.

DeGrazia, Alfred. 1951. *Public and Republic: Political Representation in America*. New York: Alfred A. Knopf.

Fairlie, John A. 1940. "The Nature of Political Representation." *American Political Science Review* (April and June): 236–48 and 456–66.

Fiorina, Morris P. 1989. *Congress: Keystone of the Washington Establishment*, 2nd ed. New Haven: Yale University Press.

Hinckley, Barbara. 1990. *The Symbolic Presidency: How Presidents Portray Themselves*. New York: Routledge.

Hirschfield, Robert S., ed. 1973. *The Power of the Presidency: Concepts and Controversy*, 2nd ed. Chicago: Aldine Publishing Co.

Kendall, Willmoore. 1985. "The Two Majorities in American Politics." In *The Conservative Affirmation in America*. Chicago: Regnery Gateway, pp. 21–49.

Link, Arthur S., ed. 1974. *The Papers of Woodrow Wilson*, Vol. 18. Princeton: Princeton University Press.

McConnell, Grant. 1976. *The Modern Presidency*, 2nd ed. New York: St. Martin's Press.

Moe, Terry M. 1991. "The Politicized Presidency." In *The Managerial Presidency*, ed. James P. Pfiffner. Pacific Grove, CA: Brooks/Cole, pp. 135–57.

Morgan, Ruth P. 1970. *The President and Civil Rights: Policy Making by Executive Order*. New York: St. Martin's Press.

Neustadt, Richard. 1990. *Presidential Power and Modern Presidents*. New York: Free Press. Originally published in 1960.

Peterson, Merrill D., ed. 1977. *The Portable Thomas Jefferson*. New York: Penguin Books.

Pitkin, Hannah. 1967. *The Concept of Representation*. Berkeley: University of California Press.

Richardson, James D., ed. 1903. *Messages and Papers of the Presidents*. Washington, DC: Bureau of National Literature and Art.

Rose, Richard. 1991. *The Postmodern President: George Bush Meets the World*, 2nd ed. Chatham, NJ: Chatham House Press.

Rossiter, Clinton. 1960. *The American Presidency*, rev. ed. New York: Mentor.

Smith, Kathy B. 1981. ''The Representative Role of the President.'' *Presidential Studies Quarterly* (Spring): 203–13.
Vogler, David J. and Sidney R. Waldman. 1985. *Congress and Democracy*. Washington, DC: CQ Press.

Chapter 3

Washington and/or Versailles: The White House as a Court Society

DANIEL P. FRANKLIN

This chapter is about the politics internal to the presidency. It is not, however, about an "imperial presidency." In the aftermath of the Nixon administration, Arthur Schlesinger wrote of *The Imperial Presidency*, suggesting that the power of the presidency had eclipsed the power of Congress and the courts (Schlesinger, 1974). Recent events, subsequent to the end of the Cold War and the congressional elections of 1994, have demonstrated that Schlesinger's predictions of the demise of the separation of powers was premature. Therefore, in this chapter the politics of the royal court refers *not* to Schlesinger's Imperial Presidency but to the politics *internal* to the presidency that resemble a royal court.

WHAT IS A ROYAL COURT?

To define a "royal court" it is necessary to distinguish court politics from those of a legislature, bureaucracy, or corporation. A royal court is an organization centered around the authority of a single individual (see also Dexter 1977: 267–68).[1] Every person who holds a position in court is completely dependent for his or her place in the hierarchy on the individual in charge. A court is not a formal hierarchy. Formal titles, organizational charts, and formal rules of procedure do not generally give an accurate indication of where the real power of the organization lies. In that sense, courts are not highly institutionalized (Polsby 1968: 145). They have little or no institutional memory. They have few permanent and fixed rules of procedure. Court politics are fluid—formed and re-formed from one administration to the next and can, in fact, be completely reconstituted at the whim of the person in charge.

Thus, the court is not a bureaucracy. With structured organization, firm hierarchy, and organizational memories, bureaucracies are highly institutionalized. The head of a bureaucracy is hardly master of his own house. Employees are hired, fired, and advanced in a bureaucracy according to a firm, fixed set of organizational guidelines. Thus, the incoming director of a bureaucracy will inherit a ponderous set of institutional procedures for implementing policy, an organizational structure from another era, and a staff that is more likely to be loyal to the organization than to the person at the helm.

Neither is a legislature a court. In legislatures, members serve at the pleasure of their constituents. Power emanates from the bottom up, and the legislative leadership has very little leverage to enforce its will. After all, the leadership cannot (except in the most extraordinary of circumstances) unelect a member of a legislature.

Corporations may bear a superficial resemblance to a royal court. But as powerful as the president or CEO of a corporation may be within the context of his own organization, that organization is controlled by powerful outside forces such as the market, a board of directors, the government, and stockholders. A corporate CEO who ignores the market does so at the risk of bankruptcy. A CEO who ignores his or her board of directors or stockholders runs the risk of losing his job.

THE WHITE HOUSE AS A ROYAL COURT

The presidency as an institution is almost unique to the American context. (Other American governmental executives, mayors or governors, may be more or less similar.) Ever since the creation of the Executive Office of the Presidency (EOP) in 1939, the president has administered a large pyramidical organization. Most essential employees of the EOP are in one way or another personally beholden to the man who sits in the Oval Office. The EOP has a budget that is theoretically checked by the legislature. However, as a practical matter there is an unspoken agreement between the branches which forbids the reduction or veto of each other's budgets as long as a certain degree of decorum is maintained. While the president does not serve for life nor does he ascend "to the throne" by reason of birth, he serves for virtually uninterrupted intervals of at least four years and, in a second term, serves without the prospect of, or need for, reelection. Thus, the president cannot be removed (except in the most extreme circumstances) during his term of office.

Consequently, within the context of his four-year term, and especially during a second term, the president's power within the Executive Office of the Presidency goes virtually unchallenged. That is the organizational description of a court. Therefore, it would be accurate to describe the politics of the presidency as the politics of the court. It is important to note, however, that parallels between the presidency and the royal courts of the past can be taken too far. For the players involved, the stakes of White House politics are not as high as they were for courtiers of a true monarch. Failure at the court of, say, Louis XIV could mean total loss of status, livelihood, and even life itself. Disgrace in the Executive Office may lead to jail, public approbation, and the like, but it can also result in lucrative book contracts, lobbying jobs, candidacies for election, and even a job as radio talk show host. Furthermore, because the president serves for a set term with an end date certain, he has less leverage with his staff. Recalcitrant or self-serving staffers can simply wait out the president, safe in the knowledge that the boss will be out of office in, at most eight years, never to return (as a result of the Twenty-Second Amendment).

Nevertheless, within those boundaries, the politics of the White House parallel the politics of the royal court. Thus, an understanding of court politics past and present will give us a much better understanding of the ways and means of presidential decision making today and tomorrow.

THE INTERNAL POLITICS OF A ROYAL COURT

Perhaps the best place to start our examination of the politics of the court is to review the political life of one of history's most highly developed royal courts: that of the "Sun King," Louis XIV of France. For such a review, we can turn to the memoirs of Louis de Rouvroy, the second Duc de Saint-Simon (de Gramont 1963). "Le Duc" was born in 1675, the son of a modestly successful peer in the court of Louis XIII. From 1694 until 1723 (Louis XIV died in 1711), Le Duc compiled and wrote one of the most complete and insightful documentations of court life and politics in existence. Ironically, Le Duc, who was a committed monarchist, became after his death a hero of the French Revolution. Pirated editions of his memoirs (suppressed for obvious reasons) began to appear in 1781 and were used to illustrate the corruption of the Court at Versailles.

According to the Duc, there were three basic paths to power in the Court of the Sun King: persuasion, access, and assassination. We will review each of these techniques in turn and relate them to the modern presidency.

Persuasion

For the supplicant at court, persuasion is a very subtle art. In his seminal work on *Presidential Power*, Richard Neustadt (1960) discusses the art of persuasion at the presidential level. He finds that the skillful use of persuasion by the president is the most successful path to power. However, he almost exclusively focuses on persuasion as a two-way street (28)—one in which both sides have something the other wants. Only in passing does he acknowledge the position of the White House staff and others, who "have no 'powers' in their own right, or depend on the president for status, . . . their counter pressure may be limited indeed" (32).

This passage suggests that the only path to persuasion is leverage. However, that construction may be too limiting. The Duc de Saint-Simon, who lived the life of a supplicant, was very much aware of the courtier's potential for influence through persuasion. In one passage, the Duc recounted his attempt to influence the Dauphin (heir to the throne) on the matter of the "dignity" (or position) of persons of ducal rank. As the Duc described his technique:

My main intention was to sound him on everything concerning our dignity. I therefore gently broke off any subject that led away from this goal, bringing the conversation back to all the different chapters of this theme. . . . I then followed him, leaving him the pleasure of speaking, showing me that he was educated, and allowing him to persuade himself. . . . I tried less to press the arguments and parentheses than to lead him on to other subjects, in order to show a moderation that might appeal to his reason, his justice, his conviction arrived at by himself, and his trust, and to have time to sound him on all points and to impregnate him gently and thoroughly with my feelings and views on all these matters. (Elias 1983: 107)

Within the context of the Royal Court, the Duc had no leverage, especially in relation to the heir to the throne, but he could make use of certain techniques for persuasion to his advantage.

In the White House, persuasion of this kind is quite useful, and those who are adept at it reap the rewards of power and influence. While there are many examples that illustrate this point, one of the best is recounted by Jeb Stuart Magruder, aide to President Richard Nixon:

Nixon normally ignored staff people who sat in on meetings, but it was not easy to ignore [Chuck] Colson. He's one of the most persuasive men I've ever met. He could always see which way the President was leaning, and he would state brilliantly whatever the President wanted to hear. He could devastate those who disagreed with him. His tactic was always the same: he only wished to help the President, so if you disagreed with him, you must be disloyal to the President. From the first he would challenge any of the senior advisers if he thought they were wrong—that is, he would challenge anyone except Haldeman and Nixon, who were never wrong. (Magruder 1974: 65)

Magruder remarks that because of his persuasive skills Colson became the only newcomer from outside Nixon's immediate circle of advisers to gain direct access to the president (65).

Beyond persuasion there are other ways advisers can use their positions to influence decisions. Because the president is dependent on his advisers for information, any manipulation of that information can result in a skewed decision-making process. For example, Dick Morris wrote regarding President Clinton's relationship with his staff: "In the conflict between the President and his staff, each side had its powers. The staff's foremost weapon was the ability to select information the president received" (Morris 1997: 98–99).

It is possible to package an argument in such a way that leaves out important options and details.[2] This is a dangerous game however. To be perceived as something other than an honest broker by the ruler is to risk the legitimacy and access of position. For example, in authorizing the Bay of Pigs operation, the plan's architects in the Central Intelligence Agency did not give President Kennedy important details about the potential pitfalls of the operation (Janis 1982: 19–27) When the 1961 operation devolved into disaster and a major embarrassment for Kennedy, CIA Director Allen Dulles was dismissed.

Finally, and most directly, subservients can manipulate policy in their favor by simply blocking the access of those with opposing points of view. Donald Regan, chief of staff to President Ronald Reagan, is reported to have viewed himself as the president's prime minister with independent policy-making authority that included controlling and blocking access to the Oval Office. H. R. Haldeman apparently played the same role in the Nixon administration, as do most presidential chiefs of staff to some degree.

Access

In all his years in the court of Louis XIV, Saint-Simon had only three brief interviews with the king. His access improved with the death of the king because of his close friendship with the new king's regent, the Duc d'Orleans. (Louis XV was still a child when he ascended to the throne.) As a result, for a brief period in his life, Saint-Simon's career flourished. However, until then, Le Duc was either out of favor and therefore denied access, or too low in the pecking order to gain the king's attention.

In order to understand the dynamics of access in a court, it is important to remember that *titles mean nothing*. This is not to say that titles *always* mean nothing. Rather, a title will only reflect the true position of the titleholder if that person has actual access to and is well regarded by the leader. Thus, organizational charts are largely irrelevant in mapping out the politics of the court. Unfortunately, in the absence of an organization guideline, trying to know who is "in" and who is "out" of power is very difficult.

Louis XIV encouraged his noble families to live at Versailles. The king took great pleasure in personally allocating the housing accommodations for those who were living at court. Of course, not all accommodations were equal. Besides the obvious variations in size and comfort, the most important indicator of status was the proximity of an apartment to the king's own quarters. Saint-Simon writes of a nobleman's fall from favor when the unfortunate fellow returned to his apartment at the end of the day only to find someone else (Le Duc, himself) living in his quarters (de Gramont 1963: 50–51).

It was not just through living accommodations that the king bestowed his favors. The court was constantly alert to the slightest sign of the king's regard. Who was to travel with the king to Marly (the king's "hunting lodge," a smaller palace nearby)?[3] Who was to hold the king's candle during morning prayer? Who would be asked to attend the king's lunch? Who was to help the king dress in the morning? In retrospect, all of this may sound ridiculous. However, in court society, every indication of the king's favor is at the same time an indication of status.

Gaining access to the decision maker is another problem. It was commonly known at Versailles that in the course of his daily routine the king would walk along certain corridors or paths in the garden. If they could not obtain a personal audience, courtiers who wished to approach the king made sure that they were on the king's route during his daily activities. In that way, an impromptu audience could be arranged. For his first audience with the king in 1699, the Duc waited until the king's bedtime and "stood near the sitting room fire place, and followed the King when he went to get undressed. As he stood with his back to the hearth, saying good night as usual to all those who did not have full access . . . I went up to him" (de Gramont: 206–207).

In the modern context location, proximity to the president, and staff size are all indicators of access and status. In the court of the White House politics, office space has a special meaning. During the administration of Harry Truman, Clark Clifford reports;

[Harry] Vaughan compounded his growing problems by a unilateral act of office imperialism. On his own authority, Vaughan took over [Sam] Rosenman's spacious office. Washington has always been a city which pays special attention to such perquisites, and Vaughan's new office, with its proximity to the Oval Office, seemed to convey an increase in power. From it, Vaughan proceeded to attempt to spread his influence still further, and this led both [Navy Secretary] Forrestal and Judge Robert Patterson, who had just succeeded Colonel Stimson as Secretary of War, to complain to President Truman. (1991: 67)

Later, Jeb Magruder reported a White House promotion in this way;

When I joined the Office of Communications early in 1970 I moved from the White House basement across Executive Avenue to an office in the Executive Office Building. . . . I was assigned a big high-ceilinged corner office on the first floor, one with a view of both the White House and Lafayette Park. . . . I was told that my office had once been Cordell Hull's. . . . Nixon's own "hideaway" office was in the middle of our corridor, with Colson's office past it and Len Garment's at the far end of the corridor. (91–92)

In the White House, indicators of status are as varied and as arcane as those of the Court of the Sun King. For example, during the Nixon presidency, Communications Director Herb Klein was a particular target for ridicule and humiliation. According to one report, while Klein was out of town on an extended trip, Henry Kissinger—who had the adjacent office—broke down the wall to Klein's private bathroom (the only one in the West Wing besides that of the president) and walled up Klein's bathroom door (Burke 1992: 47). Most of Nixon's staff considered Klein disloyal because he held the attitude that the press was not necessarily an adversary but that, with proper management, could be enlisted as an ally for the president's benefit. When it became evident that the president did not support this point of view, Klein was fired in 1973.

There are many other signs of status in the White House. Among documented White House status symbols are priorities on the White House tennis court, seatings at state dinners, tickets to the president's box at the Kennedy Center, trips, seating and, apparently, exits from Air Force One.[4] Status rankings are evident from the very beginning of a presidential administration. For example, any number of inaugural balls are held on the evening of a president's swearing-in.[5] Each one of these balls has its own ranking, and an invitation to one or the other of these parties is a sure sign of one's initial status in the administration. All of this may sound petty, but competition for such trifles is a deadly serious business in Washington. Status is the only currency worth having at court. Any indication of the ruler's favor or disfavor can have enormous repercussions for a person's position in the court hierarchy.

Assassination

Besides the obvious route of gaining the king's attention and favor, getting ahead at court may involve maneuvering around or through obstacles imposed by rivals. To be less oblique, it may be necessary to kill your enemies. While Saint-Simon never referred, indelicately, to assassination at court, it is probably the case that Louis XV's ascension to the throne was influenced by the untimely death of others in the line of succession. There is evidence that the Duc de Bourgogne, the grandson of Louis XIV who became heir to the throne in 1711, died (by poisoning) at the hands of the Duc d'Orleans in 1712. The Duc d'Orleans then became prince regent during the childhood of Louis XV upon the death of Louis XIV in 1715.

While it is less likely that actual assassinations occur in the White House court—the stakes are somewhat lower and getting caught is a greater possibility—metaphorical "assassinations" probably occur. How would one "assassinate" a rival at the White House? The path to power at court is based on a personal relationship with the ruler. That personal relationship is useful only insofar as it is a relationship of mutual respect and benefit. If an aide loses the respect of or becomes a liability to his president, he will lose his access to the president and perhaps his job as well. The best way to destroy a rival in this way is through leaks to the press.

At Versailles, the Duc reports that courtiers commonly played elaborate practical jokes on one another. While some of this was just horseplay, it often had a harder edge. The Duc reports that several members of the king's court essentially disappeared, rarely to be seen again, as the result of being the butt of one practical joke or another.

In the modern context, assassination or embarrassment of one's rival through a practical joke has been replaced by destruction of one's rival through the press.

Former Chief of Staff Donald Regan made just that point when he wrote the following.

Without stretching things too far, it can be suggested that the most popular poison in twentieth-century Washington is bad publicity. In massive doses it can destroy a reputation outright. When leaked slowly into the veins of the victim it kills his public persona just as certainly, but the symptoms—anger, suspicion, frustration, the loss of friends and influence—are often mistaken for the malady. The victim may realize that he is being poisoned; he may even have a very good idea who the poisoners are. But he cannot talk about his suspicions without adding a persecution complex to the list of faults that is daily being compiled in the newspapers. A good many people—National Security Advisor Richard Allen, former Secretary of the Interior James Watt, and former Secretary of State Alexander M. Haig come to mind—have left the Reagan Administration after whispering campaigns broke into the press and destroyed their dignity and, with it, their effectiveness. (Regan 1988: 55)

While it is difficult to document actual leaks to the press, it is probably the case that in the Clinton administration, presidential confidant Dick Morris, a rival to presidential advisers—especially Chief of Staff Leon Panetta, George Stephanopoulos, and, particularly, Harold Ickes[6]—was "outed" by someone at the White House. The relatively conservative Morris had become too great a threat to White House liberals—not only in terms of his ideology but also because of his back-channel access to the president. In July 1996, prostitute Sherry Rowlands was for some reason motivated to come forward and sell her story of a year-long (business) relationship with Morris to *The Star*, a supermarket tabloid. While it would be difficult to know what caused Ms. Rowlands to come forward at just that time (immediately prior to the 1996 Democratic Convention, marking the kickoff of the 1996 general election), the end result was that Morris was fired and Ickes's status was restored.[7]

There have been other notable incidents of leaks to the press. In the Nixon administration, the White House "Plumbers Unit" was set up precisely in order to stem this sort of thing. The actual event that set the Plumbers in motion was a leak to the press about Henry Kissinger's conduct as national security adviser. Apparently, a "mole" in Kissinger's office was stealing documents and feeding them directly to newspaper columnist Jack Anderson—probably with the knowledge and perhaps at the behest of Alexander Haig (who eventually became Nixon's chief of staff). And, of course, no discussion of leaks in the White House would be complete without at least a mention of "Deep Throat," Bob Woodward and Carl Bernstein's source for information about the Watergate affair.[8] The events that are collectively known as Watergate would be little more than a few campaign tricks were it not for a source of information close to the president.

THE ROLE OF WOMEN AT COURT

A word or two needs to be said about the position of women at court. At Versailles, a number of women achieved status because of their relationship with the king. Nevertheless, the court was by and large a patriarchal community. The queen or one of the king's mistresses could be counted on to use her access to gain influence or facilitate the interests of others. In particular, the king's long-time mistress (and eventual wife), Madame de Maintenon, who had started her career at court as a governess to the king's illegitimate children, eventually became as powerful as any courtier. Nevertheless, no woman at Versailles exercised influence except through her personal and intimate relationship with the king.

Not much has changed at the president's court. No woman has ever advanced very far into the inner circles of the White House as a professional in her own right. This is not to say that women are without influence at the White House.[9] Nevertheless, the influence of women in the White House is mainly limited to the role of First Lady. Presidents' wives have exercised varying degrees of influence (see Chapter 11 for further discussion of the First Lady). Prominent among influential presidential wives of recent years was Nancy Reagan. According to Don Regan's own account, while he was chief of staff to the president, Regan fought a battle with the First Lady (and her astrologer) for control of the president's schedule. Regan lost.

It is important to reiterate that court politics are a reflection of politics as they are, not as we would like them to be (or outlined by an organizational chart). While we would like to think that there is no "glass ceiling" in our modern democracy, the White House court is a stark example of the limits to power for women in politics. Dee Dee Myers, former press secretary to Bill Clinton, found that, despite promises to the contrary, she was never admitted to the inner circle of Clinton advisers that she and other women on the staff referred to as the "White Boys Club" (Birnbaum 1996).

Because court politics are a function of informal relationships, participation in the activities and relationships that throw individuals together are the paths to success. Clark Clifford was a naval aide on the presidential yacht, *Williamsburg*, in charge of planning the menus for President Truman's dinners—that is, until one evening when he was asked to sit in on one of the president's nightly shipboard poker games. It was at that game that Clifford became friendly with Truman and acquainted with Lyndon Johnson, Averell Harriman, and Dean Acheson (a nonpoker player). According to Clifford, "The poker weekends were stag affairs: President Truman, while always courteous to women, was rarely relaxed and comfortable in their presence" (p. 70). Until a woman is elected to the presidency in her own right, or overall relationships between men and women change, women in the White House will probably continue to serve in a secondary role.

SUPERVISING THE COURT

Influence is a two-way street. While the supplicants at the president's court are trying to gain influence, the president is trying to maintain control. Saint-Simon reports that while Louis XIV was a man of limited intelligence (and compassion), the king had a special skill for managing relations at court. There were three keys to the king's control over his court: information, uncertainty, and convincing the aristocracy that there was no status outside of court.

For information, the king employed any number of spies. Their job was made easy by the fact that almost all nobles at the higher levels of the French aristocracy resided at court. Any modern-day visitor to Versailles will notice not only the size of the palace, but also the fact that it is situated well outside of Paris. The king disliked Paris and, at times, was actually in fear of the Parisian mob. The geographical effect of having the king's palace so far outside of the capital city was to make it virtually impossible for members of the aristocracy to attend the court without living there as well. That hothouse environment made it easier for the king not only to spy on his subjects, but also to manipulate the court through the distribution of what were often petty favors. In the isolated environment of court politics, the bestowal of favors or even the occasional word, glance, or nod was magnified and had the effect of elevating or lowering one's status. The Duc reports that the king was masterful at the art of interpersonal nuance. In fact, Saint-Simon reports breathlessly (which was quite out of character) every nuance of his very brief and generally inconsequential meetings with the king.

In the modern context, it may be difficult to imagine why anyone would want to live at Versailles and negotiate all of the risks and indignities of the king's whims. In order to understand this reasoning, it is important to penetrate the aristocratic mind. In a class-oriented society, especially one in which the king exercises unchallenged authority, there is no place to be except at court. Besides the practical concerns that nobles had in achieving satisfactory treatment of their claims before the king, to be out of the king's favor or not at court was to relinquish most of their status. In a class-oriented society, where there is no social mobility, status is everything and a fall from the king's grace is a fall to nothingness. Because such value was placed on living at court, the king was able to use banishment as a sufficient threat to maintain control.

Finally, the king was very inconsistent in his award of favors. Whether by design or intuition, this behavior created an atmosphere of uncertainty about the state of the court hierarchy. In turn, in an atmosphere of uncertainty, members of the king's court had trouble forging alliances (especially against the king himself) with allies of uncertain status and allegiance. Instead, court intrigue consisted mainly of rivalries among and between courtiers who were themselves uncertain of their status.

At the White House, successful presidents can maintain order in the same way. However, there are certain obstacles to the president's control of his own house, some of which are generic to court politics and others of which are specific to the American presidency. Perhaps the four most pernicious problems for the leader at court are sycophancy, isolation, inexperience, and the sheer size of the Executive Office. These are certainly problems for the American president.

Sycophancy

On the basis of his experience in the Johnson administration, George Reedy (1997) wrote:

There is built into the presidency a series of devices that tend to remove the occupant of the Oval Room from all of the forces which require most men to rub up against the hard facts of life on a daily basis. The life of the White House is the life of a *court* [emphasis in original]. It is a structure designed for one purpose and one purpose only— to serve the material needs and the desires of a single man. (419)

Because the president is without equal in his own office, it may be difficult for him to elicit honest opinions and evaluations of his own policies.[10]

Fortunately, in the United States, we do not have the overlay of a formal class structure. Thus, at least in theory, we are a society of equals. However, in reality, because the presidency is invested with so much symbolic import and because the modern chief executive has at his disposal such an enormous array of formal and informal powers, it is not a stretch to suggest that the powers and position of the modern presidency are "imperial" (Schlesinger). Furthermore, this sycophancy is reinforced by the sometimes necessary isolation of the occupant of the office.

Isolation

The era of Harry Truman's daily strolls through downtown Washington is over. The Kennedy assassination began a transformation in presidential security. Later, there were no less than two attempts on Gerald Ford's life. Ronald Reagan actually was shot, and there have been at least two attempts on the life of Bill Clinton. For no other reason than the president's personal safety, he is isolated from the general public. The effects of this isolation are all too obvious. In one instance, President George Bush did not even know what a bar-code price scanner was at a supermarket. But he could not have known. For obvious reasons, as president and vice president before that, Bush had not shopped at a supermarket since at least 1980.

Inexperience

The president may try to overcome these problems of court politics, but another obstacle, specific to the American presidency, may hamper any type of reform. By design a certain degree of inexperience is built into the American presidency. By virtue of the Twenty-second Amendment to the Constitution (which limits presidential terms), there is a constant, artificial churning of personnel in the presidency. Louis XIV was king of France for *seventy-two* of his seventy-seven *years*. He was born to be king, and his heirs were groomed for the monarchy. By contrast, no American president can expect to serve more than two terms. Furthermore, inexperience (outside Washington, that is) seems to be one of the informal prerequisites for election to the post–Watergate presidency.

As a result, almost every new president has to reinvent the presidency—especially when there is a presidential transition from one party to the other. American presidents may be able to design their offices to minimize the pernicious effects of sycophancy and isolation, but their terms of office are so short and their range of experience tends to be so limited that even the most carefully refined staff structure will remain in existence for only a finite period time—and that is generally at the end of a presidential term when the chief executive tends to be least effective. Thus, the effects of isolation and sycophancy are likely to be a problem in most presidential administrations.

To control the effects of sycophancy and isolation, a president needs to structure his office in such a way as to encourage debate and bring in outsiders to the decision-making process. This so-called collegial structure is fine except that it may result in a certain degree of presidential "overload" and a tendency for presidents to become involved in the minutiae of decisions that are outside their province. This was particularly the case for the collegial administration of Jimmy Carter (Burke 1992: 55–58).

Alternatively, in order to control and structure the flow of information, the president may choose a more formal structure, with a powerful chief of staff serving as gatekeeper to the presidential office. The problem with this approach is that the president may become the prisoner of his own staff structure. A powerful chief of staff may become a pseudo-president controlling access and flow of information to the president. The danger here is that the chief of staff may have his own personal ambitions or may be as inexperienced as the president. The powerful chief of staff structure has more often than not been a failure. H. R. Haldeman (Nixon), and John Sununu (Bush) seemed to have their own personal agendas. Donald Regan (Reagan) and Mack McClarty (Clinton) found that running the White House was nothing like running Merrill-Lynch or Arkla Gas. The notable successes of the formal chief of staff structure all seem to be related to experience—either that of the president or of the chief of staff himself. Dwight Eisenhower, who had extensive experience in heading large bureaucratic organizations at the federal level, worked well with his chief aide, Sherman Adams. James Baker (first Reagan term) was experienced in the ways of Washington and was held in check by Reagan loyalists Michael Deaver and Edwin Meese. Nevertheless, with these few exceptions, the president is constantly at risk of losing control of his own staff. The result of such a loss is disorder or isolation.

Size of the Court

Ultimately, the weakest link in the chain of command in any court is the leader himself. Louis XIV was skilled and experienced in court politics, but his descendants were not. It is the eventual fate of any monarchic dynasty to fall into the hands of an incompetent king. Recognizing this problem, the framers of our Constitution set out to design a government of "laws, not men." It is ironic, therefore, that the presidency has become an institution of men. As James Madison pointed out in *Federalist* 10, the problem of a government of men will be not that all leaders will be corrupt but that corruption (and incompetence) will be inevitable. Not all presidents will be Richard Nixon, but a Richard Nixon (or someone like him) will eventually come along. Thus, a government of men is bound to fail.

Court politics are an inevitable result of a presidential system. A presidential system, in contrast to a parliamentary system, is one in which the chief executive is independent of the legislature and serves for a set term. Consequently, a president, like a king, is in charge for at least four years. Court politics do not exist in a parliamentary system where a prime minister can be removed at any time by his own party or by national elections. Consequently, one solution to the problem of court politics in the presidency would be to move to a parliamentary system where the president would be dependent on his party and its legislative members for his position in office. Of course, getting rid of the presidential system in the United States would also mean truncating the separation of powers, which may not be desirable.

As an alternative, it may be desirable to shrink the court. The present study seems to indicate that the creation of the Executive Office of the President accentuated court politics in the presidency. Prior to 1939, when the EOP was created, the president was master of his own house to be sure. But his "house" consisted of a small number of stenographers and clerical staff.[11] Prior to that time, if the president wanted expert advice, he called upon a variety of outsiders, friends, cabinet members, professional bureaucrats, and members of Congress for advice. It was much more likely, therefore, that the president would receive advice and counsel influenced by factors outside the president's office. It was a collegial system without the formality of a White House plan.

In order to accomplish the goal of reducing the influence of court politics in the White House it may be possible simply to limit the funding of the EOP to pay for only a few clerical staff. Other essential functions of the White House would then be performed by the permanent bureaucracies of the federal government. The president would therefore be forced to go outside the White House for advice and counsel. He would have to rely on bureaucracies, Congress, and private sources for information untainted by loyalty struggles in the EOP. This dramatic reduction in size would help deal with problems of sycophancy and isolation. There is little we can do about the problem of presidential inexperience short of getting rid of the Twenty-second Amendment or grooming our presidents from birth. But, then again, there is no guarantee in this suggestion that the president will choose wisely those with whom he wishes to consult. Presidents Grant and Harding were hardly poster children for the premodern presidency. However, shrinking the EOP would at least remove one inefficiency bias from the presidential decision-making process.

CONCLUSION

Even if we choose to do nothing about limiting court politics in the presidency, this chapter presents us with a unique way of understanding and analyzing politics internal to the White House. The politics of the court should be understood as an alternative explanation to the politics of bureaucratic, legislative, or corporate structures. Court politics are rare and, in fact, may be only associated with a limited range of governmental structures—monarchies, dictatorships, and presidential systems. Nevertheless, there are distinct enough patterns of behavior in court societies, there are enough presidential systems, and there are certainly enough dictatorships to warrant a reexamination and a modern reapplication of the theory of the royal court.

NOTES

1. While we tend to focus on the mode of selection (primogeniture) as being a crucial determinant of the politics of a royal court, I am arguing that primogeniture is an important principle in the selection of *kings*. However, the power resources of the individual in a position of leadership are a much more important determinant of court politics. Thus, we can speak of "court" politics without necessarily referring to a "royal" court.

2. Whether this type of behavior is "ethical" is quite another matter (Burke 1984).

3. Much to the king's displeasure, the Duc had resigned his commission in the Army. The king displayed his displeasure by inviting Madame Saint-Simon to Marly but not the Duc. The Duc's wife had no choice but to comply and travel without her husband.

4. In one noted example of this, House Speaker Newt Gingrich complained about his seating assignment on Air Force One and the fact that he was asked to de-plane out of the back exit of the aircraft (*New York Daily News*, 1995, p. 1).

5. In January 1997 the Presidential Inaugural Committee sponsored fourteen official balls.

6. The *New York Times* identified Ickes as the "untitled" campaign manager of the Clinton reelection campaign (Mitchell 1996).

7. Morris commented in his own book (but not in direct reference to the Rowlands affair), "Since I discouraged press attention, I believed that most stories about me were the result of leaks or plants by my adversaries in the White House or in the Republican Party" (Morris 1997: 114). While it is possible, it is unlikely that someone in the Republican Party "outed" Morris. After all, Morris had had a professional relationship with

Jesse Helms and Trent Lott. Furthermore, the timing of the affair, just prior to the Democratic Convention, indicates that the leak was stimulated by an intramural dispute. Had the Republicans been responsible, it is much more likely that the leak would have occurred during the general election campaign.

8. There are many rumors as to the identity of Deep Throat. Clearly, Deep Throat would have had a personal interest in embarrassing the administration. For example, H. R. Haldeman thinks that Fred Fielding, a deputy to John Dean, acted as Deep Throat to retaliate and to protect himself against the attempt to use his boss as a "fall guy" for the Watergate Affair (Ehrlichman 1982: 85).

9. In particular, Alice Rivlin, Laura Tyson, and Dee Dee Myers have all had formal positions of prominence in the Clinton White House. Nevertheless, by the second term they were all gone. Furthermore, while they worked in the White House, they were never reported to be in a position of great influence in the president's court.

10. Bruce Buchanan notes that deference not only has a negative effect in the short term, but also has a cumulative, deleterious effect in the long term (Buchanan 1978: 53–75).

11. Prior to 1939 when the EOP was created, President Roosevelt had a total staff of thirty-seven. In 1995 the presidential branch had eleven separate divisions, a budget of $172 million, and a staff of 1,600 (Hart, 1995: 5).

REFERENCES

Birnbaum, Jeffrey H. 1996. *Madhouse: The Private Turmoil of Working for the President.* New York: Random House.

Buchanan, Bruce. 1978. *The Presidential Experience: What the Office Does to the Man.* Englewood Cliffs, NJ: Prentice-Hall.

Burke, John P. 1984. "Responsibilities of Presidents and Advisers: A Theory and Case Study of Vietnam Decision Making." *Journal of Politics* (46): 818–45.

———. 1992. *The Institutional Presidency.* Baltimore, MD: Johns Hopkins University Press.

Clifford, Clark with Richard Holbrooke. 1991. *Counsel to the President.* New York: Random House.

de Gramont, Sanche, ed. and trans. 1963. *The Age of Magnificence: The Memoirs of the Duc de Saint-Simon.* New York: Capricorn Books.

Dexter, Lewis A. 1977. "Court Politics: Presidential Staff Relations as a Special Case of a General Phenomenon." *Administration and Society* 9(3): 267–83.

Ehrlichman, John. 1982. *Witness to Power: The Nixon Years.* New York: Simon & Schuster.

Elias, Norbert. 1983. *The Court Society.* Trans. Edmund Jephcott. New York: Pantheon Books.

Hart, John. 1995. *The Presidential Branch: From Washington to Clinton*, 2nd ed. Chatham, NJ: Chatham Publishers.

Janis, Irving L. 1982. *Groupthink*, 2nd ed. Boston: Houghton Mifflin.

Magruder, Jeb Stuart. 1974. *An American Life.* New York: Atheneum.

Mitchell, Alison. 1996. "A Political Troubleshooter Is Clinton's Point Man." *New York Times*, August 26, NYT Internet Web Site.

Morris, Richard S. 1997. *Behind the Oval Office: Winning the Presidency in the Nineties.* New York: Random House.

Neustadt, Richard E. 1960, 1980. *Presidential Power: The Politics of Leadership from FDR to Carter.* New York: John Wiley & Sons.

New York Daily News. 1995. "Cry Baby: Newt's Tantrum." November 16, p. 1.

Polsby, Nelson W. 1968. "The Institutionalization of the U.S. House of Representatives." *American Political Science Review.* 42(1): 144–68.

Reedy, George E. 1997. "The American Monarchy." In *Understanding the Presidency,* ed. James P. Pfiffner and Roger H. Davidson. New York: Longman Press, pp. 419–23.

Regan, Donald T. 1988. *For the Record: From Wall Street to Washington.* New York: Harcourt Brace Jovanovich.

Schlesinger, Arthur M. 1974. *The Imperial Presidency.* New York: Popular Library.

Woodward, Bob. 1996. *The Choice: How Clinton Won.* New York: Simon & Schuster.

Chapter 4

Electing Presidents and Other Potentates

JODY BAUMGARTNER

Presidential campaigns and elections are inherently personal, or candidate-centered. This was true in the United States even in the era of party dominance (Dinkin 1989). However, the idea that presidential selection has become more personalized, especially since the 1960s, is to some degree taken for granted in both the press and in academia.[1] On the surface the claim seems to match reality, but few studies empirically demonstrate that the relationship between candidate and party in presidential selection has changed.[2] Does it matter? And what of other systems? Are candidate-centered politics unique to the United States, or are they a structural characteristic of all presidential systems? If the latter is true, is it wise that many countries in this "Third Wave" of democracy (Huntington 1991) are adopting presidential government (Easter 1997; Linz and Valenzuela 1994)? Viewing presidential selection through a comparative lens can help us better understand these questions.

Most studies concerned with candidate-centered campaigns focus either on the electorate or on the campaign as political communication. Few quantify the relationship between party and candidate.[3] In this chapter I take a different approach, looking at the campaign organizations of candidates and parties. Are candidate organizations, relative to party organizations, becoming more important during presidential campaigns in the United States? If it can be established that candidate-centeredness in this organizational sense is increasing in the United States, what of other presidential systems? Is candidate-centeredness a phenomonen unique to the U.S. political system, or is it being diffused elsewhere? If so, why?

Here presidential selection is defined broadly as the process by which a country chooses its president; by campaign is meant the strategy (the blueprint) and tactics (its implementation) designed to capture public office (see Arterton 1993:

75; Wayne 1997: 213–34). Our attention is restricted to the national party organization. The idea is to cast a net widely to include all phases of presidential
selection (recruitment, prenomination, nomination, general election) and any significant actors.

The characteristics of candidate-centered presidential selection are well re-
hearsed. Technological advances in transportation and communications (especially television) have reduced presidential candidates' reliance on party
organization(s) for national political communication. Crafting appeals (images,
messages) is aided by improvements in polling, whereas targeting appeals (e.g.,
mass mailings) is made easier by widespread availability of increasingly sophisticated personal computing equipment. Political consultants are important in
both developments. Changes in political parties are also noted, including the
decline of parties in the electorate; loss of control over the party label brought
on by direct primaries; the increased electoral prominence of the political action
committee (PAC), single-issue, and ideological groups; and campaign finance
laws that put money in the hands of the candidate as opposed to the party.[4]

The analysis in this chapter is organized as follows. After highlighting what
students of the American political system have argued with regard to the implications of a more personalized style of political campaigning, we look at
candidates and parties in American presidential selection. Then we review what
students of comparative politics have written about presidential government and
selection in other countries. Presidential scholarship is, in general, focused on
the American presidency; this is a myopic approach. Accordingly, the French
presidential selection is briefly presented. Both cases are organized around three
categories of the characteristics outlined above: (1) technological advances, including use of campaign professionals; (2) campaign finance laws; and, (3) the
decline of party.

PERSONALIZED PRESIDENTIAL SELECTION

Three general areas of concern can be discerned in the literature focusing on
presidential selection in the United States: (1) Executive qualification, including
patterns of recruitment and learning; (2) policy direction and accountability; and
(3) patterns of governance.[5] Obviously, all of these questions touch on the role
of political parties, especially vis-à-vis candidates and elected officials. Thus,
the impact of personalized presidential selection on system effectiveness is explicitly tied into the larger question of the role of political parties.

Executive Qualification

In his examination of political executives, King (1975) noted that studies of
executive recruitment and selection tend to cluster around either the social structure or partisan mechanics of selection.[6] If we categorize presidential qualifications in terms of disposition, campaign skills, and background and experience,

it is evident that good campaigners are chosen president.[7] Nelson (1982), using Barber's (1977) typology, asserted that contemporary candidates may be psychologically better fit. But what of background and experience? Does the process produce qualified officeholders? Does it test or teach the qualities that presidents should have? Are capable but uncharismatic people disadvantaged in presidential selection?

Analysis of selection and qualification "remains at a fairly soft level" (Rockman 1986: 118). This is partly because these questions are intimately tied to assumptions regarding qualifications a president *should* have; as Rockman noted, this is a "highly subjective" matter. Nelson (1982) asserted that there is a body of evidence which suggests that candidates under the "new" system are as qualified as those in the "old" (pre-1968). Most of the work that addresses this issue is found tangentially in party scholarship. Polsby (1983), for example, claimed that "what it takes to achieve the nomination differs . . . [very] sharply from what it takes to govern effectively" (89). In his classic study, Ceaser (1979) claimed that the biggest failure in the modern system is its failure to deal adequately with political ambition.

Matthews (1973) examined executive selection in several countries; the idea that selection processes affect governance and system performance is explicit. Heclo's (1973) "entrepreneurial" (U.S.) and "apprentice-oriented" (Britain) modes of selection are useful for understanding selection processes as different systems of learning; the implication is that the U.S. system discourages "team-oriented" governance. Similarly, Rose (1987) suggests that five tasks confront presidents (and prime ministers), two of which, "sustaining popular support and party management—are directly related to success in campaigning for office" (55). His conclusion? Presidents generally "learn to campaign" rather than govern.

It is hard to say if the modern selection process produces better qualified presidents. Certainly the self-recruitment considerations of potential aspirants have changed (Wayne 1997: 182–83). The type of prior governmental experience is also different; the road to the White House increasingly favors governors and vice presidents. Personal and family characteristics are more important than they used to be. Money-raising potential and style (physical and verbal) matter more than previously; ability to build party support and knowledge of government (specifically, Washington, D.C.) matter less. Finally, increased scrutiny from the media probably repels some, although how many it is hard to say.[8]

What of skills brought to, or learned from, the campaign? Modern candidates must demonstrate an ability to build and maintain public support; this can be of some use in governance. Organizational skills, which ostensibly are not task-specific, are important during campaigns and thus are also useful in office. And a successful candidate must be able to build coalitions, though these no longer need be strictly party coalitions. (We address this subject in more detail later in this chapter.)

Policy Direction and Accountability

Most serious students of American politics realize that the ideal of responsible party government (as supposedly found in the British system) is just that—an ideal. But recalling Schattschneider's claim that "modern democracy is unthinkable save in terms of the parties" (1942: 1), there remain important questions about candidate-party linkages with regards to the direction of, and accountability for, public policy. How do political campaigns affect policy direction, and, given political campaign styles, can elected officials be held accountable for policy success or failure? Politics remains a peripheral concern for most (Rosenstone and Hansen 1993); in the extreme, a candidacy unconnected to a political party runs a danger similar to that which the Founders feared, namely, demagogic or populist politics.[9] Moreover, a less partisan citizenry is more volatile, and a president's ability to maintain long-term public support suffers.

Short-term electoral considerations of personalized campaigns seem increasingly to drive policy direction and may also raise false expectations about presidential performance (Matthews 1973). Lowi (1985) claimed that all presidents eventually fall victim to a cycle of high expectations which they can never fulfill. Heard and Nelson (1987) speculated that because the American selection process is loosely structured, pollsters may encourage candidates to adopt policy stands that diverge from the party line. Polsby wondered how and if a "new elite" of political consultants, and so on, can be held accountable; "what values animate and constrain [their] behavior. . . . [And] how do these compare with whatever the values were that animated and constrained the old?" (1983: 75).

Ceaser (1979) noted an increase of less-than-principled appeals by candidates and an increasing potential for factional division within parties in the modern system.[10] More optimistically, others note that successful candidates generally keep (or try hard to keep) their campaign promises (Klingemann et al. 1994; Pomper and Lederman 1980; Ware 1996). While this does not guarantee accountability, it does offer some solace, especially to party-oriented political scientists.

Patterns and Styles of Governance

Does presidential selection affect how, and with whom, a president sets out to accomplish his policy agenda? It must be stressed that a successful presidential candidate cannot ignore his party organization; at issue is whether personalized campaigns marginalize the party so greatly that coalition-building efforts after the election are compromised (Ceaser, 1990). Several factors suggest that the gap between candidate and party may be widening. First, primary struggles, as noted previously, may widen factional divisions within parties. Second, candidates recruit themselves, as opposed to being recruited by party notables. Third, the increased prominence of interest groups (including single-issue and ideological groups) in electoral politics and the money their PACs bring to the process suggest that coalition building during the campaign is increasingly done outside conventional party bounds.

Jones believes that party linkages are valuable "political capital . . . [badly] needed under conditions of distributed power" (1996: 4). An "extraordinarily self-centered" (Jones 1994: 294) election process has the potential to exacerbate messianic and self-reliance tendencies in a new president, leading to party exclusion afterward. This idea fits with Kernell's notion of "going public" as a strategy for building support (1993). Seligman and Covington (1989) noted that presidents find it increasingly difficult to translate electoral support into governing support; alliances between presidents and parties are shorter and more volatile (see also Milkis 1993).

It seems incontrovertible that a more personalized presidential selection process has serious consequences for the larger political system. Now let us move to an examination of the U.S. case.

PRESIDENTIAL SELECTION IN THE UNITED STATES

In this section we look at presidential selection in the United States since the 1960s, limiting our attention to the candidacies of the two major parties. Is presidential selection becoming more personalized, as measured by the relationship between party and candidate? The strategy is straightforward. Personalized presidential selection is characterized by an increased use of advanced technology (including political consultants),[11] changes in campaign finance which privilege the candidate, and a decline of the national political party organizations. We will examine various aspects of these characteristics. Taken together, the body of evidence that follows embodies a strong case for asserting that, relative to party, candidates are becoming more important in the presidential selection process.

Such a finding should not be a total shock. Candidate involvement in the selection process is largely a product of this century but has increased over time (Wayne 1997). Asher (1987) conceptualized modern presidential campaigns in terms of the campaign of the candidate, the party, and the independent; he asserted that the candidate, though not solely in charge, is now the dominant player. Troy's (1996) reference to the "changing role" of modern presidential candidates is similar, whereas Thurber (with Nelson 1995) asserted that the "most important" change in modern campaigns is that strategy and tactics, formerly the "sole domain" of the party, is increasingly in the hands of the candidate and his handlers.

Technology and Professionalization

The impact of communication and transportation technology on political campaigning hardly needs rehashing here.[12] Image-making is exceedingly important in contemporary campaigns; and is especially facilitated and reinforced by television. The days of "whistle-stop" campaigning seem quaint in this era of modern, airport-tarmac schedules that put candidates in multiple cities or states in a single day. Although these technologies have limits, it is incontrovertible that candidates have increasingly taken advantage of them and increasingly craft campaign strategy assuming the national scope that they provide. Political consultancy belongs in this category, primarily because of the advances in computer technology and survey methodology with which they practice their profession. In short, the way we fashion and deliver political messages has become increasingly sophisticated.

Professionalized campaigns are receiving more attention from scholars of late (Sabato 1981, 1989; Shea 1996). Consultants are increasingly "calling the shots" in modern, professionalized campaigns, and they are proliferating and specializing. The American Association of Political Consultants has grown from its founding in 1969 from 25 to 550 members;[13] *Campaign and Elections*, a magazine for the trade, has over twenty categories (and sixty subcategories) in its "Products and Services" listings (Polsby and Wildavsky 1996: 189). Since these services are, in the main, controlled by the candidate and are an alternative (or supplement) to party efforts, it seems safe to conclude that since the profession is both growing and diversifying, the candidate's control over the campaign, relative to the party, is increasing. Simply put, now that they have the services of campaign professionals, candidates no longer need the party to carry their message to a national audience (which, it could be argued, was the original *raison d'être* for American political parties).

Finance

Nor do candidates rely on parties to finance their campaigns; this is thanks to the campaign finance laws of the 1970s which privilege the candidate over the party (Alexander 1992; Corrado 1997; Sorauf 1988). A series of data can demonstrate this effect. The first set is somewhat deceiving, showing that the party, relative to the candidate, was actually better off in 1996 as opposed to 1976. The ratio of candidate to party spending (through all phases of the election season) was 6.1:1 in 1976, decreasing to 3.8:1 in 1996.

This is less than half the story, however, which of late revolves around the growing importance of "soft" money (Wayne 1997: 50–52, Box 2–3). Although technically controlled by the political parties (national, state, and local), dispensation is controlled largely by the candidates. And even though soft money cannot be used for advocacy, there are increasingly sophisticated ways around this restriction (Alexander 1992; Sorauf 1988). From Table 4.1, we can see that soft money expenditures far outstrip either party or candidate "hard" money.

Again, soft money is generally associated with, and benefits, the candidate. Another, albeit indirect, measure of the increase in the candidate's financial independence is the increase in PAC activity. The number of PACs grew sevenfold from 1974 to 1992 (608 to 4,195).[14] Although not all of these PACs

Table 4.1
Candidate, Party Spending (1976–1996), and Soft Money (1980–1996), in Millions of Dollars

	Candidate		Party		
	Primary	**General Election**	**Convention**	**General Election**	**Soft Money**
1976	$10.90	21.80	2.20	3.20	19.1*
1996	31.00	61.80	12.40	11.60	405.0**
% Increase	2.84%	2.83	5.64	3.63	21.2

*Figure for 1980
**Estimated total through September 30, 1996.

Source: Compiled from Wayne 1997: 47, 49, tables 2-4, 2-5.

contribute to presidential campaigns, a great many do so through the soft money option referred in the preceding. To repeat, the candidates' need for political parties as sources of funding is far less than before; parties remain important, however, as coordinators and conduits, a fact that must not be overlooked.

Parties

Changes in technology and finance are not unrelated to the decline of party. There is conflicting evidence with regard to the organizational decline of American political parties. The decline of the party-in-the-electorate is well documented. It makes some sense to argue that since people identify with parties less than previously, their electoral importance has diminished, and thus, their strength relative to the candidate has also been reduced. The extent of this decline is another question. Certainly, national party organizations have grown (Herrnson, 1988). From 1972 to 1988, the staffing in the Republican National Committee grew from 30 to 160, the Democratic National Committee, from 30 to 145 (Beck and Sorauf 1992: 105).

The recent tendency for vice presidents to become presidential nominees probably argues for the importance of party service; party activists now seem to regard party service as more important in presidential nomination than before (see Table 4.2).

It needs to be recognized that party seems to matter more for Republicans; for example, it was widely recognized that 1996 was Dole's "turn." And although Goldwater and Nixon ran without party, Reagan and Bush were party men (Wayne 1997: 208–209).

To get at the idea that presidential candidates increasingly self-recruit, the number of candidacies during the 1968–1992 was tabulated. Theory suggests

Table 4.2
How Important Is Party Service for Presidential Aspirants?

Party activists should . . .	1972		1988	
	Democratic	Republican	Democratic	Republican
Weigh party service very heavily in selecting candidate for nomination	3.2	23	24.8	29.4

Source: Kessel 1992: 86, table 3-3, ''Activists' Feelings of Obligations about Party Work.''

that in the post-reform (1968) era, there are increased numbers of candidates and in-party factions. See Table 4.3, where the data do not demonstrate any trend whatever.

While the number of candidacies has not increased (or decreased), it is clear that candidates are building their prenomination organizations earlier. It is well established that early organization is increasingly critical in attaining the party nomination (Kessel 1992: 7; Polsby and Wildavsky 1996: 68–69). An early start depends on early money; early money makes for early exposure and coverage, which enhances the chance of winning early primaries, which in turn attracts more money. In addition, early fund-raising potentially denies others money for matching funds if the pool runs dry. Table 4.4 tracks the average number of months before September of election year that presidential candidates announced.

While this table is somewhat ambiguous,[15] it shows, at the least, a slight upward trend. When we consider that the media began speculating, and potential aspirants began posturing, about election 2000 (Gephart, Gore) immediately after the 1996 returns were in, we can safely conclude that candidacies are starting earlier. Again, early starts are necessary to get the party nomination, which now has little to do with the national party organization. All this reinforces the candidate's, and his organization's, role. Finally, candidates are increasingly employing, or tied to, activists (as opposed to ''party hacks''), ad hoc citizen groups (e.g., Citizens for Kennedy), PACs, single-issue, and ideological groups (Asher's ''independent'' campaign).

Two other indicators help demonstrate that the national party organization is increasingly impoverished in relation to the candidate. First, after the election, presidents have an increasing tendency to appoint people from their personal circle to cabinet and White House staff posts (Wayne 1997: 212). This is not to say that party is insignificant in presidential appointments; rather, the winning candidate's ''debts to party'' have been smaller as the century has worn on (Mackenzie 1994; the Twenty-second Amendment is important in this regard also). Second, there is some reason to believe that the congruence between the party platform and the president's implementation of it has declined (Pomper and Lederman 1980).[16]

Table 4.3
Total Number of Candidacies, 1968–1992

Year	1968	1972	1976	1980	1984	1988	1992
Democratic	5	12	12	3	8	8	6
Republican	4	3	2	7	1	6	3
Total	9	15	14	10	9	14	9

Source: Niemi and Stanley 1994: 96–97.

Much ink has been spilled about the increased number of primaries and the concomitant decrease in the significance of the national convention in the nomination process. In 1960 fifteen states held Democratic primaries; in 1992 the number rose to thirty-nine (Republicans, sixteen and forty, respectively). ''Unaffiliated'' delegates at the end of the primary season comprise only 9 percent of total convention delegates in the post–1968 period as opposed to 38 percent earlier. In addition, the relationship between delegate count of the eventual nominee at the end of the primary season and the first ballot vote for him is .75 in the post–1968 time period and .48 for pre–1968 (Kamarck and Goldstein 1994: 190–91). These facts, taken together, reinforce what most people already know, that the nomination is now decided by the time the convention—where party notables formerly made final bargains—begins. Simply put, at the presidential level, the party has almost no control over its primary product: its label. The party is almost entirely absent from the nomination process.[17]

The evidence in this section, though somewhat ambiguous, suggests that from 1960 onward, presidential candidates have increasingly centered their strategy and tactics on their own organizations to the exclusion of their parties. Technological factors, including the use of political consultants and professionals, have made it easier for candidates to fashion and deliver increasingly sophisticated messages for a national—or as the case demands, a specialized—audience. With regard to finance, while candidate to party ''hard'' money spending has decreased, increases in soft money spending favors candidates.

Looking at the national party organizations, we find contradictory evidence. While candidates have strengthened their organizations and capacity to conduct their campaigns without party help, the number of candidacies has not increased, national party organizations have grown, and party service seems to be more important to party activists when they are considering presidential aspirants. However, pointing to decreased party strength is the well-documented decline in the party-in-the-electorate. Candidates are building their organizations earlier; they are increasingly employing, or tied to, nonparty political groups and individuals; the nomination is decided well before the convention; presidents show

Table 4.4
Announcement of Candidacy, 1968–1992, in Months before September (Average)

Year	1968	1972	1976	1980	1984	1988	1992
Value	3.78	8.60	12.86	13.30	9.43	14.64	10.00

Source: Compiled by author; data from Niemi and Stanley 1994: 96–97.

an increased tendency to appoint their personal circle to cabinet and White House staff posts; and finally, the congruence between party platform and the president's implementation of it has declined somewhat.

To sum, presidential candidates have increased their power relative to their party organizations during the selection process. Parties are not unimportant, but their relationship to presidential aspirants has changed. It would seem that parties are less in control of the campaign than previously. This is no revelation; the main point here is that it is possible to quantify the relationship.

CANDIDATE-CENTERED CAMPAIGNS IN COMPARATIVE PERSPECTIVE

By looking at the presidential selection process in other countries, we can begin to determine if a personalizing trend is inevitable, a structural aspect of presidential systems; this could inform students of presidential government in the United States and otherwise. In this section we lay a base for crossing the intradisciplinary bridge from the literature on the American Presidency to a growing body of comparative literature that deals with presidentialism. In this regard, Riggs correctly asserted: "Sad to say, most Americanists know little, in depth, about other systems of government, and American comparitivists typically ignore American politics. Without further inquiry I dare say that this limitation applies to comparitivists working outside the United States" (1988: 247). Most Americanists seem to believe that "the [American] presidency does not lend itself (except in limited fashion) to comparative study" (Waldo 1975: 91). While there is a body of work we can identify as "American-comparative presidency" literature, in the main it deals with either leadership or the structure, organization, and efficiency of political executives in general, much of it contrasting presidential and parliamentary models.[18]

Most (non-American) comparative presidential scholarship is in the neo-institutional tradition of the recent transitions to democracy literature[19] most does not compare across systems.[20] It is a literature concerned with the effects of presidential (as opposed to parliamentary) regimes on democratic consolidation, specifically, system stability, rigidity, legitimacy, and effectiveness.[21] While almost no work specifically addresses presidential selection in a comparative fashion, ample impressionistic evidence exists suggesting that candidate-centeredness in presidential elections may be on the increase in other countries. As in the American literature, casual usage of the term is peppered throughout studies of comparative presidentialism. There is little reason to expect otherwise. While in many countries the government still controls the mass media,[22] sophisticated communications technology is increasingly available to those with sufficient funding. Moreover, parties in many of these countries are weak and rife with corruption.

Linz and Valenzuela (1994) make and test certain hypotheses in their work which bear on the personalized nature of presidential selection; each is inherent to presidentialism, and according to them, contributes to the breakdown of democratic regimes:

1. *An Exaggeration by the President of His Mandate and Power*: The tendency of presidents to interpret their election as a mandate and the subsequent tendency to fashion themselves as messiahs.

2. *Paralyzing Conflict between the Legislature and Executive*: Due partly to the first hypothesis and to a weakening of the executive as leaders prepare for the next election.

3. *Political Polarization*: Winner-take-all presidential elections that are inherently dramatic and personal.[23]

THE CASE OF FRANCE

Virtually no research has been done in the English language on the French (or any other) presidency (King 1993: 416). Therefore, much of the evidence presented here is fragmentary, gathered from general sources. First, let us present a quick overview of the French Fifth Republic.

The ideas that animated the creation of the French Fifth Republic were in one respect similar to those that were dominant in the formation of the United States, namely, to check tyranny. In the French Fourth Republic (1946–58) the power of the Assembly, in general, and specifically the political parties in the Assembly (Safran 1997: 7–15) was dominant. The upper chamber of the Assembly, the Council of the Republic, was weak, as were both executives (a figurehead president elected by parliament and a somewhat more powerful prime minister).

Charles de Gaulle, called upon to lead France out of its crisis, was more than suspicious of political parties; in a 1965 interview, he admitted that he had "proposed the Constitution of 1958 to the country . . . with the intention of ending the rule of the parties" (quoted in Toinet 1988: 12). His answer to the partisan and legislative immobility of the previous regime was the proposed constitution for the Fifth Republic, which was institutionally similar to its predecessor but had a dramatically different balance of power. If the Fourth Republic shortchanged the executive, its successor privileged it; the powers of both president and prime minister were greatly enhanced.[24] But if de Gaulle's intention was to end the *rule* of political parties, he did not end the *role* of parties (nor, incidentally, is there any indication that he wanted to).

Only five men have held the office of French president in the Fifth Republic: Charles de Gaulle (1958–1969), Georges Pompidou (1969–1974), Giscard d'Estaing (1974–1981), François Mitterand (1981–1993), and Jacques Chirac (1995–present). The term, seven years, is not fixed.[25] There is no vice president, so in the event of resignation (de Gaulle in 1969), death (Pompideau in 1974), or disability, the president of the Senate assumes the office in what is fundamentally a caretaker role, and elections are held within thirty-five days. This constitutional provision provides an initial clue as to the relationship between candidates and parties. Presidential aspirants must be ready for an election at any moment; France, in one sense, is in a continual presidential campaign.

A 1962 referendum (initiated by de Gaulle) provided for direct election of the French president. Legal requirements for candidacy are exceedingly simple. (For example, although citizenship is required, there is no residency requirement, nor must a candidate be French-born.) Although rules governing access to the first ballot were amended in 1976 to make it more difficult, it remains remarkably easy.[26] If no candidate receives more than 50 percent of the vote in the first round, the leading two votegetters move to a second round. (As of yet, no candidate—even de Gaulle—has won in first-round voting.)

The party system during the Fifth Republic has changed; the cause of the change is another matter. For Sartori, party politics in the Fourth Republic were a prime example of polarized pluralism (1976). Competition was centrifugal; there were many parties, several of which (on both the left and the right) were opposed to the regime. The party system has been consolidated: nineteen parties were represented in the Assembly in the middle 1930s, and by the early 1970s there were only four (Safran 1997: 69). The four main parties typically ally along a left-right axis in second-round voting. The party furthest on the right (with the exception of Le Pen's National Front [NF]) is the Rally for the Republic (RPR), the main heirs to the Gaullist Party; Chirac belongs to the RPR. The Union of French Democrats (UDF), though rightist, is more to the center than the RPR; this is the party of d'Estaing. These two parties, occasionally with the NF, are the French right. The left consists of the French Communists (PCF), the last of the "true believers" in Western Europe. They are (sometimes uneasy) allies with the Socialists (PS), who are the party of Mitterand. Let's now look at presidential selection in France, using the same indicators as in the American case.

Technology and Professionalization

Modern transportation technologies, important in election campaigns in a country as vast as the United States, are far less significant in a smaller country like France. However, as regards communications (television), Gaffney (1989) noted an increasing emphasis on candidate rallies and their coverage by the mass media (23). Furthermore, the televised debate is now the "most mediatic event" of round two (Hayward 1989) and revolves exclusively around the image and wit of each candidate. Some consensus has been reached that there has been a drift in the direction of image-based politics in French presidential campaigns. Some see this change as favoring parties (Ware 1996), but it can easily be argued that it privileges candidates.

What of campaign professionals? Gaffney also referred to an increasing need to refine media-handling techniques (1989: 26–27); Hayward (1989) saw the same need. We can therefore conclude that there is an increased reliance on campaign and media specialists (Hayward 1989: 79 n.13), although there is little ready data (at least in English) to substantiate this assumption. The discussion of candidates and communications technology would not be complete without mentioning media regulation in France. Although regulation of electronic media and government ties once made the French media less than pluralistic (to say the least), since the 1980s it has perhaps become the most privatized in all of Europe (Humphreys 1996), largely eliminating the potential for government bias. Moreover, political advertising is not allowed in France, and all candidates receive the same two hours of free air time during the campaign. In sum, it is a fairly level playing field.

Finance

France, like many other European countries, had no campaign finance laws until the 1980s. This meant, among other things, that there was little transparency (and thus, of course, little data). Corruption was widespread. There are now limits on contributions to both parties and candidates, for both corporations and individuals; caps have been set on how much candidates may spend in the twelve months before an election; and public funding has increased: Money is certainly more important. However, most of the public money is channeled to the parties, not directly to the candidates. In all, changes in campaign finance laws seem on the surface to have disadvantaged candidates (Whitney 1997).

Parties

There is conflicting evidence regarding the relationship between French political parties and presidential candidates. Here again English-language research is quite limited; much of the literature on French parties focuses on individual parties or their leaders.[27] Almost nothing has been written specifically on presidential campaigns. One feature of French parties must be made explicit. "It is the nature of French politics that parties may arise principally out of a shared support for a particular leader rather than out of strongly held and coherently formulated beliefs" (Raymond 1994: 110 n. 23). Though subject to factional struggle and takeover, French parties generally belong to the party leader; all presidents have been the long-time leader of their parties. This follows the French/Gaullist tradition of strong leadership

Most observers agree that the entire system has to some large degree become "presidentialized" (Pierce 1995; Raymond 1994). The ambiguity arising from the close relationship between a party and its leader(s) is highlighted in the relationship between parties and presidential aspirants during presidential campaigns. The "four major parties orient their strategy and adjust their tactics on the basis of" the presidential elections (Toinet 1988: 13). The uncertain position of parties is highlighted in this quote:

[Parties] focus on the presidency . . . almost certainly bringing with it personalization, supporters loyal to the candidate who have not worked well with the rest of the party, and methods of publicity and financing that have drawn interest and energy away from the party's program to promote electoral activism. . . . [However], the parties have remained the special arena for electoral competition and mass action. Without parties there would be no credible candidates . . . even in a choice so personalized . . . no candidate has a chance of gaining adequate backing without the support of an organized party. (Toinet 1988: 12)

In this sense, it may not be appropriate to ask if presidential selection is becoming more personalized in France. In fact, Pierce noted that both modes of selection that Heclo (1973) identified (apprentice and entrepreneurial, or "self-promotion," in Pierce's words) are available to aspiring presidential candidates in France (1995: 218). Of the three sets of indicators used earlier in the American case, party organization may be the least illuminating for the French. It may, in the end, confirm the idea that presidential systems are inherently personal and say nothing about trends. Arguments are made both for an increase in the importance of parties and in personalized candidacies; neither, as a rule, makes much distinction between the party and the candidate organizations.

The parties-are-more-important argument revolves around the presidentialization of the system. Suleiman (1980: 98; see also Machin and Wright 1982: 17–18) noted, perhaps obviously, that a candidate needs the support of one (or, more accurately, two) of the major parties. Perhaps more to the point, party capital is necessary if a president wants another term. Thus, party ties are key. Szarka (1996) agreed; taking on the party-candidate question directly, he argues that there has been an increase in party strength, based on the candidate's electoral needs. Moreover, positions within the party and other levels of government (municipal, the NA; see Kaminsky 1973) are exceedingly important.

Arguments have also been made for increased personalization. Like the United States, a good deal of evidence exists for a decline of the party-in-the-electorate; from the mid-1970s until the late 1980s, the percentage of nonpartisans in France increased (Dalton 1996: 209, Figure 9–3). Others speak to the notion that party ideology is becoming more centrist and, thus, that image is becoming more important. A decrease in ideological politics further enhances personal politics, although the rise of Jean-Marie Le Pen in the 1980s reminds us that ideology is decidedly not dead in France.[28] Second-round and factional struggles within parties are another indicator of increased candidate strength (Gaffney 1989; see also Hayward 1989). The complement to this literature is the political communications perspective referred to earlier. One analyst (Hayward 1989); noted Chirac's "profound mistrust" of television prior to 1995; we presume this attitude changed in 1995.

Safran (1997) implies that party–candidate linkages in France are weak, that French politics at the top is closed elite bargaining. Presidential politics are marked by leaders in collusion ("unnatural alliances") and party switching ("political wanderings"; 108–109); neither necessarily suggests strong party ties. Others explicitly suggest that running against party is increasingly a sound strategy; Raymond asserted that "the winning strategy of Mitterand the politician and Mitterand the president [involved, in part], framing his utterances in a way that reflected on his own function as the republican persona above all partisan interests and considerations" (1994: 90). Others note that parties are generally reluctant to make their policies binding on their candidates (see, for example, Macridis 1975).

Still others point to institutional features of the system as evidence that presidential campaign politics is becoming more personalized. Two features stand out. First, while parties are in nominal control of who will represent them (governed by party, as opposed to state rules), they typically ratify the candidate who has jockeyed for and won the spot by other means. This leads to a second point, the variance in the length of time in both nomination and election seasons. Thus, the jump a particular candidate has is important in building his image. Successful candidates generally jump in early, declaring themselves independent of party—while welcoming their support (Kaminsky 1973). Cole (1993) also sees the party as subordinate in what is essentially a permanent election campaign.

In sum, the evidence points to a slight increase in personalized presidential campaign politics in France. Parties are still very important with regard to finance; prior government experience is almost a necessity; and support of two of the major parties is pivotal in winning the presidency. However, image politics and professionalization of the campaign seem to be on the rise, and partisan identification has declined, which favors individual candidates. At the same time, movement in other aspects of candidate-centered campaigns is less than clear. Communications and transportation technology is probably less important in a smaller country; in addition, there are strict rules governing political use of television. Elite bargaining, outside of party, has been a constant, as have the "permanent election campaign" and the fact that parties usually ratify the candidate who has won the nomination by other means. Accordingly, they are reluctant to force their platforms on the candidates.

DIRECTIONS FOR FUTURE RESEARCH

This chapter has been less an effort to point to a research frontier then a
tentative step into it. While easier in this first cut in the case of the United States
than in the French, the relationship between candidate and party in the presidential selection process can, as has been demonstrated, be quantified. Various
aspects of technology, including political professionals, campaign finance, and
the party organization, can be operationalized so that the balance between party
and candidate can be quantified.

In the United States, presidential selection is becoming more personalized.
While national party organizations are a larger presence, the campaign efforts
of candidates seem to be increasingly independent of those parties. Parties are
still important, but to some degree they are becoming the tools of their candidates (as opposed to the converse). It is somewhat less clear that French presidential selection is following a trend toward personalized selection. This may
be at least partly because the relationship between French parties and their presidential candidates has always been more equal. And while certain technological
advances, namely, the professionalization of campaigns, may privilege candidates, the campaign finance laws of the late 1980s did not. It must also be
remembered that campaign professionals, too, can be employed by parties.

Impressionistic observations bear out the idea that candidate-centeredness may
be on the rise in other systems. Russia's one democratic election (1996) is one
example. The Communist Party candidate (Gennadi Zyuganov) was linked
closely to party, but as the campaign wore on, it became clear that any success
he might have would be tied to a certain disassociation from the party line
(which voters and others saw as a return to the Communist past; see Orttung
1996). And whether one accepts Kramer's (1996) version of Yeltsin's campaign
(American-style, complete with American consultants), or Remnick's repudia-
tion of this account (1996), what is clear is that in no way was the Yelstin
victory dependent on party. Indeed, how could it be? He does not belong to
one. Of course, the Russian party system is in its infancy, but as we have seen
in the French case the way presidential elections are conducted has an impact
on the development of party systems.

What can be made of this preliminary examination? Perhaps obviously, rules
matter. Americanists, at least impicitly, know this, with their constant advocacy
of procedural reform. However, examination of other systems could inform these
efforts. To take a simple example, efforts to design campaign finance so that
parties are not marginalized (as per Corrado 1997) could benefit from a cross-
country examination, of which there are few. Furthermore, it makes a difference
whether parties are regulated internally or by the state. Further research in this
vein could inform reform endeavors with solid evidence rather than impressions.

There is much to be learned about democratic consolidation from studying
presidential campaigns. Unlike the new nation of the post–World War II era,
emergent democracies of the post–Cold War era have shown a decided ''pref-

erence for presidentialism'' (Easter 1997). What effect will this change have on democratic consolidation or the development of a stable party system in these countries? Examination of Latin American and French cases (at least) invites examination into the process of institutionalizing charasmatic leadership—which may not be such a different question than the previous one in the case of presidential systems.

NOTES

1. The dean of modern presidential studies, Richard Neustadt, summed it up nicely: "We have . . . left the age of [party] barons and entered the age of candidates'' (1990: 199).

2. To be sure, there are studies that illustrate the increasing importance of candidates vis-à-vis political parties in the eyes of the electorate (Hess 1988; Wattenburg 1991) and in political messages (Denton and Stuckey 1994; Troy 1996). There is no shortage of literature debating Broder's (1971) claim that the "party is over'' (Kayden and Mahe 1985; Polsby 1983; Ranney 1975; Sabato, 1988; to name only a few).

3. Herrnson's (1988) study of congressional campaigns stands out as a notable exception.

4. On the role of television in American politics, see Frantzich (1989); for accounts and implications of the rise of political consultants, see Sabato (1981) and Luntz (1988); on campaign finance, see Alexander (1992) and his quadrennial accounts (for example, Alexander and Corrado 1995). It must be stressed that is the purpose here is not to explain candidate-centered politics; depending on the scholar, many of the characteristics noted are identified as being either the cause or consequence of personalistic campaigns.

5. Aldrich (1993) provides an excellent discussion of this.

6. Lamenting the lack of attention paid to connections between selection and governance, King focused on eligibility (availability), recruitment (methods and criteria), and tenure (1975: 183–96). As implied, prime ministers and their cabinets were included in his examination.

7. À la Bryce (1893); see also Aldrich (1987), who noted that changes in technology introduce a bias that favors those who can use it.

8. For the difficulties involved here, see Fowler and McClure's study of congressional ambition and noncandidacies in Rochester, New York (1989).

9. Even more extreme is the potential for authoritarian government (see the mass society literature of Arendt 1951; Kornhauser 1959), a fear that can perhaps be easily dismissed in the United States but historically and in other settings, only with difficulty.

10. The "candidate-supremacy,'' or plebiscitary model, since the 1960s.

11. See Note 3.

12. For a summary see Dinkin (1989: 164–74); also see Frantzich (1989).

13. As per Amy Mercenaro, Executive Director; conversation with the author, June 3, 1997.

14. From Conway and Greene (1995: 157, Table 7–1). Information from FEC; "All PACs'' is the combined total of the following categories: corporate; labor; trade; membership; health; cooperative; corporation without stock; nonconnected.

15. Factoring in incumbency and other values that help determine entrance into the race would likely give a clearer picture.

16. The study compared the periods of 1944–1966 and 1968–1976.

17. See also Polsby and Wildavsky (1996: 146–49).

18. The list of scholars who engage in this type of comparison is small. A fairly comprehensive search would uncover King (1975, 1993); Campbell (1983, 1993; with B. Guy Peters 1988; with Margaret Jane Wyszomirski 1991); Macridis (1968); Mathews (1973); Meynaud (1958); Plowden (1987); Rockman (1995); Rose (1980, 1987); and Simeon (1991).

19. Neo-institutionalism centers around the proposition that the incentive structures created by institutions affect political behavior; elites accommodate themselves to political institutions, which are relatively fixed in stable democracies. See March and Olsen (1984).

20. Powell (1982), Duverger (1984); and Riggs (1988, 1993) are notable exceptions; Lijphart (1992) sums this scholarship up neatly in an edited collection.

21. In his seminal work, Juan Linz (1990; expanded, and with Valenzuela 1994) warned of the "perils" of presidentialism, namely, that the fixed term of office and winner-take-all elections of these regimes contribute to rigidity in political processes, inadequate representation for society, dual bases of authority, and fragmentation of the party system. Also weighing in on the dangers of presidentialism are Stepan and Skach (1993). Presidential government is not without its supporters. Horowitz (1990) argued that Linz's study inadequately represented presidential democracy; parliamentarianism was the "insurgent villain" behind failed democracies, resurgent authoritarianism, and unstable polities in postcolonial Africa and Asia. Others have noted that the relationship between stable democracy and parliamentarianism is not as cut and dry as Linz claims (O'Donnell 1995; Shugart and Carey 1992).

22. In Latin America, for example, see Skidmore (1993).

23. They further posit that the rigidity of the electoral schedule (fixed term of office) does not allow for the removal of a failed president; see McClintock (1994: 286). Mainwaring (1990), looking specifically at Latin American presidencies, comes to similar conclusions about the deleterious effects of presidential government on multiparty systems.

24. Lijphart (1992) provides a succinct synthesis of the debate over what "type" of regime the French Fifth Republic is (parliamentary, presidential, semipresidential, etc.). The prevailing wisdom, particularly after the "cohabitations" of 1986–1988 and 1993–1995 (and currently in the midst of the third), is that the French system is none of these—nor is it a synthesis. It is, rather, an alternation, dependent on whether the president enjoys a parliamentary majority. (The Weimar Republic, Finland, and Portugal fit the definition of "true" semipresidential systems.)

25. Nor is the term of the National Assembly, which sits for five years unless dissolved by the president.

26. See Pierce (1995: 3–16), for a good summary of the institutional framework (constitutions, party and electoral systems, etc.) of both the French and U.S. presidencies.

27. Cole (1993: 50), provides a nice summary of the French party literature.

28. The Le Pen phenomenon is a good example of increased personalization in presidential politics.

REFERENCES

Aldrich, John H. 1987. "Methods and Actors: The Relationship of Processes to Candidates." In *Presidential Selection*, ed. Alexander Heard and Michael Nelson. Durham, NC: Duke University Press.

———. 1993. "Presidential Selection." In *Researching the Presidency: Vital Questions, New Approaches*, ed. George C. Edwards III, John H. Kessel, and Bert A. Rockman. Pittsburgh: University of Pittsburgh Press.

Alexander, Herbert E. 1992. *Financing Politics: Money, Elections, and Political Reform*, 4th ed. Washington, DC: CQ Press.

——— and Anthony Corrado. 1995. *Financing the 1992 Election*. Armonk, NY: M. E. Sharpe.

Arendt, Hannah. 1951. *The Origins of Totalitarianism*. New York: Harcourt, Brace.

Arterton, F. Christopher. 1993. "Campaign '92: Strategies and Tactics of the Candidates." In *The Elections of 1992: Reports and Interpretations*, ed. Gerald M. Pomper. Chatham, NJ: Chatham House.

Asher, Herb. 1987. "The Three Campaigns for President." In *Presidential Selection*, ed. Alexander Heard and Michael Nelson. Durham, NC: Duke University Press.

Barber, James David. 1977. *The Presidential Character: Predicting Performance in the White House*, 2nd ed. Englewood Cliffs, NJ: Prentice-Hall.

Beck, Paul Allen and Frank J. Sorauf. 1992. *Party Politics in America*, 7th ed. New York: HarperCollins.

Broder, David S. 1971. *The Party's Over: The Failure of Politics in America*. New York: Harper & Row.

Bryce, James. 1893. *The American Commonwealth*. Vol. 2. New York: Macmillan.

Campbell, Colin, S. J. 1983. *Governments under Stress: Political Executives and Key Bureaucrats in Washington, London, and Ottawa*. Toronto: University of Toronto Press.

———. 1993. "Political Executives and Their Officials." In *Political Science: The State of the Discipline II*, ed. Ada W. Finifter. Washington, DC: APSA.

——— and B. Guy Peters, eds. 1988. *Organizing Governance, Governing Organizations*. Pittsburgh: University of Pittsburgh Press.

——— and Margaret Jane Wyszomirski, eds. 1991. *Executive Leadership in Anglo-American Systems*. Pittsburgh: University of Pittsburgh Press.

Ceaser, James W. 1979. *Presidential Selection: Theory and Development*. Princeton: Princeton University Press.

———. 1990. "Political Parties—Declining, Stabilizing, or Resurging?" In *The New American Political System*, ed. Anthony King, 2nd ed. Washington, DC: American Enterprise Institute.

Cole, Alistair. 1993. "The Presidential Party and the Fifth Republic." *West European Politics* 16(2): 49–66.

Conway, M. Margaret and Joanne Connor Greene. 1995. "Political Action Committees and the Political Process in the 1990s." In *Interest Group Politics*, ed. Allan J. Cigler and Burdett A. Loomis, 4th ed. Washington, DC: CQ Press.

Corrado, Anthony. 1997. "Financing the 1996 Elections." In *The Election of 1996*, ed. Gerald M. Pomper. Chatham, NJ: Chatham House.

Dalton, Russell J. 1996. *Citizen Politics: Public Opinion and Political Parties in Advanced Industrial Democracies*, 2nd ed. Chatham, NJ: Chatham House.

Denton, Robert E., Jr. and Mary E. Stuckey. 1994. "A Communication Model of Presidential Campaigns: A 1992 Overview." In *The 1992 Presidential Campaign: A Communication Perspective*, ed. Robert E. Denton, Jr. Westport, CT: Praeger.

Dinkin, Robert J. 1989. *Campaigning in America: A History of Election Practices*. Westport, CT: Greenwood Press.

Duverger, Maurice. 1984. "Presidential Elections and the Party System in Europe." In *Political Parties and the Modern State*, ed. Richard L. McCormick. New Brunswick, NJ: Rutgers University.

Easter, Gerald. 1997. "Preference for Presidentialism: Postcommunist Regime Change in Russia and the NIS." *World Politics* 49: 184–211.

Fowler, Linda L. and Robert D. McClure. 1989. *Political Ambition: Who Decides to Run for Congress*. New Haven, CT: Yale University.

Frantzich, Stephen E. 1989. *Political Parties in the Technological Age*. New York: Longman.

Gaffney, John. 1989. "Introduction: Presidentialism and the Fifth Republic." In *The French Presidential Elections of 1988: Ideology and Leadership in Contemporary France*, ed. John Gaffney. Aldershot, UK: Dartmouth.

Hayward, Susan. 1989. "Television and the Presidential Elections April–May 1988." In *The French Presidential Elections of 1988: Ideology and Leadership in Contemporary France*, ed. John Gaffney. Aldershot, UK: Dartmouth.

Heard, Alexander and Michael Nelson. 1987. "Change and Stability in Choosing Presidents." In *Presidential Selection*, ed. Alexander Heard and Michael Nelson. Durham, NC: Duke University Press.

Heclo, Hugh. 1973. "Presidential and Prime Ministerial Selection." In *Perspectives on Presidential Selection*, ed. Donald R. Matthews. Washington, DC: Brookings Institution.

Herrnson, Paul S. 1988. *Party Campaigning in the 1980s*. Cambridge, MA: Harvard University Press.

Hess, Stephen. 1988. *The Presidential Campaign*, 3rd ed. Washington, DC: Brookings Institution.

Horowitz, Donald L. 1990. "Comparing Democratic Systems." *Journal of Democracy* 1: 73–79.

Humphreys, Peter J. 1996. *Mass Media and Media Policy in Western Europe*. Manchester, UK: Manchester University.

Huntington, Samuel. 1991. *The Third Wave: Democratization in the Late Twentieth Century*. Norman, OK: University of Oklahoma.

Jones, Charles O. 1994. *The Presidency in a Separated System*. Washington, DC: Brookings Institution.

———. 1996. "The Clinton Administration in the Separated System: A Presidency at Risk." *Extensions: A Journal of the Carl Albert Congressional Research and Studies Center* (Spring): 3–9.

Kamarck, Elaine Ciulla and Kenneth M Goldstein. 1994. "The Rules Do Matter: Postreform Presidential Nominating Politics." In *The Parties Respond*, 2nd ed., ed. L. Sandy Maisel. Boulder, CO: Westview Press.

Kaminsky, Elijah Ben-Zion. 1973. "The Selection of French Presidents." In *Perspectives on Presidential Selection*, ed. Donald R. Mathews. Washington, DC: Brookings Institution.

Kayden, Xandra and Eddie Mahe, Jr. 1985. *The Party Goes On*. New York: Basic Books.

Kernell, Samuel. 1993. *Going Public: New Strategies of Presidential Leadership*, 2nd ed. Washington, DC: CQ Press.

Kessel, John H. 1992. *Presidential Campaign Politics*, 4th ed. Pacific Grove, CA: Brooks/Cole.

King, Anthony. 1975. "Executives." In *Handboook of Political Science*, Vol. 5, ed. Fred I. Greenstein and Nelson W. Polsby. Reading, MA: Addison-Wesley.

———. 1993. "Foundations of Power." In *Researching the Presidency: Vital Questions, New Approaches*, ed. George C. Edwards III, John H. Kessel, and Bert A. Rockman. Pittsburgh: University of Pittsburgh Press.

———. 1997. *Running Scared: Why America's Politicians Campaign Too Much and Govern Too Little*. New York: Martin Kessler Books.

Klingemann, Hans-Dieter, Richard I. Hofferbert and Ian Budge. 1994. *Parties, Policies, and Democracy*. Boulder, CO: Westview Press.

Kornhauser, William. 1959. *The Politics of Mass Society*. Glencoe, IL: Free Press.

Kramer, Michael. 1996. "Rescuing Boris." *Time*, July 15, pp. 28–37.

Lijphart, Arend, ed. 1992. *Parliamentary Versus Presidential Government*. Oxford, UK: Oxford University.

Linz, Juan. 1990. "The Perils of Presidentialism." *Journal of Democracy* 1: 51–69.

———, and Arturo Valenzuela. 1994. *The Failure of Presidential Democracy*. Vols. 1 and 2. Baltimore, MD: Johns Hopkins University Press.

Lowi, Theodore J. 1985. *The Personal President: Power Invested, Promise Unfulfilled*. Ithaca, NY and London: Cornell University Press.

Luntz, Frank I. 1988. *Candidates, Consultants, and Campaigns*. Oxford: Basil Blackwell.

Machin, H. and V. Wright. 1982. "Why Mitterrand Won: The French Presidential Elections of April–May 1981." *West European Politics* 5(1).

Mackenzie, G. Calvin. 1994. "Partisan Leadership Through Presidential Appointments." In *The Parties Respond*, 2nd ed., ed. L. Sandy Maisel. Boulder, CO: Westview Press.

Macridis, Roy C. 1968. "Political Executive." In *International Encyclopedia of the Social Sciences*, ed. David L. Sills. New York: Macmillan.

———. 1975. *French Politics in Transition*. Cambridge, MA: Winthrop. Chapter 4, "The Presidential Election," May 5–19, pp. 96–128.

Mainwaring, Scott. 1990. "Presidentialism in Latin America." *Latin American Research Review* 25: 157–79.

——— and Timothy R. Scully. 1995. "Introduction: Party Systems in Latin America." In *Building Democratic Institutions: Party Systems in Latin America*, ed. Scott Mainwaring and Timothy R. Scully. Stanford, CA: Stanford University Press.

March, James G. and Johan P. Olsen. 1984. "The New Institutionalism: Organizational Factors in Political Life." *American Political Science Review* 78: 734–49.

Matthews, Donald R. 1973. "Introduction." In *Perspectives on Presidential Selection* ed. Donald R. Matthews. Washington, DC: Brookings Institution.

McClintock, Cynthia. 1994. "Presidents, Messiahs, and Constitutional Breakdowns in Peru." In *The Failure of Presidential Democracy*, Vol. 2, ed. Juan J. Linz and Arturo Valenzuela. Baltimore, MD: Johns Hopkins University Press.

Meynaud, Jean. 1958. "The Executive in the Modern State." *UNESCO: International Social Sciences Bulletin* 10: 171–99.

Milkis, Sidney M. 1993. *The Presidency and Political Parties: The Transformation of the American Party System Since the New Deal*. Oxford, UK: Oxford University Press.

Nelson, Michael. 1982. "Sentimental Science: Recent Essays on the Politics of Presidential Selection." *Congress and the Presidency* 9: 99–106.

Neustadt, Richard E. 1990. *Presidential Power and the Modern Presidents: The Politics of Leadership from Roosevelt to Reagan*. New York: Free Press.

Niemi, Richard G. and Harold W. Stanley. 1994. *Vital Statistics on American Politics*, 4th ed. Washington, DC: CQ Press.

O'Donnell, Guillermo. 1995. "Delegative Democracy." *Journal of Democracy* 5(1): 55–69.

Orttung, Robert W. 1996. "Rejecting Communists, Voters Return Yeltsin to Office." *Transition* 2(15): 6–7.

Patterson, Thomas E. 1994. *Out of Order*. New York: Vintage Books.

Pierce, Roy. 1995. *Choosing the Chief: Presidential Elections in France and the United States*. Ann Arbor: University of Michigan Press.

Plowden, William, ed. 1987. *Advising the Rulers*. New York: Basil Blackwell.

Polsby, Nelson W. 1983. *Consequences of Party Reform*. Oxford, UK: Oxford University Press.

——— and Aaron Wildavsky. 1996. *Presidential Elections: Strategies and Structures in American Politics*, 9th ed. Chatham, NJ: Chatham House.

Pomper, Gerald M. and Susan S. Lederman. 1980. *Elections in America: Control and Influence in Democratic Politics*, 2nd ed. New York: Longman.

Powell, G. Bingham. 1982. *Contemporary Democracies: Participation, Stability, and Violence*. Cambridge, MA: Harvard University Press.

Ranney, Austin. 1978. "The Political Parties: Reform and Decline." In *The New American Political System*, ed. Anthony King. Washington, DC: American Enterprise Institute.

Raymond, Gino. 1994. "The Decline of the Established Parties." In *France During the Socialist Years*, ed. Gino Raymond. Brookfield, VT: Dartmouth.

Remnick, David. 1996. "The War for the Kremlin." *New Yorker*, July 22, pp. 40–57.

Riggs, Fred. 1988. "The Survival of Presidentialism in America: Para-constitutional Practices." *International Political Science Review* 9(4): 247–78.

———. 1993. "Fragility of the Third World's Regimes." *International Social Science Journal* 45(2): 199–244.

Rockman, Bert A. 1986. "Presidential Studies: The One, the Few, and the Many." In *Political Science: The Science of Politics*, ed. Herbert F. Weisberg. New York: Agathon.

———. 1995. "The American Presidency in Comparative Perspective: Systems, Situations, and Leaders." In *The Presidency and the Political System*, ed. Michael Nelson. Washington, DC: CQ Press.

Rose, Richard. 1980. "Governments and Sub-Governments: A European Perspective on Washington." In *Presidents and Prime Ministers*, ed. Richard Rose and Ezra N. Suleiman. Washington, DC: American Enterprise Institute.

———. 1987. "Learning to Govern or Learning to Campaign?" In *Presidential Selec-*

tion, ed. Alexander Heard and Michael Nelson. Durham, NC: Duke University Press.

Rosenstone, Steven J. and John Mark Hansen. 1993. *Mobilization, Participation, and Democracy in America*. New York: Macmillan.

Sabato, Larry J. 1981. *The Rise of Political Consultants: New Ways of Winning Elections*. New York: Basic Books.

————. 1988. *The Parties Just Begun: Shaping Political Parties for America's Future*. Boston: Little, Brown.

————, ed. 1989. *Campaigns and Elections: A Reader in Modern American Politics*. Glenview, IL: Scott, Foresman.

Safran, William. 1997. *The French Polity*, 4th ed. New York: Longman.

Sartori, Giovanni. 1976. *Parties and Party Systems: A Framework for Analysis*. Cambridge: Cambridge University Press.

Schattschneider, E. E. 1942. *Party Government*. New York: Farrar & Rinehart.

Seligman, Lester G. and Cary R. Covington. 1989. *The Coalitional Presidency*. Chicago: Dorsey.

Shea, Daniel M. 1996. *Campaign Craft: The Strategies, Tactics, and Art of Political Campaign Management*. Westport, CT: Praeger.

Shugart, Matthew S. and John M. Carey. 1992. *Presidents and Assemblies: Constitutional Design and Electoral Dynamics*. Cambridge: Cambridge University Press.

Simeon, James C. 1991. "Prime Minister's Office and White House Office: Political Administration in Canada and the United States." *Presidential Studies Quarterly* 21: 559–80.

Skidmore, Thomas E., ed. 1993. *Television, Politics, and the Transition to Democracy in Latin America*. Washington, DC: Woodrow Wilson Center.

Sorauf, Frank J. 1988. *Money in American Elections*. Glenview, IL: Scott, Foresman/ Little, Brown College Division.

Stepan, Alfred and Cindy Skach. 1993. "Constitutional Frameworks and Democratic Consolidation: Parliamentarianism and Presidentialism." *World Politics* 46: 1–22.

Suleiman, Ezra N. 1980. "Presidential Government in France." In *Presidents and Prime Ministers*, ed. Richard Rose and Ezra N. Suleiman. Washington, DC: American Enterprise Institute.

Szarka, Joseph. 1996. "The Winning of the 1995 French Presidential Election." *West European Politics* 19(1): 151–67.

Thurber, James A. and Candice J. Nelson. 1995. *Campaigns and Elections American Style*. Boulder, CO: Westview Press.

Toinet, Marie-France. 1988. "The Elections of 1981: Background and Legal Setting." In *France at the Polls, 1981 and 1986: Three National Elections*, ed. Howard R. Penniman. Durham, NC: Duke University Press.

Troy, Gil. 1996. *See How They Ran: The Changing Role of the Presidential Candidate*. Revised and Expanded Edition. Cambridge, MA: Harvard University Press.

Waldo, Dwight. 1975. "Political Science: Tradition, Discipline, Profession, Science, Enterprise," In *Handbook of Political Science*, Vol. 1. *Political Science: Scope and Theory*, ed. Fred I. Greenstein and Nelson W. Polsby. Reading, MA: Addison-Wesley.

Ware, Alan. 1996. *Political Parties and Party Systems*. Oxford: Oxford University Press.

Wattenberg, Martin P. 1991. *The Rise of Candidate-centered Politics: Presidential Elections of the 1980s*. Cambridge, MA: Harvard University Press.

Wayne, Stephen J. 1997. *The Road to the White House: The Politics of Presidential Elections*. New York: St. Martin's Press.

Whitney, Craig R. 1997. "Do Francs and Yen Corrupt? Absolutely." *New York Times*, March 4, Section 4, pp. 1, 5.

Part II

New Insights on Power and Policy

Chapter 5

The Overlooked Relevance of the Pardon Power

MARK MORRIS

The 1996 presidential campaign brought the executive pardon power into the public spotlight once again. Two examples demonstrate this point. First, Republican nominee Bob Dole challenged President Clinton to issue a public pledge that he would not pardon any of the individuals associated with the Whitewater investment scandal. Unlike President Bush who was driven to make the "read my lips" pledge, President Clinton did not surrender to election-year challenges and issue a no pardon pledge. Second, Susan McDougal, one of the individuals convicted and sentenced for crimes related to the Whitewater partnership, proclaimed that she would not accept a pardon if offered by President Clinton. Clearly Ms. McDougal was unaware that the issuance of a presidential pardon is not subject to the recipient's acceptance or declination; the pardon is an executive action over which the president has total authority.

Both of these examples demonstrate the general lack of understanding of presidential pardon power. The potential use of pardon power has become a topic in newspapers, on talk radio, and on television news shows. Proponents defend the pardon as a legitimate use of presidential power, whereas opponents link the use of the pardon to conspiracy and self-protection from unsavory or even illegal activities of the past. It appears that the pardon has been inextricably linked with coverup and political self-preservation. President Ford's pardon of President Nixon in 1974 may have forged this initial connection in the minds of many. President Bush's 1992 Christmas Eve pardon of six individuals allegedly linked to the Iran-Contra affair further solidified this nexus between conspiratorial coverup and a timely presidential pardon.

Despite two high-profile pardons issued by Presidents Ford and Bush, only limited scholarly interest has been shown in this unique and increasingly controversial presidential power. The apparent lack of interest in the executive pardon creates something of a void within presidential studies. For example, many are unfamiliar with the Office of the Pardon Attorney in the Department of Justice which administers the pardon process, or would be surprised to learn that President Nixon himself granted 863 pardons and another 63 commutations during his tenure as president (Office of the Pardon Attorney 1996). This chapter seeks to stimulate academic interest in this area by providing the reader with a better understanding of presidential pardon power, its evolution, use, and future. The pardon power, it is argued, does have relevance in presidential research. The power to pardon is relevant because of its all but absolute nature. Chief Justice William Howard Taft wrote that only impeachment can constrain presidential pardon power (*Ex parte Grossman* 1924). No other executive power is as unrestrained as the power to pardon. The absolute nature of the pardon power will be demonstrated in this chapter through a review of the historical and judicial record.

The historical record helps identify the scope of presidential pardon power, but it does not tell the entire story. The second section of this chapter presents an overview of the administrative elements of presidential pardon power. The frequency of approved pardon actions is somewhat surprising and is included in this section. The final section of the chapter offers a number of areas for future research that may help to clarify and expand our understanding of the pardon power. Finally, we turn to one particular area of interest, the trend toward disuse of the pardon, as an example of how this type of research might be structured.

EVOLUTION AND DEVELOPMENT

For over two hundred years, presidential power has evolved and taken the shape we now recognize as the modern presidency. A combination of constitutional provision, individual will, political precedent, and judicial determination have all played roles in the development and evolution of the presidency. Over time, the power to pardon has also been influenced by these same factors. Judicial review has played an especially important role in defining presidential pardon power as it is now understood. Rather than limiting pardon power, judicial challenges have resulted in the further solidification of the absolute nature of the pardon power. A brief review of the history of pardons is useful in developing a general understanding of its place in the American political system.

Historical Foundations

The power to pardon has a long and multifarious history. Pardons are part of all cultures and are included in the constitutions of all countries except China (Moore 1989: 7). "Retributive justice and pardon were bound together in the oldest known legal code—the Code of Hammurabi, developed by the Babylonians around the eighteenth century B.C." (Moore 1989: 15). Over its long history, the power to pardon has been used to achieve both charitable and dubious ends. The inconsistent use of pardons was due in large part to the discretion available to the grantors. However, inconsistencies and abuses did not entirely preclude the usefulness of pardon powers. History provides a record of the evolution of primitive legal systems and the important role of pardons within these systems. The specific origins of the U.S. legal system and presidential pardon power are rooted in the English common law heritage.

The English monarchy's power to pardon first appeared in law in the seventh century (Moore 1989: 17). However, it was not a power exclusively held by the king. Earls, church officials, and local leaders all claimed the right to and exercised the power to pardon. Generally, if an individual had the power to mete out punishment, he also possessed the power to pardon. This diffuse structure of justice and retribution created conflicts between those who had power and influence. The power to pardon could be a useful political tool for one looking to consolidate a position of authority. Timely demonstrations of mercy, whether or not sincere, were effective means of solidifying public acceptance of one's authority. In 1536 the parliament put an end to multiple pardon authorities by placing the power to pardon exclusively with the king (Humbert 1941: 10). We should not read the historical record as if the pardon were simply a tool of self-serving and devious politicians. The pardon did serve important purposes.

Those of us familiar with the modern-day judicial system would not recognize the foundations from which the power to pardon arose. The days of an eye-for-an-eye have long since been replaced—to the chagrin of some—by parole, good behavior reductions in sentences, and outplacement rehabilitation. Without these modern-day methods, the pardon became a rudimentary legal system's tempering mechanism. The pardon provided a mechanism to balance the harshness of inchoate legal systems lacking clarity and experience. Emerging legal systems lacked "distinctions between manslaughter and murder . . . intentional and accidental harms . . . excuses or justifications" (Humbert 1941: 18). Thus, a legal system was allowed to develop and evolve over time with the knowledge that seemingly inappropriate "justice" could be corrected with an executive pardon. In this fashion, the common law tradition began its slow but steady case-by-case development.

As the powers of the English monarchy consolidated, so too were the powers to pardon strengthened. The king found the pardon to be a particularly useful tool in advancing his consolidation of power. The record here provides fewer examples of mercy and more numerous examples of abuse of the pardon power. Prior to the establishment of specific punishments for specific crimes, common law justice often settled disputes with some form of financial compensation. An offender could provide a monetary settlement to the victim (or the victim's family) as punishment for an offense. The monarchy seized on this financial opportunity and began to offer pardons for a price. The pardon, when purchased in this fashion, became a commodity for those who had the financial wherewithal to pay the necessary expense. Not only did the pardon provide the king with additional income, but it also generated a pool of individuals beholden to him. Edward I (1239–1307) was the first English king to use the pardon to entice recruitment into the military (Hurnard 1969). The implications of the recruitment of criminals into military service (discipline and loyalty were somewhat suspect) seemed to elude Edward I, but it was a highly creative use of his pardon powers. The pardon was also used to satisfy the growing demands for labor throughout the English colonies. "It is difficult to determine how many felons were sent to the New World; estimates vary between 15,000 and 100,000" (Moore 1989: 19). Regardless of the exact number, a significant number of criminals found their way to a new life in the colonies by way of an opportunistic pardon.

These examples demonstrate the less merciful and more practical side of the king's pardon. In this light, we can view the pardon as an effective political tool. However, we should not minimize or trivialize the king's use of a pardon to mitigate harsh or undeserved penalties. Pardons of this nature are more consistent with the current-day understanding of the use of the pardon power. The historical record of the king's pardon laid a solid foundation from which the American founders could draw on when designing their own system of government. As one historian of the monarchy in the Middle Ages put it, "The king's discretion to pardon was seen from the earliest times as a useful means of avoiding inequity and of reconciling public opinion to legislation extending such punishment" (Hurnard 1969: 327).

Constitutional Provision

The American Revolution created an independent nation but one steeped in the English common law tradition. The challenge for the American revolutionaries was to establish their own rules of governance and the distribution of political power. The framework to accomplish this objective was created at the Constitutional Convention held in 1787. Out of the Philadelphia convention emerged a constitution that divided power among the newly created branches of the U.S. federal system. One of the many powers debated at the convention was the power to pardon. The debate surrounding pardon powers provides a limited, albeit unsatisfactory, insight into the "original intent" of executive pardon power. The pardon debate centered on these issues: Should the power to pardon be formally established? If so, where should the power to pardon be located, and what checks, if any, should be included?

Those who gathered in Philadelphia to debate a new constitution included many of the key political leaders of the time. Most of their state constitutions included some provisions for executive pardoning power; thus, pardoning was a familiar concept to all participants. The power of state executives to pardon was often limited, but it was clearly recognized as a legitimate governmental power. For reasons unknown, the original constitutional plans submitted for debate, the Virginia and New Jersey plans, did not include provisions for pardoning power. However, both of the later plans submitted by Charles Pinckney and Alexander Hamilton included language adopting some form of executive pardoning power. John Rutledge added a clause to the Virginia plan granting pardon power to the executive, and his language established the framework for the final constitutional clause (Humbert 1941). From this point forward, the debate centered not on whether or not to include the power to pardon in the Constitution, but rather on what was to be the scope of the power.

The specific language of the power to pardon underwent several changes before reaching its final form. At issue were two key elements: where was the power to be vested; and when could a pardon be issued? The first attempt to modify the Rutledge language added a requirement for Senate consent. Hamilton expressed his preference for an executive pardon power in *The Federalist*, Number 74, and merits quoting at length:

The criminal code of every country partakes so much of necessary severity, that without an easy access to exceptions in favor of unfortunate guilt, justice would wear a countenance too sanguinary and cruel. . . . It may be inferred that a single man would be most ready to attend to the force of those motives which might plead for a mitigation of the rigor of the law, and least apt to yield to considerations which were calculated to shelter a fit object of its vengeance. The reflection that the fate of a fellow-creature depended on his *sole fiat* would naturally inspire scrupulousness and caution. It is not to be doubted, that a single man of prudence and good sense is better fitted, in delicate conjunctures, to balance the motives which may plead for and against the remission of the punishment, than any numerous body whatever.

Hamilton questioned the ability of a legislative body to determine the merits of a pardon under publicly charged circumstances. A single executive, Hamilton argued, is less likely to succumb to these public pressures. He went on to argue the most compelling aspect of executive pardon power, timeliness. "In seasons of insurrection or rebellion, there are often *critical moments, when a well-timed offer of pardon to the insurgents or rebels may restore the tranquillity of the commonwealth*" (Hamilton 1961). President Ford would use remarkably similar language in 1974 when he pardoned Richard Nixon.

A second matter was debated prior to finalizing the constitutional pardon provision: When could a pardon be granted? Luther Martin suggested that the phrase "after conviction" be included in the constitutional clause. Concerned proponents of Martin's position argued that the president might use pardon powers inappropriately "to shield his own confederates in case of an abortive attempt to subvert the Constitution, or to stop investigations and, as a consequence, to avoid detection" (Humbert 1941: 18). James Wilson countered Martin and others by arguing that a pardon can be a useful device when attempting to obtain incriminating testimony from accomplices (Humbert 1941). Aptly persuaded, Martin withdrew his motion, and no specific timing language was included. This issue of timing would resurface with both the pardon of President Nixon and the Iran-Contra related pardons granted by President Bush.

The Constitution of the United States, including the provision for executive pardon power, was ratified in 1788. Article II, Section 2, states in part, ''The President . . . shall have Power to grant Reprieves and Pardons for Offenses against the United States, except in Cases of Impeachment.'' The constitutional framers, not without debate, ultimately found that the power to pardon should reside exclusively with the executive. As with other provisions of the Constitution, the framers included a general concept and excluded definitional and usage details. The constitutional debate does suggest that mercy may have been an element of the original intent of the pardon power. However, the major areas of contention—where will the power reside, requiring Senate consent, issue before or after conviction—suggest a greater concern with functionality. The new government needed powers that were effective and operable. The framers were practical men designing a practical government, and the pardon power was not an exception to this objective (Moore 1989).

Judicial Influence

The courts have played a critical role in U.S. policy development since Chief Justice Marshall penned the concept of ''judicial review'' in the landmark case Marbury v. Madison in 1803. Under the doctrine of judicial review, the courts are the final arbiters of constitutional interpretation. The pardon power has been subjected to judicial review, scrutiny, and interpretation. A review of judicial decisions is helpful in assessing the evolution of presidential pardon power in the United States. These cases were selected because of their important precedential value. They do not constitute the entire record of judicial review of executive pardon power. The research for this chapter uncovered fourteen cases that relate to pardon or amnesty power. Some of these cases have only a tangential relationship to pardon power. For example, Brown v. Walker (1896) upheld congressional immunity, which can be viewed as a form of amnesty. However, the following five cases establish the judicial foundation for today's presidential pardon powers.

United States v. Wilson (1833). The first significant challenge to presidential pardon power occurred in 1833. George Wilson was charged with numerous counts of U.S. mail robbery. For political reasons, President Andrew Jackson pardoned Wilson of these crimes. Wilson was then charged with a second set of related charges to which he pleaded not guilty. Wilson rejected the pardon in this second instance under the popular conception that acceptance of a pardon inferred guilt (Moore 1989). Wilson's challenge to the presidential pardon was heard by the Supreme Court in United States v. Wilson (1833). The common law principle of precedent played a significant role in the Court's decision. Using the historical judicial record to explicate prior uses and traditions related to the pardon power, Chief Justice Marshall wrote the Court's opinion from which two important concepts emerged. First, the Court ruled that a recipient could reject a pardon. Marshall wrote, ''A pardon is a deed, to the validity of which delivery is essential, and delivery is not complete without acceptance" (*United States v. Wilson* 1833). This logic limited the presidential pardon power and potentially diminished its scope. A second important—albeit unrelated—principle to emerge from this case was the notion of grace. Marshall wrote, "A pardon is an act of grace, proceeding from the power intrusted [*sic*] with the execution of the laws" (*U.S. v. Wilson 1833*). Within this opinion, Marshall firmly lodged the pardon power in the traditions of English common law from which the U.S. judicial system had evolved.

Ex parte Wells (1855). A second important challenge to presidential pardon power occurred in 1855. William Wells was convicted of murder and given a sentence of death. President Fillmore granted Wells a conditional pardon that commuted his death sentence to life in prison. Wells argued that the president could grant only full pardons and demanded to be released. In *Ex parte Wells* (1855), the Supreme Court upheld the president's power to grant conditional pardons. Justice James Moore Wayne wrote the opinion and reiterated the pardon as "a work of mercy." Like Chief Justice Marshall in *U.S. v. Wilson*, Justice Wayne relied on traditional uses and accepted practices associated with the use of pardon power. He wrote: "The real language of the Constitution is general; that is, common to the class of pardons, or extending the power to pardon, to all kinds of pardons known in the law as. . . . In this view of the Constitution, by giving to its words their proper meaning, the power to pardon conditionally is not one of inference at all, but one conferred in terms" (*Ex parte Wells* 1855). Thus presidential pardon power was now judicially broadened to include conditional pardons.

Ex parte Garland (1867). An 1867 legal dispute established the heretofore unsettled issue of the timing of a presidential pardon. A. H. Garland had been a member of the Congress of the Confederate States. The post–Civil War U.S. Congress had adopted a provision requiring all lawyers who were to practice before federal courts to swear to an oath that they had never taken up arms against the United States. Garland wanted to practice law but could not legally swear to this oath. President Johnson granted Garland a conditional pardon that would waive the oath requirement for offenses he may have committed during the Civil War. The Supreme Court heard the case of *Ex parte Garland* (1867). The Court found that Garland need not violate the oath requirement prior to the granting of the pardon. Thus the Court ruled that President Johnson had issued a valid pardon. "[The pardoning power] extends to every offense known to the law, and may be exercised at any time after its commission, either before legal proceedings are taken, or during their pendency, or after conviction and judgment" (Moore 1989: 80). This case weakened the historical connection between guilt and pardon since Garland was not required to violate the law prior to receipt of his pardon. Thus, establishing guilt could not be an assumed prerequisite for a presidential pardon. And acceptance of a pardon might *infer* potential guilt but no longer guaranteed a violation had occurred. More than a hundred years later, this would be a key element in President Nixon's pardon.

Burdick v. United States (1915). Shortly after the turn of the century, the Court began to move away from the pardon as grace doctrine. George Burdick was a *New York Tribune* city editor who refused to answer grand jury questions regarding a customs fraud investigation. Rather than reveal his sources, Burdick cited his right to avoid self-incrimination. President Wilson offered Burdick a full pardon in an attempt to get him to testify. Burdick refused the pardon and refused to testify. The Supreme Court, relying heavily on *U.S. v. Wilson*, reaffirmed the right of an individual to reject a presidential pardon. However, in reaffirming the *Wilson* decision, the Court indicated, "Indeed, the grace of a pardon, though good its intention, may be only in pretense" (*Burdick v. United States* 1915). This opened the door for the Court to move away from the pardon as grace tradition and view the pardon in broader administrative terms. In what seemed to be a minor point at the time, Justice McKenna considered the relationship between guilt and the granting of a presidential pardon. In a comparison of legislative immunity and a pardon, Justice McKenna wrote in the Court's opinion, "The latter carries an imputation of guilt; acceptance a confession of it. The former has no such imputation or confession" (*Burdick v. United States* 1915). The high-profile pardons of Richard Nixon and Caspar Weinberger were both couched in terms that vigorously rejected this notion of guilt by acceptance.

Biddle v. Perovich (1927). One last case completes this review of judicial rulings affecting presidential pardon power. *Biddle v. Perovich* (1927) overturned *U.S. v. Wilson*. Perovich was sentenced to death following his conviction for murder. President Taft commuted Perovich's sentence from death to life in prison. Perovich was transferred from a jail to a penitentiary to serve out his sentence. Perovich argued that he had rejected the pardon and that the transfer had been effected without his approval. He demanded a writ of habeas corpus be issued. Justice Holmes wrote the opinion for the Court. First, the Court abandoned the grace doctrine: "A pardon in our days is not a private act of grace from an individual happening to possess power. It is a part of the constitutional scheme. When granted, it is the determination of the ultimate authority that the public welfare will be better served by inflicting less than what the judgment fixed" (*Biddle v. Perovich* 1927).

The Court then abandoned the recipient's right to reject a pardon. Referring to Perovich's commutation, Holmes wrote: "The considerations that led to the modification had nothing to do with his will" (*Biddle v. Perovich* 1915, 487). *Biddle v. Perovich* remains the key precedent with respect to the use of the presidential pardon power today.

The process of judicial review further defined and enlarged presidential pardon power. The president can now issue conditional or full pardons. A presidential pardon may be issued before, during, or after criminal or civil conviction. In fact, no specific charges need be filed prior to the issuance of a pardon. The recipient of a pardon has no say in whether the pardon will be accepted or declined. Thus, pardon power has grown to be virtually absolute. This has led to interesting speculations regarding the potential use of presidential pardon power. One hypothetical example had President Nixon pardoning himself prior to his resignation (Haig 1992). More recent speculation has President Clinton pardoning his wife, Hillary Rodham Clinton, should she be indicted for crimes related to her involvement in the Whitewater partnership. It is almost a certainty that the Supreme Court would have been asked to rule had President Nixon in fact pardoned himself. In the absence of a case for judicial review, the potential of self-pardon remains only fodder for hypothetical speculation. President Clinton might face a similar Supreme Court challenge should he pardon his wife. However, judicial rulings to date seem to indicate a constitutional basis for this highly unusual course of action. Of course, the political implications of such a choice are another matter altogether.

ADMINISTRATION OF PARDONS

The historical record presented here is both interesting and informative. Yet it tells us little about the actual use of presidential pardon power. The following presents some of the basic administrative aspects of pardon power as well as the frequency of its use since 1900.

Classification

Executives have not eschewed the judicious use of their power to issue pardons. As previously noted, prior to receiving the most widely discussed pardon in U.S. history, President Nixon himself granted 863 pardons during his tenure as president. All levels of government define the limits of the pardon powers available to their respective executives. From city mayors granting amnesty to parking violators, to a president granting a pardon to a former president, the power to pardon covers a wide range of offenses. And at all levels of government, the overwhelming majority of pardons are issued outside the spotlight with little public fanfare. Most executives probably prefer it that way. The vast majority of pardons go unnoticed because there are numerous types and degrees of pardon power. Humbert identifies ten types of clemency or pardon available to executives: full pardon, pardon to terminate sentence and restore civil rights, pardon to restore civil rights, conditional pardon, amnesty, amnesty on condition, reprieve, commutation, commutation on condition, and remission of fines and forfeitures (Humbert 1941: 22).

The first four types listed here are typically used to remedy acts by individuals against ordinary laws. For example, an executive may grant a full pardon to an individual thought to have been wrongly convicted and thus remedy an "unjust" punishment. Amnesties are usually granted to groups, rather than individuals, who have committed crimes against the state or the sovereign. The general amnesties granted following the Civil War and the Vietnam War serve as good examples. The last four types of the pardon power are used to modify punishment. A reprieve simply delays the administration of punishment or court sanctions and does not affect the court's final decision. It may, however, provide additional time for an individual to influence the court's final decision. Commutations reduce specific punishments. A common commutation is the reduction of a death penalty sentence to life in prison. Remissions are a return of fines or properties taken as part of a judicial decision. In large part, the evolution of the judicial and parole systems has reduced the need for executive involvement in these last four types of pardon power. Most presidential actions are either full or conditional pardons and an occasional commutation.

Process

The process for requesting a presidential pardon is administered in the Department of Justice by the Office of the Pardon Attorney (OPA). The pardon attorney is a political appointee serving at the discretion of the president. The OPA receives clemency and pardon petitions, reviews and investigates petitions, and makes recommendations for disposition. Since 1900, over seventy-two thousand requests for pardons or commutations have been processed through the OPA; nearly twenty thousand of these requests have been granted (Office of the Pardon Attorney 1996). This yields an average of 208 affirmative pardon actions per year, every year since the turn of the century.

At this point, we should consider why someone might request a presidential pardon or commutation. Commutations reduce a sentence and thus have obvious benefits for the recipient. For example, G. Gordon Liddy and Patty Hearst both received commuted sentences from President Carter which resulted in their early releases from prison (Berkman 1996). Pardons serve another purpose: the restoration of civil rights lost upon conviction. Rights lost with conviction may include "voting, holding public office, obtaining many jobs and occupational licenses, entering legally-enforceable agreements, maintaining family relationships, obtaining insurance and pension benefits . . . [and] possessing a firearm" (Mullins 1996). Pursuit of a pardon may also be the final avenue for clearing one's name when it cannot otherwise be accomplished through other means.

As with most governmental administrative actions, presidential pardon requests follow a codified process. The executive clemency regulations are found in section 28 of the Code of Federal Regulations. The administrative process requires, among other things, the meeting of eligibility requirements and the submission of informational forms, and may include an investigation by the Federal Bureau of Investigation. One example of the regulations in this section is a minimum five-year waiting period prior to applying for a pardon. This waiting period begins with the release from confinement or from the date of conviction if not sentenced to confinement. The OPA reviews the completed pardon application package and makes a recommendation to the president. The president is free to agree or disagree with OPA recommendations. When the OPA recommends denial of a petition, no response from the president within thirty days is considered concurrence. All petitioners are notified of the disposition of their application whether affirmed or denied. Although the pardon process is codified, 28 CFR 1.10 states that all regulations in this section are "advisory and for the internal guidance of the Department of Justice personnel." In this fashion, executive clemency regulations do not interfere or inhibit the president's constitutional power to pardon. The administrative process does not necessarily include the extraordinary pardon like the one granted to President Nixon. Because the pardon application files are created for advisory purposes, they may be exempt from Freedom of Information Act requests. This creates one hurdle for detailed research into the administrative aspects of the pardon process.

Frequency

The historical record on presidential pardons might best be categorized as incomplete but improving. To this writer's knowledge, no comprehensive record of all presidential pardon actions has yet been compiled. In *The Pardoning Power of the President*, W. H. Humbert began an effort to quantify the clemency case records of the United States. Long-hand copies of clemency actions served as the only record between 1789 and 1854. Humbert did not reconstruct this record in his work. The attorney general began keeping records in 1854. Using these records, Humbert was able to compile a record dating from 1860 through 1936 (Humbert 1941). Humbert not only counted the number of actions taken, but also sorted the actions into a number of categories. He first categorized according to the type of action taken (e.g., full pardon, conditional pardon, remission of fines, etc.). This categorization process generated an annual frequency of various executive clemency actions taken during this time period. He then sorted the clemency actions by thirty-eight "principal reasons for granting clemency as assigned by the Pardon Attorney and approved by the Attorney General and the President" and fifty-six "less frequently assigned" reasons. These two categorizations were accomplished by reviewing the written verbiage contained in each warrant. The pardon attorney often cited more than one reason. Humbert's categorizations provide the reader with a sense of why clemency actions were taken during this time period.

The reasons for offering a pardon are interesting and provide some insight into the thought processes of those administering clemency cases. Some of the reasons listed for clemency included poverty, youth, ill health, doubt as to guilt, and old age. Humbert found the following to be the top five most frequently cited reasons for granting clemency between 1860 and 1936:

1. Recognition of upright living by removal of civil disabilities
2. Recommended by the United States attorney and judge
3. Reputable living after serving sentence

4. Had served sentence

5. Recommended by the United States Attorney

The Office of the Pardon Attorney now maintains a record of all actions it has taken and has compiled a record dating back to 1900. Unfortunately, it does not release data using a typology similar to Humbert's. Instead, it provides only the number of pardons and commutations granted each year. For both Presidents Bush and Clinton, the pardon attorney does provide a list of all recipients, the type of relief granted (pardon or commutation), the date of the action, and the offense for which they were pardoned. What is most notably lacking in the data supplied by the pardon attorney is the reason(s) for executive clemency.

The pardon attorney's raw data do provide us with a number of general insights. Since 1900, nearly 20,000 presidential pardons and commutations (13,638 and 6,309, respectively) have been granted. Democrats have used the clemency power with greater frequency than Republicans. Since 1900, Democratic presidents have averaged 257 actions per year, while Republican presidents have averaged 169 actions per year. We should not be surprised to find that President Franklin Roosevelt leads all presidents, with 3,687 clemency actions (2,721 pardons and 966 commutations), since he held office for nearly twelve years. However, FDR's average of 314 clemency actions per year falls below the averages of both President Wilson (344/year) and President Coolidge (326/year). Wilson was especially active with commutations, which represented 61 percent of all his clemency actions.

An interesting trend that emerges from the data is the steady decline in the number of pardon actions granted. Since the presidency of Lyndon Johnson, the average number of presidential pardon actions taken each year has declined. This decline was most precipitous between Carter (142/year) and Reagan (51/year). Bush further reduced the average with just 18 actions per year. Clinton has maintained Bush's average, granting just 19 per year through January 31, 1996. Figure 5.1 shows the total number of pardons and commutations granted by each president this century.

MOVING BEYOND HISTORY

Thus far, we have considered the historic and administrative aspects of presidential pardon power. We will now move away from the historical record and consider avenues of research that might increase our understanding of and appreciation for the pardon power. In this section, we will suggest a research agenda for presidential pardon power. First, we present a range of general topics that merit potential scholarly attention, and then we present the rudimentary beginnings of attempts to address one of these general topics.

An obvious question that emerges from the brief historical review is, Why

Figure 5.1
Presidential Pardons and Commutations, 1900–1996

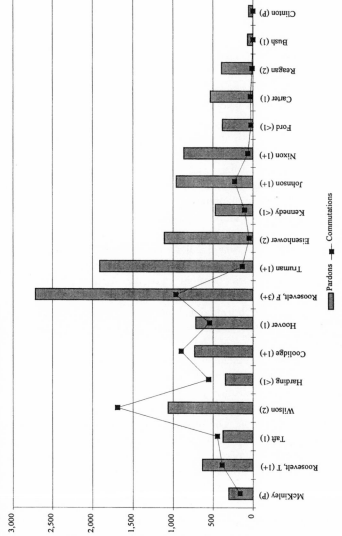

Note: Number of terms served are indicated in parentheses. (P) indicates only a partial amount of data available.

Source: Data prepared by the Office of the Pardon Attorney, January 31, 1996.

has use of the presidential pardon declined? As previously noted, the decline in usage has been a recent phenomenon and fairly precipitous. What factors might explain this shift in usage? Are these factors temporary, or do they suggest a permanent change? We will return to declining usage as we offer a set of hypotheses that might lend insight into this trend.

A second question is, Who is granted a presidential pardon? Or, conversely, Who is denied a pardon? Other than a few high-profile pardons, we know very little about the individuals who received a pardon. We can first look to the past for answers. What types of crimes were individuals pardoned for? Were the pardonees politically connected individuals? What type of socioeconomic background did they possess? Can we identify a "typical" pardon? Addressing these questions should lead to a richer understanding of the types of crimes as well as the types of individuals who were granted and denied pardons. If appropriate, we might consider these findings in the present-day context. This may lead us back to the first question posed above. The answers might also clarify the pardon as mercy and pardon as executive administration arguments.

A third area of research has a legal foundation. In this chapter we present a brief review of what are believed to be the primary legal precedents in the development of presidential pardon power. Constitutional and legal scholars might better trace this evolution and development. How many other legal challenges have there been to the pardon power? How might one challenge the pardon power today? On what legal grounds might President Clinton issue a pardon to his wife? It has been argued here that the pardon power is all but absolute; further legal research might strengthen or possibly refute this argument.

A fourth area of research available is general amnesties. Amnesties are a type of pardon granted to groups rather than individuals. Creating an historical record of presidential amnesties might be a first step. We might ask, When and to whom were amnesties granted? Are certain common factors shared by each amnesty grant? Are all amnesty grants the same? Besides group membership, how is amnesty different from a pardon?

Finally, we may want to consider presidential pardons in the broad context of administrative discretion. The discretion literature consider confining, structuring, and checking discretion (Davis 1969); accountability, responsibility and ethical administrative behavior; and issues of justice and fairness. Should the president have the power to pardon? If yes, should restraints be placed on the pardon power? Limitations placed on governors may provide alternatives if one is looking to restrict presidential pardon power. Obviously, this is a normative question with no definitive solution. However, only by further developing our understanding of this power can we begin to offer a reasoned response as to the appropriateness of presidential pardon power. Now we will offer a set of hypotheses that address one of the questions raised above, the declining use of the pardon.

Declining Use of the Pardon

The use of presidential pardon power is declining. Why is this the case? The modern presidency literature argues that a purposeful expansion of presidential power has occurred. Yet the power to pardon seems to be at odds with the general notions of an expanded presidency. What factors might we use to explain this potential inconsistency? This chapter does not attempt to directly explain the reduced number of presidential pardon actions. Instead, we offer several hypotheses that might explain the current condition of presidential pardon power.

H_1: Presidential Pardon Power Is Obsolete

Criminal justice system. The modern criminal justice system in the United States is a complex web of prevention, prosecution, rehabilitation, and punishment. Thus, the first hypothesis explaining the reduced number of pardons is that it has simply grown obsolete. The pardon may now be a relic that is no longer necessary in a modern criminal justice system. The justice system itself provides the relief formally sought through the pardon process. If this is true, we might first look at the input side of the pardon process. If fewer pardons were deemed necessary, we would expect to find a decreasing number of petitions being submitted for presidential consideration. This has generally been the case since 1945. Between 1945 and 1996, the OPA received an average of 584 petitions for pardon or commutation each year. This is well below the 966 annual average observed during the previous forty-five years. However, Nixon, Reagan and Bush all had average petitions per year well below both averages (471, 426, and 367, respectively). On the other hand, the average number of petitions increased to 765 per year through Clinton's first three years in office. This hypothesis remains attractive despite the increase in requests during the Clinton presidency.

Testing this hypothesis would be a challenging task. First, we would need to identify and quantify the types of offenses that received some form of executive clemency. We could then assess whether certain types of offenses moved from clemency to other forms of remedy. In this process, we would need to account for changes in the justice system as well. In addition to analyzing the federal level, a multistate comparative approach might also be appropriate. Although federal and state criminal justice systems are not fully comparable, we could look for clemency trends at the state level. Findings of this type would have a degree of generalizability and might better identify specific elements of the criminal justice system that have supplanted the need for executive clemency.

H_2: Administrative Changes Have Reduced the Number of Presidential Pardon Actions

Administration. A systematic study of the OPA would shed a great deal of light on the pardon process. We have very little information on the internal workings of this executive department. A second hypothesis then is that the process of administering presidential pardons has changed in a manner that reduces the number of pardons being granted. For example, in 1983 the Reagan administration increased the waiting period to apply for executive clemency to five years (Ruckman 1996). The timing of this procedural change is consistent with the rapid decline of pardons granted. However, we must be cautious before we make leaps of causality with a single factor. The general disposition of the president as well as the pardon attorney may also impact the administrative process. Ruckman has attempted to get at policy change and presidential characteristics in his work with some success (Ruckman 1996). However, much more work needs to be done in this area.

Confidentiality may hinder scholars from getting a close look at the OPA. Yet a research design structured around the personal interviews of former pardon attorneys and staff members could yield promising insights into the general process used to make these decisions. Ruckman found clemency policy to be a significant variable in his model. Yet he notes that the model does not lend any insight into the decision-making process itself. We must somehow get to the decision-making level to better understand the dynamics of presidential pardon power.

H_3: Mass Media Coverage Discourages the Use of Presidential Pardons

Media. A final hypothesis is that mass media scrutiny now inhibits the use of presidential pardon power. The high-profile pardons of President Nixon and Caspar Weinberger brought extensive media attention to this typically overlooked presidential power. The potential pardons of Oliver North and Whitewater participants have done much the same. How the media covers presidential pardons may influence the overall public perception of this power. The political price to be paid by an unpopular pardon may be too high for a president, particularly one in a first term. President Clinton had his executive clemency actions as the governor of Arkansas subjected to media scrutiny (Berkman 1996). This increased media attention may make even the routine pardon more doubtful. Negative media coverage of any kind may serve to damage a president's popular standing. The potential implications of diminished popular support are well argued in the presidential literature (Neustadt 1990).

We must first analyze media coverage of presidential pardon power before drawing any conclusions about its potential impact. One approach to this type of analysis might use a measure similar to Smoller's ''net tone'' in *The Six O'Clock Presidency*. Smoller uses content analysis to rate presidential media coverage on a scale ranging from positive to negative. The overall net tone is derived by comparing the total number of positive stories and negative stories. (Neutral stories are excluded since they have no effect on net tone.) A study of this nature might initially focus on the high-profile examples cited in this chapter (Nixon, Weinberger, North, McDougal, et al.). This sample is compelling because it includes issued pardons (Nixon and Weinberger), a potential pardon that was not issued (North), and a potential pardon that may yet be issued (McDougal et al.).

Another area of media analysis might center on gubernatorial pardons. The midnight pardons issued by outgoing governors is a popular target of media criticism. Again, content analysis seems to be an appropriate method of assessing this type of coverage. The objective of assessing gubernatorial pardons is to better understand the way the media reports pardons in general. Is the pardon reported as a viable and appropriate executive power? Or is it more often reported as an inappropriate abuse of executive power?

Research Strategies

As social scientists, we often confront difficult data collection challenges. The study of presidential pardons is no exception. In this chapter we have already discussed the data made available by the OPA. Scholarly work based on this data appears to be relatively limited. However, the limits of additional data that may be available from the OPA have not been fully tested. Confidentiality issues are one limiting factor with respect to the OPA data. Perhaps a well-defined research design that incorporates anonymity could be developed and acceptable to the OPA.

Much of the data associated with presidential pardons may be anecdotal. Personal interviews with former pardon attorneys offer one method of gathering this type of data. This approach is limited by the willingness of pardon attorneys to participate and their forthrightness if they choose to participate.

As presidentialists, we have not yet pursued a wide-ranging comparativist agenda. The use of presidential pardons in nations other than the United States offers us yet another chance to employ a comparative approach. What other nations have a constitutional or legislative power to pardon? How is the power to pardon used or not used by other presidents?

CONCLUSION

The academic study of presidential pardon power is inadequate and incomplete. Only one substantial effort to assess pardon power has been attempted (Humbert), and it was published nearly six decades ago. Since its publication, we have witnessed the pardoning of a former president. Yet even this dramatic use of presidential power drew little scholarly attention. Pardons remain primarily a topic for editorial writers and television pundits. Interest resurfaces whenever the potential of a high-profile pardon arises. Yet the apparent interest in potential pardons should serve to remind us that presidential pardon power is neither trivial nor dead. Will President Clinton pardon his wife if the need arises? Have Whitewater participants been silenced with the promise of a timely presidential pardon? These are interesting questions, but they are certainly not examples of a typical presidential pardon. We have little understanding of routine pardon actions, let alone the extraordinary ones.

The reader should not conclude that this chapter argues that presidential pardon power is a fundamental power that requires immediate scholarly attention. However, the nature of pardon power seems to suggest that some attention is warranted. The more recent trend toward disuse is particularly interesting and seems to merit an explanation. As maintained here, the power to pardon is relevant to presidential studies. The improper use of the pardon power can undermine an individual president and ultimately the presidency as an institution. Yet without a better understanding of presidential pardon power, how are we to judge what is proper and what is not? If this chapter has done little more than raise the reader's awareness of this poorly understood presidential power, than it has been successful. The reader is now a more informed student of presidential pardons and may one day find the power to pardon as intriguing as does the present author.

SELECTED REFERENCES

Berkman, Harvey. 1996. "Will the President Pardon His Friends?" *The National Law Journal* 4 (November): A01.

Davis, Kenneth Culp. 1969. *Discretionary Justice: A Preliminary Inquiry.* Urbana: University of Illinois Press.

Haig, Alexander M., Jr. 1992. *Inner Circles, How America Changed the World.* New York: Warner Books.

Hamilton, Alexander, James Madison and John Jay. 1961. *The Federalist.* Benjamin Fletcher Wright, ed. Cambridge, MA: Belknap Press of Harvard University Press.

Humbert, W. H. 1941. *The Pardoning Power of the President.* Washington, DC: American Council on Public Affairs.

Hurnard, Naomi D. 1969. *The King's Pardon for Homicide.* Oxford: Oxford University Press.

Moore, Kathleen Dean. 1989. *Pardons: Justice, Mercy, and the Public Interest.* New York: Oxford University Press.

Morris, Mark H. 1995. "Pardon Power and the Presidency." M.A. thesis, San Francisco State University.

Mullins, Jerome P. 1996. Pardon Me!—The Pardon Resource Center. [Online] available http://seamless.com/alawyer/pardonme/index.html, downloaded 19 June 1996.

Neustadt, Richard E. 1990. *Presidential Power and the Modern Presidents.* New York: Free Press.

Office of the Pardon Attorney, U.S. Department of Justice. Presidential Clemency Actions by Administration 1900–1996 (through 1/31/96).

Ruckman, P. S., Jr. 1996. *Federal Executive Clemency in the United States, 1934–1994: An Empirical Analysis.* Paper presented at the Annual Meeting of the Southern Political Science Association, Atlanta, Georgia, November 6–9, 1996.

Smoller, Fredric T. 1990. *The Six O'Clock Presidency.* New York: Praeger.

Selected Legal Cases

Biddle v. Perovich, 274 U.S. 480 (1927).
Burdick v. United States, 236 U.S. 79 (1915).
Garland, Ex parte, 4 Wallace 333 (1867).
Grossman, Ex parte, 267 U.S. 87 (1924).
United States v. Wilson, 32 U.S. 150 (1833).
Wells, Ex parte, 15 L.Ed. 421, 423 (1855).

Chapter 6

The Presidency and Social Policy

BYRON W. DAYNES AND GLEN SUSSMAN

Although *social policy* has been referred to in various ways—as policies of "emotive symbolism" (Smith 1975), as a type of *regulatory policy* (Tatalovich and Daynes 1988), as a variant of regulatory policy, namely, *social regulatory policy* (Tatalovich and Daynes 1988), or as *morality policy* (Mooney and Lee 1995)—it is basically public policy possessing legal authority that has the potential of affecting moral practices, individual standards of behavior, as well as community values. The *social policies* we will refer to in this chapter will include pornography, abortion, gun control, homosexuality, school prayer, affirmative action, and environmental policy.[1]

Each of these social policies has at one time or another become politicized. Thus, it is surprising that scholars have basically ignored social policies in their research on the presidency. Several reasons may account for this oversight. To begin with, despite recent attention paid to social issues and presidential politics in 1996,[2] no social issue has ever been a determining factor in a presidential campaign. Not until 1992, for example, was abortion—one of the more visible social issues—considered a contributing factor to a presidential election outcome (Wattier, Daynes, and Tatalovich 1997: 69). Nor can one always find social policy to be part of a president's program. A president realizes that social policy politics can often result in a "no-win" situation, losing as many votes as are gained. Moreover, when a president has become involved with social policies, it has not always been his own choice but has been the result of a position forced on him. This occurred with both Presidents Ford and Carter who only reluctantly took a position on abortion. Or the president has taken such a posture because of an unusual circumstance or because of a crisis situation.

Social issues have also provided some presidents with an avenue to strengthen their political bonds with certain constituencies, as Lyndon Johnson found from

Figure 6.1
Presidential Roles and Their Relative Power

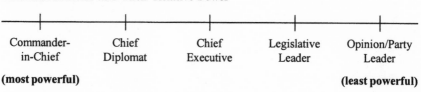

Commander- in-Chief	Chief Diplomat	Chief Executive	Legislative Leader	Opinion/Party Leader

(most powerful)   **(least powerful)**

the support he received from African Americans as a result of his civil rights policies; and as Bill Clinton found in the support he received from homosexual groups because of his gays in the military policy. At the very least, then, social policies have had an effect, if only indirectly, on presidential politics. Moreover, at the state level, activist constituencies tied to social policy have worked to elect members to the Congress who have ultimately either constrained presidential activity, influenced the president's agenda, or solidified a president's support.

Some presidents, when confronted with social issues, become assertive in their advocacy, much as Ronald Reagan did in promoting a pro-life stance on abortion. Others are more passive, while still others are "personally committed" to one position, while "publicly" articulating another. This was the case with Jimmy Carter and Gerald Ford, each of whom suggested he was personally against abortion but supported a woman's right to choose.

PRESIDENTIAL ROLES AND SOCIAL POLICY

Whether a president appears assertive or passive in response to social issues may depend in part on the *role* he assumes. We will examine contemporary presidents in five basic roles as they have responded to the seven social issues previously listed,[3] defining a *presidential role* as a president's responsibilities within a given policy area. Tatalovich and Daynes (1984) identified the five presidential roles that we will use, namely: (1) *Commander-in-Chief*—the only role named in Article II of the Constitution—that refers to a president as the nation's highest military leader; (2) *Chief Diplomat*—a role allowing a president to define our nation's relationship to other countries; (3) *Chief Executive*—a role involving a president's relationship with the bureaucracy, his administrative staff, and domestic policy-making; (4) *Legislative Leader*—a role suggesting a relationship with the Congress, and (5) *Opinion/Party Leader*—a combined role suggesting a president's relationship to the public.

These roles are not equally powerful. A commander-in-chief who leads the nation into war is normally a more significant political figure than a legislative leader who asks Congress to approve an annual budget. Based on formal authority and the resources a president can rely on, we would argue that the five presidential roles can be placed along a power continuum from the most powerful role—commander-in-chief—to the least powerful role—opinion/party leader—as Figure 6.1 makes clear.

The individual president's ability to alter the placement of these roles and maximize a normally weak political role, as Ronald Reagan did as opinion/party leader, depends on the president's individual skill, but it is a strength that cannot normally be passed on to a successor.

OPINION/PARTY LEADER

A president in this role attempts to generate public support for his own program, his administration, and his party. Communication with the public provides the president with the opportunity to draw attention to issues he considers important and to focus on specific issues in an attempt to set the national agenda. Of all the roles this is perhaps the weakest since the president has fewer resources available to call upon. A successful president in this role will, of necessity, rely on personal skills and influence rather than on established authority since little authority is associated with the role.

Partisan Differences

Examining the major political parties and their experiences with social policy shows how important their influence is on presidents and presidential candidates. The *party* is often important in determining a president's position on a particular social policy. It is easier for a Republican president, for example, to take a restrictive position on adult pornography than it is for a Democratic president to take the same position, given the Democratic Party's tendency to give priority to First Amendment access to information. When the party's official position conflicts with the officeholder's personal views on social policy, it is the party that is likely to win the argument, one way or another. For example, while the Republican Party has articulated a pro-life position on abortion in the party platform and party professionals have made it clear that Republicans should be pro-lifers, a pro-choice Republican president (or presidential candidate) will either hold back from publicly expressing that view or—if possible—ignore the subject of abortion altogether. Either way the party's view remains intact.

Party outlook and interest in the policy have certainly had something to do with the positions that presidents have taken on affirmative action. Lyndon Johnson frequently spoke out in support of affirmative action/equal opportunity against the backdrop of the Great Society program and the War on Poverty. Jimmy Carter publicly supported affirmative action and publicized the success of his administration in terms of the number of women and minorities he had appointed to governmental positions. So did Bill Clinton when he proclaimed that his administration has done its best to mirror the diversity of society. By contrast, two Republican presidents, Ronald Reagan and George Bush, reiterated their party's position, and spoke in opposition to the use of quotas and timetables.

Public Politics

Much of a president's strength in this role rests on the ability to persuade citizens through public appearances and speeches. The president may take an issue and "go public" with it (Kernell 1993), making the issue visible and enhancing the administration's identification with it. To do this, a president would probably want to rely on one or more of the president's major speeches—the Inaugural Address, the State of the Union message, and special addresses to the Congress and the nation—that can express the values and principles of the administration, help to set the legislative agenda, and highlight the role of the president as party leader. One study indicated, however, that social policies have not played a major role in any of these important addresses, comprising no more than 20 percent of any of them (Cohen 1995: 1–13). But several presidents have used major speeches to emphasize the significance of selected social policies. Lyndon Johnson would frequently emphasize affirmative action/equal opportunity and gun control in his major addresses as he did in 1964 when he committed himself and his administration to increased opportunities in employment ("Annual Message to the Congress on the State of the Union, January 8, 1964": 112–18). Ronald Reagan, moreover, referred to school prayer in six of his State of the Union messages and to abortion in three of them ("Address Before a Joint Session of the Congress on the State of the Union, January 25, 1983": 102–10; and "Address Before a Joint Session of the Congress on the State of the Union, January 25, 1988": 84–90).

The president is not limited, of course, to these major speeches in communicating with the public but can use a variety of other means of contact, including news conferences, town meetings, community forums, or speeches before interest group gatherings. In his bid for reelection in 1980, Jimmy Carter effectively used the town meeting forum to address his seemingly contradictory position on school prayer. He explained that while he supported the principle of separation of church and state, he also believed that people should be able to worship as they please without government interference ("Remarks and a Question and Answer Session at a Town Hall Meeting, Independence, Missouri, September 2, 1980": 1610–25). Richard Nixon publicly opposed pornography in numerous speeches to organized interests and such partisan groups as the National Federation of Republican Women where he encouraged its membership to ask Congress to support his antipornography legislation (Daynes 1988: 50). Activity in this role would support one scholar's observation that "the president has become the primary focus of national political attention, and the president's talk has become the primary focus of the presidency" (Stuckey 1991: 134).

In both major and minor speeches, presidents from FDR to Clinton have publicly talked of the importance of the environment. Truman, Eisenhower, and Nixon all used State of the Union messages to stress the need to conserve the nation's natural resources. Richard Nixon, in fact, bragged in his 1970 State of the Union message that his environmental efforts for that year would be the most "comprehensive and costly program in this field in America's history" ("Text of President Nixon's State of the Union Message, 1970": 5–8).

Gun control received considerable attention in public speeches given by Presidents Lyndon Johnson and Bill Clinton. The assassinations of President Kennedy, and later Martin Luther King, Jr., and Robert Kennedy, heightened public concern over easy access to handguns and facilitated President Johnson's support of gun control. In Clinton's case, the public's perception of crime and the availability of semiautomatic assault weapons encouraged him to speak out in favor of the Brady bill, a statute requiring those purchasing weapons to submit to a background check.

As opinion/party leader, the president is in a rather weak position due to a lack of formal authority and fragmented resources on which to rely. By communicating with the Congress and the public, the president as opinion/party leader can make a modest difference by identifying and making visible those social issues the president considers most important for placement on the public agenda and may also suggest measures for implementing them.

LEGISLATIVE LEADER AND THE SOCIAL AGENDA

This role suggests an active relationship between the president and Congress, with policy-making at its core. It is a role of conflict—a guerrilla war, in Arthur Schlesinger, Jr.'s terms—with Congress attacking in ambush against the commanding forces and firepower of the executive (Schlesinger and deGrazia 1967: 4–5). It is a role in which Congress has a substantial advantage, if not the dominant influence (Chamberlain 1946; Moe and Teel 1970). Thus, a successful legislative leader must rely on external political resources, creativity, and political persuasion to facilitate the administration's social agenda.

Advancing a Social Policy Agenda

Although most presidents have enjoyed rather modest records of legislative achievement regarding social policy, presidents who have been most effective in this role have approached the Congress with clear priorities and persuasive messages. Richard Nixon was one such president, using his 1970 State of the Union Message to encourage passage of his antipornography legislation. In his message, Nixon echoed the theme that he would carry into the congressional districts as he campaigned for Republicans in the midterm election—namely, that government had a special responsibility to bring a halt to pornography.

While Nixon proposed several restrictive statutes against pornography, he recognized it was the power of the *bully pulpit* that would actually make the difference as to whether or not his social legislation passed. Nixon not only proposed making it a federal crime to mail unsolicited pornographic materials to youths (under the age of eighteen), but he also appealed to the public to become involved in a grass-roots movement against pornography, recognizing that statutory laws are one thing, but the people's wishes and desires were clearly most important in ridding the nation of pornography. He maintained that "when indecent books no longer find a market, when pornographic films can no longer draw an audience, when obscene plays open to empty houses, then the tide will turn. Government can maintain the dikes against obscenity, but only people can turn back the tide" ("Text of President's Message on Obscenity," May 9, 1969: 702).

Ronald Reagan was perhaps more effective than Nixon in encouraging the Congress to pass restrictive child pornography laws that would ban its production for private and commercial use as well as halt its advertising ("Toughened Child Pornography Bill," November 8, 1986: 3). Reagan, like Nixon, recognized the limits of this role and did not rely exclusively on it to achieve his social policy ends. Rather, he supplemented his legislative activity with executive orders and judicial decisions from courts that had been staffed in large numbers by Reagan himself. As Gary L. Bauer, Reagan's domestic policy adviser, suggested: "With a hostile Congress that doesn't show much sign of coming toward us on some of these issues, it behooves us to take the initiative when we can take it" (Nelson 1987: 1).

George Bush's legislative social priorities centered on the environment and on child pornography, where he lauded his administration's successful project "Postporn" for its near elimination of mail-order pornography. He was particularly concerned about the unsolicited pornography one might receive through the mails and its potential effect on children. As he stated: "Our administration is committed to the fullest prosecution of obscenity and child pornography crimes. . . . this will remain a priority" ("Remarks to the Religious Alliance Against Pornography," October 10, 1991: 1280). Clean air was Bush's primary environmental priority. In signing the Clean Air Act of 1990, he indicated that passing this law had been a year-long crusade on the part of the administration to fashion this legislation. As he pointed out: "it is my mission to guarantee it for this generation and for the generations to come. . . . mission defined, mission accomplished ("Remarks on Signing the Bill Amending the Clean Air Act," November 15, 1990).

Remember the Veto

The *veto* is the president's most effective instrument associated with this role, since only about 7 percent of all regular vetoes (1789–1996) have ever been overridden by a two-thirds vote in both houses of the Congress (*Congressional Quarterly's Guide to the Presidency* 1989: 451; *Congressional Quarterly Weekly Report* 1992: 3925–26; *Weekly Compilation of Presidential Documents* 1995–1996). In terms of social policy, the veto has most often been used by liberal Democrats protecting the First Amendment from restrictive social policy proposed by the opposition party. In October 1962, for example, one of President Kennedy's pocket vetoes was directed to a District of Columbia bill that would have required the Post Office to put up public notices to warn citizens of potentially obscene matter in the U.S. mails and to allow citizens to return questionable material to the Post Office. Kennedy believed that the bill was too broad and vetoed it, indicating that: "Such a brief delay in the enactment of this legislation seems a small price to pay in order to obtain an enforceable law which will achieve the worthy objectives which prompted the bill before me" ("Obscenity Bill Pocket Veto," October 26, 1962: 2061).

Bill Clinton found in May 1995 that the veto was about the only means he had left to use against the Republican-dominated 104th Congress to preserve the achievements in environmental policy he believed had marked his first term. Republicans set about with their unifying political covenant in hand—their "Contract with America" (Gillespie and Schellhas 1994)—to do what Carol Browner, Environmental Protection Agency head, feared they would do, namely, to "undermine virtually every public-health and environmental protection that Americans have come to depend on" (*Salt Lake Tribune*, February 17, 1995).

What Influences Presidential Success?

Crisis can serve as a reason for introducing social legislation to the Congress, if not always assuring its passage. After the Kennedy assassination in 1963, gun control measures were introduced in 1965 to limit the sale of mail-order handguns to minors. As Robert Spitzer argues, however, even a successful legislative leader like Lyndon Johnson could not assure passage of any gun control measure until 1968 (Spitzer 1995: 143).

For many reasons, presidential power in the role of legislative leader is problematic. A president lacks the authority to force Congress to enact the president's programs and, instead, must rely on other political resources to shape the legislative arena to the executive's advantage. To succeed in this role, a president must appreciate the myriad of "political" conditions that increase or decrease his ability to influence the legislative process and then must go well beyond the formal legal relationship between the president and Congress.

THE CHIEF EXECUTIVE AND SOCIAL POLICY

The chief executive may seem quite a powerful role for the president since the framers determined that the president would not share power with any advisory body. Yet the president in this role is often frustrated in establishing a social agenda because the Constitution fragments control over the bureaucracy, making it difficult for any president to control the executive branch.[4] The president *can* determine the direction of social policy through the use of executive orders, as did Ronald Reagan and Bill Clinton, in enforcing their own perspectives of abortion. In 1988, for example, Ronald Reagan imposed a moratorium on federal funding of fetal tissue research (Graber 1995: 235), as well as declaring a ban on abortion counseling for any group or agency receiving federal funding. Bill Clinton, in one of his first official acts as chief executive, reversed both of Reagan's orders through a series of five presidential orders (Craig and O'Brien 1993: 354–55).

This change in abortion law did not cause the outcry that Clinton's second attempt to honor a campaign promise did, when he issued an executive order lifting the ban against homosexuals in the military. Resistance to this policy change came from every front: from the military, because the change conflicted with military tradition (Schmitt 1993: A1, A5); from powerful members of the Senate such as Sam Nunn (D-Ga), then-chair of the Senate Armed Services Committee, who regard changes affecting military law and personnel as matters for Congress to determine (Thompson 1993: 1A, 3A); and from the electorate, with 60 percent of the public opposing the lifting of the ban (Boot 1993: 3). As a result of this and other controversial decisions, in a short time Bill Clinton became the most unpopular chief executive in history (Devroy and Marcus 1993: 12).

The Appointment Power

The appointment power is key to the president's controlling the executive branch. Once an administrative post becomes vacant, the president must find appointees who are loyal to the party and the president, and who possesses the necessary experience for the job. Most presidents do confine their search to their own party, but even here they may be limited in whom they can appoint as a result of political constraints imposed by special interests, by voter blocs, by policy focus, or by their own ideologies. Affirmative action is one of those social policies that has influenced both parties in their appointments. In recent administrations, presidents of both parties—including Presidents Johnson, Carter, Reagan, and Clinton—have recruited African Americans to head the Department of Housing and Urban Development (HUD). The Supreme Court has also been open to such appointments. Lyndon Johnson appointed former NAACP counsel Thurgood Marshall to the High Court, and upon Marshall's retirement, George Bush filled the vacant seat with another African American, Clarence Thomas. Jimmy Carter, though he was never presented with a vacancy on the Supreme Court during his term, appointed a record number of minorities and women to the federal judiciary. Carter was able to appoint 202 federal district judges and 56 appellate court judges, with African Americans increasing their representation in the federal judiciary from 4 to 9 percent (Abernathy, Hill, and Williams 1984: 106–108; Dumbrell 1993: 77; Rosenbaum and Ugrinsky 1994: 739). Clinton followed Carter's example in his appointment of 187 judges, 60 percent of whom were women or racial minorities (Rosen 1995; Rowan 1996); he was also the first president to appoint an Asian American to be assistant attorney general for the Civil Rights Division of the Department of Justice ("President Names Bill Lann Lee as Assistant Attorney General for the Civil Rights Division at the

Department of Justice'' 1997)—although that appointment encountered insurmountable opposition in the Republican-controlled Senate.

Abortion politics was also persuasive in staffing decisions made by Ronald Reagan, who let his desires to encourage his pro-life views on abortion influence his judicial appointments. Following the 1980 Republican Platform provision calling for "the appointment of judges at all levels of the judiciary who respect traditional family values and the sanctity of innocent human life" ("1980 Republican Platform Text": 2034), Reagan was quite successful in appointing close to half of all federal lower court judges. Democrats and Republicans alike acknowledged that, in staffing the courts, Reagan was relying on an "ideological litmus test" and the appointee's views on abortion were central to filling the position (Craig and O'Brien 1993: 174–78). As a presidential candidate in 1992, Bill Clinton also tacitly acknowledged that he would use a litmus test on abortion in selecting judicial nominees.

Structural Reorganization

In past governmental reorganizations, presidents have used this role to create new agencies and departments. Franklin Roosevelt, who was first to be granted this authority, promoted his own interest in the environment and the goal of reducing unemployment by creating the Civilian Conservation Corps (CCC) to rebuild roads and visitor pathways in national parks and improve national forests. Bill Clinton demonstrated his commitment to environmental issues by inducing a number of structural changes in the executive branch, including the creation of the National Biological Service, the White House Office on Environmental Policy, and the Council on Sustainable Development.

Advisory System

While the cabinet as a collective body has little influence on the president, individual secretaries can be important in strengthening the president's social agenda. Two secretaries who were particularly close to Franklin Roosevelt— Secretary of Agriculture Henry Wallace (later vice president) and Secretary of Interior Harold Ickes—helped FDR shape his environmental programs. For Bill Clinton, Vice President Al Gore and Interior Secretary Bruce Babbitt symbolized the president's commitment to promoting an activist environmental agenda.

To avoid the pitfalls of bureaucratic inertia, presidents have at times turned to "task forces" or advisory commissions to study particular issues and recommend remedial action. Both Lyndon Johnson and Ronald Reagan used commissions to investigate the impact of pornography on society. In 1967, Johnson appointed a Commission on Obscenity and Pornography, but the group did not complete its work until 1970. Dissatisfied with the commission's report, President Nixon was moved to "categorically reject its morally bankrupt conclusions and major recommendations" ("Statement About the Report of the Commission on Obscenity and Pornography'': 940). Nixon's rejection of the 1967 Commission report encouraged Ronald Reagan to establish a second pornography commission, the 1985 Attorney General's Commission on Pornography (the Meese Commission), which determined that pornography was linked to antisocial behavior (Daynes 1988: 55).

Both authority and influence are critical to the role of chief executive and have had an effect on the president's establishing a social agenda. While a few presidents have been able to use this role to enhance social values, in general it has not been extremely productive in advancing a president's social agenda.

CHIEF DIPLOMAT/COMMANDER-IN-CHIEF AND SOCIAL ISSUES

These two roles—chief diplomat and commander-in-chief—are the president's strongest roles in terms of authority and resources. But these roles deal with a president's efforts in foreign affairs and as such have least to do with social policy.

With the possible exception of abortion and the environment, most social issues are restricted to the domestic realm. For the few issues that do have international consequences, however, constitutional authority in these roles puts the president in a very strong decision-making position. Consider the record of presidential international actions on the environment.

International Environmental Issues

One issue for international action has been that of chlorofluorocarbons and the ozone layer. Although several countries (including the United States) had imposed their own bans on ''nonessential'' chlorofluorocarbons (CFCs), and at least one international convention had called on other nations to take ''appropriate measures to protect the ozone layer,'' substantive international action did not take place until 1987. The Montreal Protocol, concluded that year, required signatories to work toward substantive reductions in the production of CFCs. In this case, the Reagan administration supported the international effort and the president signed the protocol in 1988 (''Statement on Signing the Montreal Protocol on Ozone-Depleting Substances, April 5, 1988'': 420–21).

The issue of acid rain faced a different fate. Although the subject was addressed in direct meetings between President Reagan and the Canadian prime minister, there was no resolution until 1991. At that time, President Bush signed an air-quality agreement with Canada (''Remarks by the President and Prime Minister Brian Mulroney of Canada at the Air Quality Agreement Signing Ceremony in Ottawa, March 13, 1991'': 254–57).

In that same year, President Bush worked to bring the United States into the North American Free Trade Agreement (NAFTA). In addition to citing the economic benefits of free trade between the United States and Mexico, Bush also highlighted the environmental benefits, suggesting that the trade agreement offered "the surest road to worker safety, public health, and indeed, environmental quality" ("Remarks at a Meeting with Hispanic Business Leaders in Houston, Texas, April 8, 1991": 345–48). Bill Clinton eventually won congressional support for NAFTA in 1993, convincing a Republican-led majority in both chambers that the legislation would provide both regional economic development and environmental protection.

President Bush often spoke of his concern for environmental protection in the context of national security. In a 1989 interview, he argued in favor of "prudent development" of the Arctic, indicating that "we can find a balance between environmental interests and national security interests" with regard to Arctic oil and gas resources ("Interview with Gerald Boyd of the *New York Times* and Katherine Lewis of the *Houston Post*, August 25, 1989: 13–15). But Bush's interest in the environment was not unlimited.

At the 1992 Earth Summit in Rio de Janeiro, President Bush refused to sign the multilateral biodiversity treaty, frustrating environmentalists at home and abroad (Mittermeier and Seligman 1992: 19). On winning the presidency in 1992, Clinton reversed Bush's decision and signed the agreement. Clinton appeared at the 1997 Earth Summit, proclaiming the global threat of "greenhouse gases" and promising to construct a plan for major American commitments to reduce greenhouse emissions before the end of that year. He also promised $1 billion to aid Third World countries to develop alternative energy sources and promised that the United States would increase its use of "more environmentally friendly technologies" in the future (Bennet 1997: A1, A7).

Working with and Through International Organizations

As a member of the United Nations, the United States often confronts policy conflicts with the multinational organization. This became evident during the Reagan-Bush years, as their pro-life abortion policies clashed with family planning practices promoted through the U.N. Population Fund. In the view of the Reagan administration, the program "either encouraged or permitted abortions in foreign countries" (Widensale 1997: 264). Both Reagan and Bush were particularly concerned about China's "coercive abortion policy" ("Cold War's Demise Shapes $26.3 Billion Spending Bill" 1992: 3178). While both presidents withheld funding from the U.N. program, Bush in 1989 also vetoed a foreign aid package that included assistance for the U.N. Population Fund (Rourke 1991: 555). Clinton reversed the Reagan-Bush policy regarding the U.N. Population Fund and provided financial assistance to some foreign programs that included abortion as an option (Tobin 1997: 282).

Military Personnel Matters

Military personnel matters also fall under the authority of the president as commander-in-chief. Roosevelt established a Committee on Fair Employment

Practices to encourage the full participation of all members of the armed forces regardless of race, creed, or religion, although he stopped short of ending racial segregation in the armed forces. In 1948 President Truman issued an executive order abolishing military segregation. Military personnel affairs also captured center stage when Clinton indicated in his race for the presidency in 1992 that homosexuals should not be barred from service in the nation's military. Although the "don't ask, don't tell" policy that eventually emerged from the Congress was less than Clinton wanted, he accepted the compromise stating: "As President of all the American people, I am pledged to protect and to promote individual rights. As Commander-in-chief, I am pledged to protect and advance our security. In this policy, I believe we have come close to meeting both objectives" ("Remarks Announcing the New Policy on Homosexuals in the Military, July 19, 1993": 1109).

Presidential Advantages and Disadvantages

As chief diplomat/commander-in-chief, a president has diplomatic and defensive powers that put the him at great advantage when confronting other institutions involved in foreign affairs. The problem has been, of course, that a president does not have frequent occasion to exercise this role in implementing social policy, but when social policy has reached beyond national borders, as in the case of abortion and environmental policy, the president's policy position has generally been respected. In the future, presidents as chief diplomats may be called upon to resolve the controversies posed by indecency of communications on the Internet. As one American lawyer in Germany suggested, "The Internet created a universal jurisdiction so that once you are on the Internet you are subject to the laws of every country in the world. . . . The Internet gives rise to jurisdictional problems that never happened before (Andrews 1997: A1, C2).

CONCLUSION

The last six decades or so have been characterized by an increase in the frequency of national debates over social policies. These debates have put the president, as the most prominent (and in many ways, the most dominant) elected official, in positions where the public expects the chief executive to play a key role in resolving these issues. Yet Lyn Ragsdale (1993: 363) perceived that "presidents often seem uncomfortable as leaders on social rights issues. They implicitly recognize the fallout they may experience because the policies, by definition, redistribute benefits from one group to another." Some years ago, Tatalovich and Daynes recognized that it wasn't just the president who was put in this uncomfortable position when confronted with the need for social policy resolution, but that all of our democratic institutions find themselves in similar circumstances. This situation poses a major challenge for our political system. As they observed of abortion: "Here is an issue that consistently generates conflict, an issue that refuses to disappear from the agendas of our governmental institutions, an issue that has continually evaded compromise and resolution'' (Tatalovich and Daynes 1981: v). What was said of abortion could be said of any social issue.

Although these issues are not easily resolved, presidential decisions regarding them have had significant social and political consequences. In some cases, presidents who have taken a particular interest in a social issue have acquired a new constituency. This happened in the cases of Reagan and Clinton, as they became involved with abortion policy, attracting pro-life and pro-choice supporters, respectively. Clinton also found that homosexual groups began supporting his endeavors after he fought to end the ban on gays in the military, although this enthusiasm became somewhat muted after the president refused to endorse same-sex marriages.

Presidents themselves have varied in their involvement with social policy. In part, this variation can be explained by the different roles presidents play. As opinion/party leader, a president, though in a normally weakened role, can establish links with the public in influencing their views on social policy. As legislative leader, a skillful president can use the limited resources available, along with personal skills, to successfully guide policy through Congress. As chief executive, a president's perspective on social policies has occasionally influenced the structure of government through staffing choices and reorganization efforts. Finally, as chief diplomat and commander-in-chief, some presidents have occasionally used these two powerful roles to influence international action in areas of social policy.

Our evaluation of presidential roles and social policies indicates that some presidential roles have been more important to some issues than to others (see Table 6.1). The dual role of chief diplomat and commander-in-chief, for example, has been important in negotiations over abortion and environmental policy disputes between nations. In matters of military personnel, presidents have used the commander-in-chief role to end segregation, introduce affirmative action, and alter the treatment of homosexuals. Yet these roles are largely irrelevant to other social policies, such as gun control or school prayer. In the less powerful role of opinion/party leader, some presidents have tried to win approval for their views on abortion, the environment, affirmative action, and gun control, but this role has less frequently been used to handle concerns of pornography, prayer, and homosexual rights. The legislative leader role has perhaps reached more broadly across the scope of social policy than other roles, with presidents introducing legislation in almost every area. Nevertheless, when a president has been faced with issues of school prayer and homosexual rights, they have tended to avoid legislative remedies. Finally, the chief executive role has lent itself more to abortion, affirmative action, and the environment than to the other social issues.

Presidents have used the power resources available to them in these roles to facilitate their own positioning on social policy. In this regard, some presidents

Table 6.1
Presidential Roles and Social Policy

	ROLES			
POLICY IMPORTANCE	**Opinion/ Party Leader**	**Legislative Leader**	**Chief Executive**	**Chief Diplomat/ Commander-in-Chief**
Most Important	abortion affirmative action environment gun control	pornography gun control environment abortion affirmative action	abortion affirmative action environment	abortion environment affirmative action* homosexuality* pornography**
Least important	homosexuality pornography prayer	homosexuality prayer	gun control homosexuality prayer pornography	gun control prayer

*In the military, these social policies have been fostered by presidents.

**While pornography has not yet proven to be important to the president as chief diplomat, the challenges posed by Internet pornography may in the future make it necessary for presidents to negotiate with other nations to control the pornography that may conflict with other nations' "local community standards."

have shown themselves to be more assertive than others in their involvement with social policy (see Table 6.2). Among the modern presidents, Ronald Reagan became involved with more social policies than any other modern president, setting the tone for the 1980s in his opposition to abortion, pornography, gun control, and affirmative action, and his support of school prayer. Clinton, the only socially assertive Democrat, comes in a close second, having made decisions affecting gun control, affirmative action, homosexuality, abortion, and the environment. Richard Nixon also exhibited great energy in his fight against pornography and in support of the environment.

Social policies have become an important part of the public agenda, and it is difficult for presidents to ignore them because it is difficult for the polity to ignore them. Although they have not necessarily been a defining factor in presidential electoral politics, presidents' involvement with the more controversial policies have helped to mobilize segments of the electorate to action—through polarizing politics, encouraging the involvement of political activists, and creating an issue-oriented politics.

Table 6.2
Presidential Types, Social Policy, and Individual Presidents

				SOCIAL POLICY			
TYPES	**Abortion**	**Pornography**	**Environment**	**Gun Control**	**Affirmative Action**	**School Prayer**	**Homosexuality**
Assertive	Reagan Clinton	Reagan Nixon	FDR Clinton Nixon	Clinton Bush	Reagan LBJ Clinton Carter	Reagan	Clinton
Moderately Active	Bush	LBJ	Bush	Reagan	HST	JFK Clinton Bush	
Passive		Ike					
Duplicitous	Ford Carter						

Note: If a president said nothing and paid no attention to the issues, the president is not listed. If a president acknowledged the issue but paid little attention to it, the president is listed as passive.

"Duplicitous" suggests that a president holds to one personal view while articulating another one publicly.

114   New Insights on Power and Policy

NOTES

1. George McKenna lists the *environment* as a social issue because the political dynamics are very similar to those of other social issues (McKenna 1994). We will do the same.

2. In July 1996, a *USA Today*/CNN/Gallup poll indicated that nine out of every ten persons responded that Clinton's and Dole's position on "moral values" would be important in casting their votes for the presidency. George Gallup, Jr., saw this as exhibiting more interest in moral values than had been expressed in all the sixty years of Gallup polling (Edmonds and Oldenburg 1996: 4A).

3. These five roles were previously developed by Tatalovich and Daynes (1984).

4. The powers of this role come from two clauses of Article II in the Constitution: one stating that "the executive power shall be vested in a President of the United States of America," and the other indicating that the president has the responsibility to "take care that the laws be faithfully executed."

REFERENCES

Abernathy, M. Glenn, Dilys M. Hill and Phil Williams. 1984. *The Carter Years: The President and Policy Making*. London: Frances Pinter.

"Address Before a Joint Session of the Congress on the State of the Union, January 25, 1983." 1984. *Public Papers of the Presidents of the United States: Ronald Reagan*. Washington, DC: U.S. Government Printing Office.

"Address Before a Joint Session of the Congress on the State of the Union, January 25, 1988." 1990. *Public Papers of the Presidents of the United States: Ronald Reagan*. Washington, DC: U.S. Government Printing Office.

Andrews, Edmund L. 1997. "Germany's Efforts to Police Web Are Upsetting Business." *New York Times*, June 6, pp. A7, C2.

"Annual Message to the Congress on the State of the Union, January 8, 1964." 1965. *Public Papers of the Presidents of the United States: Lyndon Johnson*. Washington, DC: U.S. Government Printing Office.

Bennet, James. 1997. "Clinton Defers Curbs on Gases Heating Globe." *New York Times*, June 27, pp. A1, A7.

Boot, Max. 1993. "First Monday in Office: Clinton Picks Take Over." *Christian Science Monitor*, January 25, p. 3.

Chamberlain, Lawrence H. 1946. *The President, Congress and Legislation*. New York: Columbia University Press.

Cohen, Jeffrey E. 1995. "Presidents, Public Opinion, and Civil Rights." In *Presidential Leadership and Civil Rights Policy*, ed. James W. Riddlesberger, Jr., and Donald W. Jackson. Westport, CT: Greenwood Press.

"Cold War's Demise Shapes $26.3 Billion Spending Bill." 1992. *Congressional Quarterly Weekly Report* (October).

Congressional Quarterly's Guide to the Presidency. 1989. Washington, DC: Congressional Quarterly.

Congressional Quarterly Weekly Report. 1992. Washington, DC: Congressional Quarterly, December 19, pp. 3925–26.

Craig, Barbara Hinkson and David M. O'Brien. 1993. *Abortion and American Politics*. Chatham NJ: Chatham House.

Daynes, Byron W. 1988. "Pornography: Freedom of Expression or Societal Degrada-
    tion?" In *Social Regulatory Policy: Moral Controversies in American Politics*,
    ed. Raymond Tatalovich and Byron W. Daynes. Boulder, CO: Westview Press.
Devroy, Ann and Ruth Marcus. 1993. "The Clutch Seems to Be Slipping." *Washington
    Post National Weekly Edition*, June 14–20, p. 12.
Dumbrell, John. 1993. *The Carter Presidency: A Re-Evaluation*. Manchester: Manchester
    University Press.
Edmonds, Patricia and Ann Oldenburg. 1996. "Morality Issues Matter More." *USA
    Today*, August 6, sec. 4A.
Gillespie, Ed and Bob Schellhas, eds. 1994. *Contract with America*. New York: Times
    Books.
"Gingrich Flashes His 'Green' Card, But Is Color Faded?" 1995. *Salt Lake Tribune*,
    February 17, sec. A1.
Graber, Glenn C. 1995. "Fetal Tissue Research Will Not Increase Abortion." In *The
    Abortion Controversy*, ed. Charles P. Cozic and Jonathan Petrikin. San Diego,
    CA: Greenhaven Press.
"Interview with Gerald Boyd of the *New York Times* and Katherine Lewis of the *Houston
    Post*, August 25, 1989." *Public Papers of the Presidents of the United States:
    George Bush*. Washington, DC: U.S. Government Printing Office.
Kernell, Samuel. 1993. *Going Public*, 2nd ed. Washington, DC: Congressional Quarterly
    Press.
McKenna, George. 1994. *The Drama of Democracy*, 2nd ed. Guilford, CT: Dushkin
    Publishing Group.
Mittermeier, Russell and Peter Seligman. 1992. "U.S. Should Take a Stand on Biodi-
    versity." *Christian Science Monitor*, July 17, p. 19.
Moe, Ronald C. and Steven C. Teal. 1970. "Congress as Policy-Maker: A Necessary
    Reappraisal." *Political Science Quarterly* (September): 443–70.
Mooney, Christopher Z. and Mei-Hsien Lee. 1995. "Legislating Morality in the Amer-
    ican States: The Case of Pre-*Roe* Abortion Regulation Reform." *American Jour-
    nal of Political Science* 39: 599–627.
Nelson, Jack. 1987. "Reagan to Use Executive Orders to Bypass Congress." *Los Angeles
    Times*, August 21, p. 1.
"1980 Republican Platform Text." 1980. *Congressional Quarterly Weekly Report* (July
    19): 2034.
"Obscenity Bill Pocket Veto." 1962. *Congressional Quarterly Weekly Report* (October
    26): 2061.
"President Names Bill Lann Lee as Assistant Attorney General for the Civil Rights
    Division at the Department of Justice." 1997. *The White House: Office of the
    Press Secretary*, June 12.
Ragsdale, Lyn. 1993. *Presidential Politics*. Boston: Houghton Mifflin.
"Remarks and a Question and Answer Session at a Town Hall Meeting, Independence,
    Missouri—September 2, 1980." 1982. *Public Papers of the Presidents of the
    United States: Jimmy Carter*. Washington, DC: U.S. Government Printing Office.
"Remarks Announcing the New Policy on Homosexuals in the Military, July 19, 1993."
    1994. *Public Papers of the Presidents of the United States: William J. Clinton*.
    Washington, DC: U.S. Government Printing Office.
"Remarks at a Meeting with Hispanic Business Leaders in Houston, Texas, April 8,

1991." 1992. *Public Papers of the Presidents of the United States: George Bush.* Washington, DC: U.S. Government Printing Office.

"Remarks by the President and Prime Minister Brian Mulroney of Canada at the Air Quality Signing Agreement Ceremony in Ottawa, March 13, 1991." 1992. *Public Papers of the Presidents of the United States: George Bush.* Washington, DC: U.S. Government Printing Office.

"Remarks to the Religious Alliance Against Pornography." 1991. *Presidential Papers, Administration of George Bush, 1991.* Washington, DC: U.S. Government Printing Office, p. 1280.

"Remarks on Signing the Bill Amending the Clean Air Act," November 15, 1990. *The Presidential Papers Infobase,* CDex Information Group.

Rosen, Jeffrey. 1995. "Mediocrity on the Bench." *New York Times,* March 17, sec. A15.

Rosenbaum, Herbert D. and Alexej Ugrinsky, eds. 1994. *The Presidency and Domestic Policies of Jimmy Carter.* Westport, CT: Greenwood Press.

Rourke, John T. 1991. *International Politics on the World Stage,* 3rd ed. Guilford, CT: Dushkin Publishing Group.

Rowen, Carl. 1996. "President Did Federal Bench a Disservice." *Salt Lake Tribune,* April 5, sec. A19.

Schlesinger, Arthur, Jr. and Alfred deGrazia. 1967. *Congress and the Presidency: Their Role in Modern Times.* Washington, DC: American Enterprise Institute for Public Policy Research.

Schmitt, Eric. 1993. "Months After Order on Gay Ban, Military Is Still Resisting Clinton." *New York Times,* March 23, sec. A1, A5.

Smith, T. Alexander. 1975. *The Comparative Policy Process.* Santa Barbara, CA: CLIO Press.

"Special Message to Congress on Forthcoming Legislative Proposals Concerning Domestic Programs April 14, 1969." 1971. *Public Papers of the Presidents of the United States: Richard Nixon.* Washington, DC: U.S. Government Printing Office.

Spitzer, Robert J. 1995. *The Politics of Gun Control.* Chatham, NJ: Chatham House.

"Statement About the Report of the Commission on Obscenity and Pornography, October 24, 1970." *Public Papers of the Presidents 1970: Richard Nixon.* Washington, DC: U.S. Government Printing Office.

"Statement on Signing the Montreal Protocol on Ozone-Depleting Substances, April 5, 1988." 1989. *Public Papers of the Presidents of the United States: Ronald Reagan.* Washington, DC: U.S. Government Printing Office.

Stuckey, Mary E. 1991. *The President as Interpreter-in-Chief.* Chatham, NJ: Chatham House.

Tatalovich, Raymond and Byron W. Daynes. 1988. *Social Regulatory Policy: Moral Controversies in American Politics.* Boulder, CO: Westview Press.

———. 1984. *Presidential Power in the United States.* Monterey, CA: Brooks/Cole.

———. 1981. *The Politics of Abortion: A Study of Community Conflict in Public Policy Making.* New York: Praeger.

"Text of President Nixon's State of the Union Message." 1970. In *Nixon: The First Year of His Presidency.* Washington, DC: Congressional Quarterly Press.

"Text of President's Message on Obscenity." 1969. *Congressional Quarterly Weekly Report* (May 9): 702.

Thompson, Mark. 1993. "Clinton Aims to End Troop Ban on Gays." *Las Vegas Review Journal,* January 26, sec. 1A, 3A.

Tobin, Richard J. 1997. "Environment, Population and the Developing World." In *Environmental Policy in the 1990s*, 3rd ed., ed. Norman J. Vig and Michael E. Kraft. Washington, DC: Congressional Quarterly.

"Toughened Child Pornography Bill Signed by Reagan." 1986. *Los Angeles Times*, November 8, p. 3.

Wattier, Mark J., Byron W. Daynes and Raymond Tatalovich. 1997. "Abortion Attitudes, Gender, and Candidate Choice in Presidential Elections: 1972 to 1992." *Women & Politics* 17: 55–72.

Weekly Compilation of Presidential Documents. 1995–1996. Washington, DC: U.S. Government Printing Office.

Widensale, Steven K. 1997. "Family Policy During the Reagan Years: The Private Side of the Conservative Agenda." In *Ronald Reagan's America*, ed. Eric J. Schmertz, Natalie Oatlof, and Alexej Ugrinsky. Westport, CT: Greenwood Press.

Chapter 7

The Other Side of War: Presidential Peace Powers

RYAN J. BARILLEAUX AND CHRISTOPHER KELLEY

American presidents like to portray themselves as peacemakers, although many of the most famous moments in the history of the office involve the making of war. Observers of the chief executive can readily point to events such as two world wars, the launching of Desert Storm, the dispatch of troops to Haiti, war in Korea and Vietnam, the invasion of Grenada, military interventions in Latin America, the confrontation over Soviet missiles in Cuba, and dozens of other incidents from American history. As commander-in-chief and guarantor of national security, the president is the official on whom rests responsibility for defense and the direction of military force.

Yet any president is likely to point with great pride to his role as a bringer of peace. Teddy Roosevelt arbitrated the Russo-Japanese War and for his efforts was awarded the Nobel Peace Prize. Dwight Eisenhower promoted "Open Skies" and "Atoms for Peace" in his efforts to reduce tensions between the United States and the Soviet Union. John Kennedy took pride in the Partial Test-Ban Treaty that he signed, while Richard Nixon regarded the SALT I Treaty as a key to the "structure of peace" that was the goal of his foreign policy. Jimmy Carter held up his success in brokering the Camp David Accords that ended conflict between Egypt and Israel, even running a campaign commercial during the 1980 election that featured an Oklahoma woman's praise of Carter for his role as "peacemaker in the world today." Bill Clinton has made much of his role in promoting peace between Israel and the Palestine Liberation Organization, while also immersing his administration in attempts to mediate the conflict over Northern Ireland.

The president, then, is both warmaker and peacemaker. A look at the scholarship on the presidency, however, tends to emphasize the first role over the second. Books on presidential war powers, such as Louis Fisher's *Presidential*

War Power (1995), Harold Hongju Koh's *The National Security Constitution* (1990), the growing list of books on the American Civil War, World Wars I and II, and the Persian Gulf War, and other works generally focus on the president's ability to commit the nation to armed conflict and direct the use of force. The journal literature, whether in law reviews or in political science organs, is also focused on the president's war powers. Even major reference works on the presidency give more attention to war than peace: Levy and Fisher's *Encyclopedia of the American Presidency* (1994) includes entries on "commander-in-chief" and related war-power issues, with only minimal attention to the chief executive's powers of recognition, diplomacy, and treaty-making; *Congressional Quarterly's Guide to the Presidency* (Nelson 1989) contains a lengthy chapter on the president as commander-in-chief, with but a brief section on the "power to end war or declare neutrality" (1989: 533). While the *Guide to the Presidency* also includes a discussion of the president's diplomatic powers, warmaking gets priority in this volume.

There are several possible explanations for this lopsided treatment of presidential power. The decision to employ force or direct ongoing military actions is a grave one, because it involves the life and treasure of American citizens. The Constitution also has more to say about war than peace, just as it is apparent that the topic of war drew more attention from the document's framers than the issue of peace. The president's role as commander-in-chief has also been an important engine in the expansion of executive power, particularly in the twentieth century. Each of these reasons suggests why war powers have been more carefully studied than peace powers.

Nevertheless, presidential peace powers warrant sustained scholarly attention. In the wake of the end of the Cold War, it is apparent that the chief executive's ability to shape and influence the relaxation of tensions, the avoidance of conflict, even the termination of military action, are all relevant to the presidency and the nation. Our purpose in this chapter is to examine presidential peace powers and, in doing so, illuminate new avenues of research for students of the American chief executive. To that end, we will review the foundations of the president's peace powers, the scope of those powers, and an agenda for future research.

FOUNDATIONS OF PRESIDENTIAL PEACE POWERS

Every student of the presidency knows that the nature and extent of executive power has been a subject of debate since the time of the Founding. The Constitutional Convention wrestled with the issue, ultimately describing "the executive power" in vague terms in Article II. In the wake of that vagueness, the nation has seen political debate, a variety of Supreme Court decisions, legislation, and a number of practical precedents established as presidents have attempted to meet their responsibility to "preserve and protect" the Constitution and the republic it created.

The Constitution and Early Republic

During the Constitutional Convention, the idea of who had the responsibility to make war was a matter hotly contested. Although we do not have the exact minutes of the meeting, we do know from memoirs and other personal notes the tone of the debates. For instance, Pierce Butler, a delegate to the Convention, suggested that the power to create war be vested in the president, which placed him in the minority (Ely 1993). James Madison believed that, in light of past abuses of the war power, the legislature should be the natural caretaker of the various instances of war. He also wanted to involve the executive or else there wouldn't be "much of a war" (quoted in Ely 1993: 3–4). In addition, Louis Henkin (1972) states that the convention defeated a motion to give Congress the power to declare peace. We know by reading the Constitution that Congress has the sole authority to declare war (an earlier draft of the document gave Congress the power to "make war"), but what is unclear is what happens once war is undertaken: who has the authority to declare "peace"?

This very question came to the fore in 1793 when President Washington issued the Neutrality Proclamation. While the Proclamation was a (controversial) unilateral action by Washington, it was done not as a seizure of presidential power, but rather as a consistent effort by Washington to keep the fledgling United States out of the historical disputes of Europe. The Neutrality Proclamation came in response to Washington's rejection of efforts by France's Citizen Genet to draw the United States into a war on the side of France against Great Britain (Koh 1990). Alhough public opinion favored the French, Washington's Proclamation received support in Congress, which enshrined its provisions in the Neutrality Act of 1794.[1]

Although Congress approved of the proclamation, some within the Washington administration believed the president's actions were improper. Secretary of State Thomas Jefferson argued that since "Congress had the sole authority to declare war, the president lacked the authority to decide *unilaterally* that the nation would not fight a war" [emphasis mine] (quoted in *Congressional Quarterly* 1997: 127). As was often the case in that first administration, Secretary of the Treasury Alexander Hamilton steadfastly opposed Jefferson's argument. Hamilton touched off a debate over executive power in a series of essays that appeared under the *nom de plume*, "Pacificus." To offset Hamilton's argument, Jefferson asked his friend James Madison to argue against the expansive nature of executive authority being championed by Hamilton. Jefferson did not wish to argue the case in public, although he was perfectly capable of doing so, noting that it would not be proper for a member of Washington's cabinet to attack Hamilton.

Hamilton's argument involved a broad interpretation of the president's executive power and of his capacity as chief executive. He argued that the president was given expansive "inherent powers" that allowed him to be active in those gray areas not addressed by the Constitution. While Congress was given the power to declare war, the power to issue proclamations that avoided war was clearly a presidential power, even if it "interfered with the free exercise of Congress's power to declare war" (quoted in *Congressional Quarterly* 1997: 128). Hamilton thus asserted that in those areas in which the Constitution is not specific or clear, the president has the authority to develop very broad powers. In fact, he conceded that this particular power is probably a concurrent power, shared by the president and the Congress, and thus was an "unavoidable conflict."

Madison's response, written under the pseudonym of "Helvidius," was framed in the language of a strict constructionist. It was also quite straightforward: the president's power was to execute laws that were passed by Congress and signed by him. Madison argued: "All his acts, therefore, properly executive, must presuppose the existence of the laws to be executed" (quoted in *Congressional Quarterly* 1997: 128). This interpretation of presidential power is a very restrictive one that reduces the office of president to one of executing faithfully all "laws, treaties, and declarations" that passed congressional muster.

The Pacificus–Helvidius debate exposed the ambiguities of presidential power. While Hamilton's arguments were never entirely accepted, they did provide future presidents with a framework through which to expand presidential power.

The U.S. Supreme Court was also divided during this period on the question of the president's power to act in minimizing hostilities without a declaration of war from Congress, or in defending U.S. interests up to the point of war. In the case of *Bas v. Tingy* (4 US [4 Dall] 37, 1 L.Ed. 731), the Court recognized that not all wars would be easy to identify. The Court then proceeded to make the distinction between "perfect war" and "imperfect" war. This case at hand involved the seizure of an American vessel and cargo that was "recaptured" from the French. While Congress had not declared war against France, the Court recognized that France's initial seizure of the American vessel was a hostile act "amounting to war." Thus, the Court recognized the principle of "an undeclared war." And it was the president who was responsible for the successful negotiation of this war as commander-in-chief as if it were declared. This opinion is significant not so much because it is a statement in favor of broad presidential war powers, but because it appears to be a general acceptance by the Court and the Congress that the president is responsible for seeing an end to hostilities, declared or undeclared—in essence, to keeping the peace (an acceptance somewhat qualified in *Talbot v. Seeman*, 1801).

The Nineteenth and Twentieth Centuries

In 1804 (and with John Marshall sitting as chief justice), the Court backed away from its broad interpretation of executive power in those situations less than declared war. The change occurred in the case of *Little v. Barreme* (6 US [2 Cranch] 170, 1804). Much like *Bas, Little* dealt with the seizure of a ship by a foreign power. In this case, there existed an instruction by the president to seize vessels, in this instance a Danish merchant vessel, that violated prohibition of commercial trade with France by an American ship, or any ship leaving from the United States and going to France.[2] This instruction by Congress was that a vessel may be seized only when the vessel was "bound to" a French port, which did not happen in this case. The Court noted that in the absence of a declaration of war, any action undertaken by the president in a state of imperfect war must be grounded in specific legislative provisions. Hence, the president does not have a free hand, as he would in a declared war, to negotiate it successfully to its conclusion. Congress must play a role.

It should also be noted that Justice Joseph Story, an important influence on John Marshall, argued in *Commentaries on the Constitution of the United States* (1851) that the power to declare war was congressional, as was the power to "make peace." Story's view was closer to that of Jefferson and Madison than to that of Hamilton.

As president, Jefferson held to his view that the president did not have independent war powers outside of congressional legislation, although he did undertake unilateral actions. In 1801, when pirates (at the behest of several Mediterranean states) were attacking American commercial vessels off the coast of Barbary, Jefferson sent American ships to the region in an attempt to offer the Barbary Coast states money to leave U.S. ships alone. If the offer of money was not enough of an inducement, Jefferson—without consulting Congress—instructed his officers to "Distribute your forces in such a manner, as your judgment shall direct, so as best to protect our commerce and chastise their insolence—by sinking, burning, or destroying their ships and vessels wherever you shall find them" (quoted in *Congressional Quarterly* 1997: 167). The president's unilateral action was made in a desire to remain at peace with the nations involved. After discovering the action (U.S. warships did engage, with a loss of foreign lives, the foreign vessels), Congress authorized Jefferson to use force. Jefferson had gone before the Congress and publicly recognized the legislature's constitutional authority to determine when and where and at what levels force should be used.

Jefferson's actions revived the question that Hamilton and Madison had debated previously. Hamilton, in keeping with his Pacificus statements, called Jefferson's action before the Congress "needless." Throughout the rest of his term, Jefferson followed the belief that Congress has the power to authorize U.S. action when hostilities arise. The logical corollary to this position holds as well that Congress possesses the power to declare when those hostilities are over.

The debate over congressional authority to define a conflict permeated throughout the nineteenth century. Consider the example of the Spanish-American War. President Grover Cleveland resisted the mounting pressure for a war with Spain over Cuba, convinced that as commander-in-chief he could resist sending troops into conflict *even* in the event of a declaration of war. Therefore, he told Congress forthrightly that he would not prosecute a war with

Spain upon their declaration. William McKinley was also reluctant to fight the Spanish, but finally acquiesced to congressional pressure in 1898 and sent forces into Cuba in a conflict that gained control of both Cuba and the Philippines for the United States.

In the early decades of the twentieth century, the idea of congressional authority over peace as well as war remained a strong one. After World War I, the Supreme Court held in *Commercial Trust Co. v Miller* (262 US 51, 1923) that "the power which declared the necessity is the power to declare its cessation and what the cessation requires. The power is legislative." As we will see later in this chapter, presidential practice after World War II would settle the issue by asserting a power of presidential control over the cessation or avoidance of hostilities.

Presidents would employ the ambiguities of presidential power to develop an array of peace powers. The precedents of the early Republic and the nineteenth century would be remembered to the extent that they bolstered executive action, rather than keeping open the question of the authority of Congress to share in issues of peace as well as those of war. In the Cold War and post–Cold War eras, control over peacemaking would become almost exclusively a presidential matter.

THE SCOPE OF PRESIDENTIAL PEACE POWERS

War is not always easy to define and identify: Is every military action, for example, an incident of war? This ambiguity has often complicated the debate over presidential war powers. In the same way, how do we identify and define peace? Is it a state of tranquility (as Webster might have it), a time for gathering forces (as V. I. Lenin put it), war by other means, or what?

In this chapter we define peace as the absence of armed conflict. In the real world of politics, not being in the middle of a "shooting war" is often the closest that we can come to peace. Peace powers are those capabilities of the president to prevent, avoid, or end armed conflict; conversely, they are powers that promote, sustain, or restore a situation in which there is not armed conflict. As we will see, these powers are extensive, for they include several dimensions: foreign policy declarations, conflict avoidance and war termination, arms control and disarmament, interventions to promote peace, and even shows of force as instruments of peace.

Foreign Policy Declarations and Initiatives

In 1799 then-Representative John Marshall told his colleagues in the House that the president was "sole organ" and "sole representative" of the United States in its conduct of foreign relations (Corwin 1984: 207–208). This monopoly in diplomacy stems from the first citizen's role as chief of state, chief executive, and chief diplomat, but it is more than just a ceremonial responsibility.

Indeed, from George Washington to our own time, presidents have found that they can make and influence American foreign policy simply by making a statement. Presidents have used the power to speak for the nation to make commitments, formalize decisions, and establish policy goals.

Declarations. In some cases, presidential declarations set national policy in a particular circumstance. In 1956 Dwight Eisenhower proclaimed that the United States would not support Britain, France, and Israel in their attempt to reverse Egypt's nationalization of the Suez Canal (Ambrose 1984). This pronouncement set American policy and effectively halted the attempt. In 1962, as part of the resolution of the Cuban Missile Crisis, John F. Kennedy pledged that the United States would never invade Cuba. In 1972 Richard Nixon announced that he would fly to China, not only altering years of American policy but effectively preempting any input on his opening to the People's Republic from Congress. As the Cold War wound down in the late 1980s and early 1990s, George Bush made a number of public statements that dictated the American response to the reunification of Germany, the breakup of the Soviet empire in eastern Europe, and the reorganization of a post–Soviet Russia. It has also become common for presidents to pledge—either through joint communiques with foreign leaders or on their own—American cooperation with one or more other nations in their efforts to combat terrorism, promote international understanding, or advance some other worthy symbolic or substantive goal.

Foreign policy doctrines. Presidents have also set policy through more general pronouncements that are intended to govern foreign relations across a number of cases and circumstances. These general statements are usually referred to as *doctrines*, largely in memory of the first and most famous of them: the Monroe Doctrine. In 1823 James Monroe declared that the Americas "are henceforth not to be considered as subjects for future colonization by any European powers" (quoted in Milkis and Nelson 1994: 115). The Monroe Doctrine, which was not approved by Congress, became a cornerstone of American foreign policy. Many of these doctrines, including the Truman Doctrine (aid to free peoples in their resistance to communism), the Carter Doctrine (which defined the Persian Gulf area as vital to American national security), and the Reagan Doctrine (which pledged support of anticommunist insurgencies in Latin America) invoke the president's war powers. Nevertheless, the Nixon Doctrine made it clear that American allies would be encouraged to rely less on U.S. troops as the nation became more selective about the conflicts in which it would become engaged.

Presidential diplomatic initiatives and actions. Scholars have tended to focus on certain aspects of presidential diplomacy, such as treaty-making and involvement in international summits. Presidents have used these activities as peace powers, from Warren Harding's initiatives at the Washington Disarmament Conference (1921) to John Kennedy's promotion of the Partial Test-Ban Treaty and the work of several recent presidents on arms-control treaties.

There are also other diplomatic actions that presidents have taken in order to promote peacemaking goals. President Clinton attempted to avert a divisive battle in NATO—and between NATO and Russia—over the admission of new states to the North Atlantic alliance. His Partnership for Peace proposal helped defuse the tension over the issue by offering a kind of associate status in NATO to several former Soviet-bloc countries.

One of the most successful diplomatic actions by American presidents to promote their peace agenda has received little attention from scholars: the use of parallel unilateral policy declarations (PUPDs) by two administrations to implement arms-control agreements (see Barilleaux 1986 and 1987). From 1977 to 1986, the United States observed limits on its nuclear arsenal under the terms of two treaties; yet during this period neither treaty was actually in force according the Constitution and statutory law.

The story of PUPDs is instructive for understanding the extent of presidential peace powers. In 1977 the SALT I treaty limiting American and Soviet nuclear arms expired, but negotiations on a SALT II agreement were incomplete. President Carter wanted to maintain the force levels of SALT I until the new treaty was ready, but the Arms Control and Disarmament Act of 1961 required that he obtain affirmative congressional action before the United States could participate in any arms-control agreement. (Continuation of an existing treaty past its own deadline is the same as a new treaty.) Therefore, the United States and the Soviet Union issued separate statements, identical in language, stating that each would continue to abide by SALT I provided that the other nation did likewise. By means of this "nonagreement," the terms of the treaty were in force without the acknowledgment of Congress. In 1980, when Carter was forced by circumstances to ask the Senate to suspend consideration of the SALT II treaty (because of the Soviet invasion of Afghanistan), he called upon the 1977 precedent to implement the new treaty through a similar "nonagreement." When Ronald Reagan took office, he confirmed the continued use of PUPDs to implement SALT II, although he severely criticized the agreement while campaigning for the presidency. In 1985, when the force limits of the unratified-but-in-force SALT II treaty were due to expire, Reagan even extended the life of SALT II. Then in 1986 Reagan decided to end U.S. compliance with the undead treaty. In the course of less than a decade, arms control had gone from being an area of policy determined jointly by Congress and the executive to a matter of presidential fiat.

Conflict Avoidance and War Termination

Political observers, practicing politicians, and scholars have devoted considerable time and energy to questions of how wars begin. Similarly, research on the president's ability to involve the United States in armed conflict has been a fixture of the scholarship on the office. But little attention has been given to presidential actions to avoid conflict or terminate ongoing conflict.

Actions to avoid conflict. Washington's Neutrality Proclamation (1793) made it clear that the young United States was not going to become involved in the

European conflict started by the French Revolution. It also stimulated the Pacificus–Helvidius debate between Hamilton and Madison. Other presidents also asserted the power, as both commander-in-chief and chief diplomat, to avoid conflicts rather than become embroiled in them. Grover Cleveland told Congress in 1893 that he would not mobilize the army no matter what the legislature did about declaring war on Spain (Riccards 1995).

In 1896 and 1897 William McKinley engaged in a number of diplomatic maneuvers to avoid war with Spain over Cuba, even resisting calls for a declaration of war in the wake of the explosion of the U.S.S. *Maine*. He frustrated members of Congress who wanted war by continually warning of the dangers of conflict and seeking legislative support for his attempts to find a peaceful resolution to the issues dividing the two countries. It was not until April 1897 that the president concluded that a diplomatic solution was unachievable, and he reluctantly asked Congress for a declaration of war.

Other presidents also resisted military interventions in conflicts that they believed were unwise or unnecessary. In 1954 Dwight Eisenhower faced a situation in which American-backed French troops in Vietnam were in imminent danger of being defeated by communist forces. Rather than intervene and immerse the United States in a war, the president decided to keep the country out of the war and allowed Vietnam to be partitioned (Greenstein and Burke 1989). In a pair of crises over Berlin in 1958–1959 and 1961, Presidents Eisenhower and Kennedy resisted using American military force in responding to Soviet activities to secure control over East Berlin and limit NATO access to West Berlin (George and Smoke 1974). George Bush resisted pressure to intervene militarily in the tragedy of Bosnia, arguing that it would lead to a large and long-term involvement that would cost the United States heavily in the number of lives lost. Just as the record of the presidency has been one of forces deployed, there have also been chapters about forces withheld from conflict.

War termination. The president can not only choose to stay out of a military conflict, but can also bring an end to an ongoing war. War termination was once regarded as a matter that—like war declaration—involved both the president and Congress. For much of American history, wars were usually concluded by treaties that were negotiated by the executive and approved by the Senate. The War of 1812, the Mexican War, and the Spanish-American War each ended with a treaty.

The twentieth century ushered in a new era: one in which wars would be terminated by congressional action and, later, by unilateral presidential action. World War I produced the ill-fated Treaty of Versailles, which the U.S. Senate rejected. Therefore, to formally close American participation in the conflict, Congress voted to repeal its declaration of war. A dispute erupted over the constitutional propriety of such an act. Writing in 1921, E. S. Corwin championed the "Power of Congress to Declare Peace:" "Congress has the right, then, simply by virtue of its power to repeal its previous enactments, to declare hostilities with Germany to be at an end, and its declaration to this effect, once duly enacted, will be binding upon the Courts and the Executive alike'' (1921: 674). In reply, John M. Mathews of the University of Illinois asserted the power of the president unilaterally to terminate war. He pointed to several incidents in which the executive had declared a halt to hostilities in advance of congressional action, such as the presidential proclamation of 1898 that called a cease-fire in the Spanish-American War (Mathews 1921). Only after this executive action was a treaty submitted for Senate approval.

As the century wore on, however, control over war termination shifted toward the presidency. Congress participated in the end of World War II, with the Senate approving the treaty ending the war in the Pacific theater and the whole Congress repealing the declaration of war against Nazi Germany in 1951. But then presidents began acting in a more unilateral fashion. In the Korean War, in Grenada, in Panama, and in the various bombing pauses and cease-fires in Vietnam, the president controlled the cessation of an ongoing war. Congress did legislate the end to the Vietnam War (see Franck and Weisband 1979), but under highly unusual political circumstances. President Nixon's decision to expand the Vietnam War into Cambodia in 1970, and then to end that expansion several months later, was an executive matter altogether. (Congress debated but did not act on a resolution to halt the Cambodian incursion.) In the Persian Gulf War, President Bush exercised unilateral control over the termination of the conflict, deciding on his own to end the war one hundred hours after the beginning of an Allied ground offensive. Congress, like the American public glued to CNN coverage of the war, was essentially a bystander in the ending of the conflict.

Third-Party Interventions to Promote Peace

In the pursuit of peace, American presidents have often intervened as third parties trying to resolve or expedite negotiations between international adversaries. Theodore Roosevelt's successful arbitration of the Russo-Japanese War was the first of these efforts, resulting in the so-called Peace of Portsmouth. Later presidents, particularly in the period since the 1970s, have followed this path.

One conflict that has been the subject of considerable presidential attention has been the ongoing problem of Arab-Israeli relations in the Middle East. Under Richard Nixon, Henry Kissinger's efforts at brokering peace between Israel and its Arab neighbors introduced the term *shuttle diplomacy* to the political lexicon. Jimmy Carter was successful at helping to bring about the Camp David Accords (1978) that led to peace between Egypt and Israel, while subsequent administrations tried to build on that success. Bill Clinton took great pride in assisting the conclusion of an agreement between Israel and the Palestine Liberation Organization, a deal that, like the Camp David agreement, was signed on the White House lawn.

The United States has also been a third party working for peace elsewhere. In the wake of the Cold War, American presidents became involved in the

Bosnian conflict, with the Clinton administration sponsoring talks in Dayton, Ohio, to seek some kind of resolution. Similarly, Bill Clinton took an interest in the question of Northern Ireland, sending former U.S. Senate majority leader George Mitchell to be his special envoy in trying to broker a peace agreement between the Protestant and Catholic factions in that troubled territory. American presidents have also worked on disputes in Africa, South Asia, and Latin America, with varying degrees of success.

In each of these cases, however, the executive has been fairly free to pursue a diplomatic course on its own and without congressional involvement. In general, Congress has come into the picture only when a president needed money to help facilitate a peace deal that he helped foster, such as when Jimmy Carter asked for an appropriation to help make the Egypt-Israeli peace deal a reality. At that point in the process, however, Congress has little choice but to acquiesce in the diplomatic victory scored by the chief executive.

Putting Force at the Service of Peace

Presidents have also taken actions or adopted positions that have employed their powers in diplomacy and military affairs to promote peace or deter conflict. An action of this sort sits in the place at which peace powers and war powers converge: the president is putting force in the service of peace.

Alliances and commitments. Since World War II, chief executives have made a number of commitments on behalf of the United States to create informal alliances with other nations. Such actions often take the form of a pronouncement by the president that pledges American support for a regime or policy without the formal involvement of Congress. In 1941 Franklin Roosevelt signed the Atlantic Charter with Winston Churchill, a document that laid the groundwork for American entry into World War II. During the war, FDR committed the United States to support the Allied war effort and not to sign a separate peace with the enemy. Indeed, the Allied decision to seek unconditional surrender by the Axis powers framed not only the circumstances for ending the war but the entire postwar order as well; the president unilaterally made this commitment for the United States. After the war, both Truman and Eisenhower used executive agreements to expand NATO into a unified defense organization with a standing military force. During the Cold War, American commitments to support several nations came in the form of executive agreements or presidential pronouncements rather than treaties, with the intent of deterring Soviet aggression against governments considered friendly to the anti-Soviet cause.

Shows of force and military exercises. Not all deployments of military force are intended to engage an adversary in armed conflict. Rather, governments often seek to deter adversaries, support allies, and strengthen their bargaining positions through demonstrations of their potential force. In the nineteenth century, the dispatch of an armada of ships on a "show the flag" tour was used to impress friends and potential foes alike of a nation's power. Indeed, Theodore Roosevelt sent the Great White Fleet on such a tour in 1907, despite congressional objections that the undertaking was a waste of money.

American presidents have often acted in this way to advance an agenda of peace, international cooperation, and stability. Millard Fillmore sent Commodore Perry to Japan with a squadron of ships, a move intended to impress upon the Japanese government the wisdom of cooperating with the United States. As a result, the Treaty of Kanagawa declared friendship between the two nations and opened Japanese ports to American commerce. Ronald Reagan sent American troops to Honduras in 1988 to demonstrate support for that country in the face of incursion by Nicaraguan forces. His secretary of state, George Schultz, explained that the American soldiers were not near the fighting but were in Honduras to underscore U.S. resolve. Clinton dispatched American troops to Kuwait to demonstrate a similar resolve when Iraqi troop movements near the Kuwait border made that government nervous about another invasion by Baghdad. He also sent American forces to Haiti to help ease the transition from a military to a civilian government, in the process of which he achieved one of the few foreign policy victories of his first term.

In these and other shows of force, the goal has been to avoid conflict rather than engage in it. Such actions rely on the president's power as commander-in-chief to deploy and direct American military power, but because they do not involve actual combat, they usually fall within the scope of executive power free from congressional control. Only if Congress can muster the will to cut off funding for such shows of force can it limit the president. When TR proposed to send the Great White Fleet around the world, some senators threatened to deny him funding. Roosevelt replied that he had enough money to send the fleet halfway around the world, and if Congress wanted the Navy back it would have to fork over the rest of the money.

Participation in international peacekeeping efforts. A final use of American military forces in the service of peace has been the nation's participation in international peacekeeping and humanitarian operations. Most of these endeavors have been under the auspices of the United Nations, in which the United States has often been an active supporter of these peacekeeping efforts. (Through diplomacy; America's position as leader of the West during the Cold War meant that it was not always a good choice for contributing to a "neutral" military force.) For example, in 1993 Clinton dispatched three hundred American ground troops to Macedonia to join a U.N. force already there. Clinton neither sought congressional approval for such action nor even formally notified Congress under the War Powers Resolution of 1973 (arguing that the soldiers, as peacekeepers, were not in harm's way) (Rourke, Carter, and Boyer 1994). Peacekeeping operations of this sort will continue in the future; American participation in them will most likely continue to be a matter of presidential discretion.

The Broad Scope of Peace Powers

Presidential peace powers are clearly significant to the conduct of foreign affairs, especially in the post–Cold War world. For all the attention that has been given to the executive's power to commit American forces to hostile situations, militarily intervene in foreign conflicts, start wars, and place U.S. forces in harm's way, surprisingly little systematic attention has been given to the other side of war. By having a better sense of peace powers, we can develop a fuller picture of the president's resources for advancing the overall goals of American foreign policy. As our survey of the scope of peace powers makes clear, presidents do not possess contentious and specific war powers on the one hand and nebulous peace powers on the other. Rather, the president possesses an array of fairly specific powers to promote peace, powers that have expanded in the same period that war powers have grown larger.

What should we do to correct our poor understanding of presidential peace powers? To answer that question, we shall now turn our attention to an agenda for future research.

A PEACE POWERS RESEARCH AGENDA

This survey has shown that the subject of presidential peace powers offers a different perspective on the presidency than can be found in most literature on foreign affairs. We argue that a fuller understanding of presidential power and its exercise, especially in the environment of a post–Cold war international order, requires that we examine more aspects of the chief executive's power than before. As we have seen, the rise of presidential peace powers has accompanied the rise of war powers, and both serve as important devices by which American chief executives seek to influence world events.

Where does a recognition of the relevance of peace powers leave us, then? Just saying that they are important is not enough. Rather, now that we can see this frontier of the presidency, we can point to a number of issues and questions that are ripe for future scholarly exploration. We will consider a few suggested by our prospecting.

The sources of presidential peace powers. Our work has suggested that the development of presidential peace powers has come largely through executive actions taken in the light of events, constitutional ambiguity, and presidents' desire to shape policy. But just as with the case of war powers, why is it that peace powers have become almost exclusively presidential in the face of a body of authoritative evidence that both Congress and the president ought to be involved in such decisions? Scholars have pored over the war-powers provisions and precedents in search of an answer to that question. If we further investigate the sources of presidential peace powers—in the Constitution, in law, in practice—we can better understand the overall development of presidential power.

The use of presidential peace powers. Our work has provided a number of examples of the use of peace powers, but it is by no means a systematic attempt to build a database of cases and incidents of the practice of power in this area. Scholars have given considerable effort to cataloguing incidents of "presidential war," uses of force, and related actions. Much work needs to be done with the historical record to begin building a catalogue of the uses of peace power. The records of the early Republic, nineteenth, and early twentieth centuries are available to scholars, both in original source materials and a voluminous body of American historical scholarship. For twentieth-century presidents, especially in the period since World War II, secrecy has been a cloak that has covered all kinds of executive actions. With a mountain of original materials available in presidential libraries and archives—much of it increasingly available on the Internet—scholars can turn to the task of mining the record in search of evidence of uses of peace powers. Given the urgency of foreign policy decisions and actions in the Cold War, there ought to be a host of interesting and perhaps poorly known instances of presidential peace-power actions. As we saw earlier, there are some well-known episodes: the Suez Crisis of 1956, the Camp David accords, and others. As part of a project to catalogue the uses of peace powers, probably other cases can be found and examined.

The varieties of peace powers. This chapter has focused on areas of presidential power that have not received much attention before now. In consequence, we have given little attention to better-known powers, such as treaty making, appointment and use of ambassadors, involvement in international organizations, and traditional methods of diplomacy. We have not even considered subtle and creative uses of diplomacy to promote peace, such as the "ping-pong diplomacy" that was used to assist a defrosting of Sino-American relations in the 1970s. There is still work to be done linking the kinds of powers we have examined here to more traditional—as well as more creative—means of presidential diplomacy.

The legitimacy of presidential peace powers. Promotion of peace has often been interpreted as a self-justifying activity. Indeed, some observers have come fairly close to defending executive actions of questionable constitutionality if they are successful in promoting the cause of peace. For example, research on PUPDs has demonstrated that these "executive nonagreements" raise interesting and important questions under the Constitution, statutory law, and international law. Yet a number of members of Congress, political pundits, and political scholars have tended to act is if their use to achieve arms control in the absence of a treaty that could pass the United States Senate qualifies PUPDs for a free pass on constitutional and legal questions. Is peace a sufficient justification to sidestep legal and constitutional strictures? If so, why not presidential war in the name of national security?

Certainly, other issues and questions may be raised by our analysis. Our purpose has been to call attention to the subject of peace powers, to demonstrate their relevance, and to suggest avenues for future research. We believe that work in this area is both needed and worth doing.

NOTES

1. That Act, which is still on the books, went further than what Washington proposed by "[imposing] criminal penalties, enforceable by the courts, upon person within the United States who begin, or provide the means for, a military expedition against any country with which the U.S. is at peace" (Koh 1990: 79).

2. Section 1 of the Neutrality Act (1794) "broadly outlawed Americans from using their vessels, or employing other vessels, to go from anywhere to any French port, and from being employed in any traffic or commerce with any person within the jurisdiction of France; it authorized seizures of such vessels within the jurisdiction of the United States" (Franck and Glennon 1987: 547).

REFERENCES

Ambrose, Stephen. 1984. *Eisenhower: The President.* New York: Simon & Schuster.

Barilleaux, Ryan J. 1987. "Parallel Unilateral Policy Declarations: A New Device for Presidential Autonomy in Foreign Affairs." *Presidential Studies Quarterly* 17 (Winter): 107–17.

———. 1986. "Executive Non-Agreements, Arms Control, and the Invitation to Struggle in Foreign Affairs." *World Affairs* 148 (Fall): 217–28.

Congressional Quarterly. 1997. *Powers of the Presidency.* Washington, DC: Congressional Quarterly.

Corwin, Edward S. 1984. *The President: Office and Powers, 1979–1984,* 5th rev. ed., ed. Randall Bland, Theodore Hindson, and Jack Peltason. New York: New York University Press.

———. 1921. "The Power of Congress to Declare Peace." *Michigan Law Review* 18: 669–75.

Ely, John Hart. 1993. *War and Responsibility: Constitutional Lessons of Vietnam and Its Aftermath.* Princeton: Princeton University Press.

Fisher, Louis. 1995. *Presidential War Power.* Lawrence: University Press of Kansas.

Franck, Thomas and Michael J. Glennon. 1987. *Foreign Relations and National Security Law.* St. Paul, MN: West Publishing Co.

——— and Edward Weisband. 1979. *Foreign Policy by Congress.* New York: Oxford University Press.

George, Alexander and Richard Smoke. 1974. *Deterrence in American Foreign Policy.* New York: Columbia University Press.

Greenstein, Fred and John Burke. 1989. *How Presidents Test Reality: Decisions on Vietnam, 1954 & 1965.* New York: Russell Sage Foundation.

Henkin, Louis. 1972. *Foreign Affairs and the Constitution.* New York: Foundation Press.

Koh, Harold Hongju. 1990. *The National Security Constitution: Sharing Power after the Iran-Contra Affair.* New Haven: Yale University Press.

Levy, Leonard W. and Louis Fisher. 1994. *Encyclopedia of the American Presidency.* New York: Simon & Schuster.

Mathews, John. 1921. "The Termination of War." *Michigan Law Review* 18: 819–34.

Milkis, Sidney and Michael Nelson. 1994. *The American Presidency: Origins and Development, 1776–1993.* Washington, DC: CQ Press.

Nelson, Michael, ed. 1989. *Congressional Quarterly's Guide to the Presidency.* Washington, DC: CQ Press.

Riccards, Michael P. 1995. *The Ferocious Engine of Democracy: A History of the American Presidency*. Lanham, MD: Madison Books.

Rourke, John, Ralph Carter and Mark Boyer. 1994. *Making American Foreign Policy*. Guilford, CT: Dushkin Publishing Group.

Story, Joseph. 1851. *Commentaries on the Constitution of the United States*. Boston: Little, Brown.

Chapter 8

The President and
Federal Reserve Nominations

RUSSELL LIGHTFOOT AND SCOTT HUFFMON

The nomination and confirmation of members of the Board of Governors of the Federal Reserve System has been largely overlooked in the study of the presidency and executive branch. Considerable interest has been shown, however, in other federal positions requiring Senate confirmation, especially the courts. Nominations to the Board of Governors, on the other hand, have received very little attention. Despite the obvious importance of the Fed to economic policy and to the personal finances of individual Americans, the literature on presidential nominations tends to focus on the high-profile positions in the cabinet and the judiciary. We argue that it is time to redirect scholarship toward positions that carry considerable power, albeit less celebrity.

WHY THE LACK OF INTEREST IN THE FED?

There are several possible explanations for the apparent lack of interest. First, much of the work of the Board of Governors and the Federal Open Market Committee (FOMC) is not very visible. While decisions to raise or lower the discount rate receive considerable attention, the process leading up to the decision to raise or lower interest rates has, until recently, gone largely unnoticed.

The second explanation for the lack of attention is that much of the work of the Board of Governors is poorly understood by the public, pundits, and perhaps even members of Congress. While changes in the discount rate receive considerable attention, this is only a fraction of the work of the Board of Governors. The Board of Governors is also responsible for day-to-day management of the money supply through open market operations (the buying and selling of government securities). The Board drafts regulations that influence daily operations of the banking industry. The Board also supervises the operations of the regional Federal Reserve banks.

In addition to the ignorance of the Board's functions, the structure of the Board and of the entire Federal Reserve System is not well understood by even politically attentive Americans. The Board of Governors is designed to be independent of political pressure. The seven members of the Board are appointed to fourteen-year terms, with one term expiring every two years. The chair of the Board of Governors is appointed to a renewable four-year term. This arrangement helps insulate members from political pressure and prevents any one president from packing the Board.[1] Clearly, the work of the Board of Governors is both diverse and pervasive. The lack of understanding of the Board's functions, operations, and structure has been accompanied by a corresponding lack of interest in the confirmation of its members.

Another possible explanation is that Congress has little influence over what the Board of Governors does. Members of Congress may be less interested in who sits on the Board of Governors since this is an organization that Congress has little influence over and members are, perhaps, less likely to be penalized by voters for confirming a given nominee. Havrilesky (1988), for example, found that the president has influence over the decision-making process of the Federal Reserve, whereas Congress does not. Using an index of administration signaling, Havrilesky found that the administration did have an effect on narrow definitions of the money supply while a similar index for Congress did not.

Considerable work has been done on the decision-making processes of the Board of Governors (see, for example, Khoury 1990; Lombra and Karamouzis 1990; Munger and Roberts 1990). The decision-making processes of the Federal Open Market Committee have also been well researched (see Gildea 1990; Havrilesky and Schweitzer 1990; Mayer 1990). Finally, considerable work has been done on the history of the Federal Reserve System (Kettl 1986; Moore 1990) and monetary policy in the United States (Timberlake 1993). Little has been done, however, on the selection of people to sit on the Board of Governors. This is a curious omission in the research, given the importance and authority of the Board.

Much of the literature we will be using is derived from work on the nomination and confirmation of U.S. Supreme Court justices. In many ways there are parallels in the role of the two institutions. We will deal more with this literature later in this chapter.

Given the importance and pervasiveness of the work of the Federal Reserve System, an understanding of how its highest officials are selected merits much more attention than the scholarly community has given it. However, examining the selection process of members of the Board of Governors requires the examination of more than just the nominating president. In order to fully analyze the process, one must account for the nominating president, the senators voting on confirmation, and the nominees themselves. The lack of information and data concerning all of these actors has proven to be a major stumbling block for the study of this process.

In this chapter, we will examine the confirmation of nominees to the Board of Governors by Presidents Carter, Reagan, and Bush. We will use a unique data set that will allow us to model the confirmation process, taking into account the influence of the president, the ideology of the nominees and senators, partisanship, and other outside influences.

WHAT FACTORS AFFECT CONFIRMATION?

Having already noted the surprising paucity of research on Federal Reserve members despite their enormous role in the economic welfare of the United States, we propose a theory concerning those factors that contribute to the confirmation of members of the Board of Governors. How are the people who guide our economy chosen? Do senators consider each nominee in individualistic terms, or do they merely look to the nominating president for cues as to the nominee's potential behavior?

We believe that senators are influenced by both individual and institutional factors when deciding how to cast their vote for nominees to the Board of Governors. Perhaps the most important consideration is the nominating president. If Neustadt is correct, then the most important factor in a president's confirmation battles is his ability to persuade and we believe that a president's persuasiveness flows, in part, from his institutional strength. It has been demonstrated that popular presidents who are in a strategically advantageous position are much more likely to win confirmation battles for nominees to the Supreme Court (Cameron, Cover, and Segal 1990; Huffmon and White 1996; Segal, Cameron, and Cover 1992).

Presidential Popularity

When a president is suffering from low approval ratings, members of Congress may be less afraid of public ire if they challenge his agenda. Accordingly, a senator might feel freer to vote against the nominees of an unpopular president because his or her constituency would not necessarily view such an action unfavorably. Conversely, it should follow that a president who is riding high in approval ratings would have an easier time pushing his agenda, including nominees, through Congress. Senators would fear their constituents' anger at attempting to thwart the agenda of a popular president. Therefore, we hypothesize that the higher a president's approval rating, the more likely senators are to vote for his nominee to the Board of Governors.

All politicians, however, are aware of the vapid nature of public favor. Events both calamitous and mundane can temporarily swing political approval ratings in any direction. Several scholars have noted that presidential approval springs from the events of the day, among other things (Kernell 1978; MacKuen 1983;

Ostrom and Simon 1985, 1988; Ostrom and Smith 1992; Weisberg and Kimball 1995). Popularity may reach peaks or dip to valleys, but these changes are often just the "bumps and wiggles" that surround a larger trend (Ostrom and Smith 1992). We believe that it is not the "bumps and wiggles" that affect senators' voting; rather, they look to the trends of presidential popularity for their cues. These trends set a *benchmark* of presidential popularity; when deciding how to cast their ballots, we believe that senators will look beyond the president's immediate popularity, opting instead to rely on the more accurately reflective information provided by a president's recent history of approval ratings. A president whose trend, or "benchmark," of public approval is high should be more likely to win the confirmation of a nominee to the Board of Governors (other things being equal).

Partisanship and Presidential Strength

If popularity provides a president with more resources to bring to bear on a confirmation vote, other factors mitigate the effectiveness of this and other resources. When the party of the president does not hold the majority in the Senate, or when the president is in the fourth year of his term, either as a lame duck or as a performer in the ballet of reelection, he is in a weakened position relative to the Senate. Both situations force the president to temper his agenda with practical necessity.

Conversely, when a president is not in the fourth year of his term, and his party holds a majority in the Senate, he is in an advantageous position relative to the Senate. When a president has such a favorable forum in which to bring his resources to bear, it should follow that senators would be more hesitant in voting against his position. Accordingly, we hypothesize that senators are more likely to vote for the confirmation of a nominee to the Board of Governors when the nominating president is in a position of strength (other things being equal).

High approval ratings and holding a partisan advantage in a year when the president can best use that advantage provide the president with an edge over the Senate and should have a positive effect on senators' voting behavior. In addition to these institutional influences, some individual factors influence a senator's vote on the confirmation of nominees to the Board of Governors. The most obvious factor that might sway a senator's vote is partisanship. Senators of the same party of the president should be more likely to support his nominees than senators of the opposition. We hypothesize that senators of the same party as the president will be more likely to vote to confirm his nominee than those who are not of his party (other things being equal).

Ideology

Finally, senators should logically vote to confirm those nominees to whom they are ideologically similar. Most senators would assume that the ideology of a nominee prior to the confirmation vote would provide a reliable indication of probable behavior on the Board of Governors if confirmed. If this is the case, then we might expect the senators to employ a spatial voting model in their decision-making process. According to our theory, senators will vote for those nominees who are ideologically close and against those who are ideologically distant.

Ideologically distant from whom? According to neo-institutional theories, senators cast their ballots with the goal of reelection in mind and, therefore, would attempt to match the ideology of a nominee with the ideology of their constituencies. While we do not dispute the goal-oriented notion of congressional voting provided by the neo-institutional model, we do not think that using the ideology of the constituency alone accurately reflects the spatial calculation made by senators in the voting calculus of Federal Reserve nominations.

Nominees to the Board of Governors deal with monetary policy that is beyond the scope of comprehension, or at least interest, of most Americans. Because of the subtle nature of the Federal Reserve's work, we contend that senators will rely less overtly on constituent ideology than for a more visible nomination, such as that of a Supreme Court justice. Studies in this vein often try to separate the ideological preferences of the constituents from those of a senator (see Cameron, Cover, and Segal 1990; Segal, Cameron, and Cover 1992). However, because of the nonobvious nature of the work of the Board of Governors and the Federal Open Market Committee, we believe that an ideological measure based on a senator's voting behavior, which would naturally reflect a combination of constituent and personal preferences, would provide a more accurate yardstick to measure the ideological distance from a given nominee.

Our theory posits that a senator's confirmation vote for a nominee to the Board of Governors is a function of individual and institutional influences. Our chief hypothesis is that a senator's vote is the function of ideological distance from the nominee, whether the senator is of the same party as the president, the benchmark popularity of the nominating president, and the strength of the nominating president.

DATA AND MEASURES

Dependent Variable

The dependent variable consists of the 685[2] recorded votes for the nominees to the Board of Governors by Presidents Carter through Clinton (Clinton's first term only). The votes include the nominations of Paul Volcker and Alan Greenspan to the position of chairman of the Board of Governors and the nominations of Janet Yellen, Laurence Meyer, and Alice Rivlin as members of the Board of Governors. All of the other votes for confirmation of nominees to the Board of Governors during this period, except that of John LaWare,[3] were voice votes and had to be excluded from the model. The variable was coded 0 for a vote *against* confirmation and 1 for a vote *for* confirmation.

Critics might argue that, by excluding such a large number of votes, we are biasing our sample in that we are only examining those votes in which a sizable portion, one-fifth, of the floor requested a roll-call vote. However, we do not believe this to be the case. In order for our sample to suffer from serious selection bias, there must be a systematic difference between those votes that were chosen to be analyzed and those that were not; that is, there must be a systematic difference between those nominations for which roll-call votes were taken and those that were acted on with only a voice vote.

One might claim that votes in which a portion of the floor demanded a roll-call were conflictual, while those in which only a voice vote were needed were consensual, and this is where the bias is introduced. Fortunately, this is not the case. Of the recorded votes, while some certainly were conflictual, many were consensual. Also, according to reports in the *CQ Weekly*, many of the voice votes drew heated debate. For these reasons, we do not believe that our sample suffers from serious selection bias.

Variable: Ideological Distance

This variable is the squared difference between the ideology of a given senator and the perceived preconfirmation ideology of the nominee. The ideology of the senators reflects their liberalism ratings as calculated by the Americans for Democratic Action (ADA). These scores are scaled from 0 to 100, with 100 being the most liberal position. We recoded the scores so that they ranged between 0 and 1, with 1 being the most liberal position. The ideology of the nominees was constructed from a content analysis of stories and editorials concerning each nominee prior to the confirmation vote.

The stories and editorials were examined for mentions of monetary conservatism, liberalism, or moderation. This content analysis was conducted on two of the nation's leading newspapers, one with a liberal viewpoint, The *New York Times*, and one with a more conservative viewpoint, The *Wall Street Journal*. The ideology scores for the nominees were also coded to range between 0 and 1, with 1 being the more liberal position. The ideologies we calculated for the nominees used in this analysis may be found in Table 8.1. We expect the relationship between the squared difference of the ideologies of the senators and the nominee and the probability of a senator to vote for the nominee to be negative; that is, the greater the ideological distance between the senator and the nominee, the less likely that senator will be to vote to confirm the nominee.

Variable: Partisanship

This is a dummy variable coded 0 if the senator is not of the same party of the president and 1 if the senator and the president are of the same party. We expect the relationship between this variable and a senator's vote to be positive.

Table 8.1
Presidential Nominees to the Federal Reserve Board on Whom Recorded Votes Were Taken in the U.S. Senate, 1979–1996

Nominee	Year	Ideology
Paul Volcker	1979	.273
Paul Volcker	1983	.311
Alan Greenspan	1987	.250
Janet Yellen	1994	.250
Alan Greenspan	1996	.389
Laurence Meyer	1996	.500
Alice Rivlin	1996	.667

Other things being equal, a senator should be more likely to vote for the nominee of a president from his or her own party.

Variable: Benchmark Approval

This variable measures the mean approval rating for the nominating president for one year prior to the nomination. The data for this measure came from Gallup poll surveys that asked respondents whether they approved or disapproved of the way the president was doing his job. Taking the mean of the previous year instead of the last approval rating prior to the confirmation vote should give a more accurate picture of the president's standard, or benchmark, of approval, unclouded by temporary, vacuous issues that might have a significant, but ephemeral, effect on popularity. Senators should be less willing to oppose a president who is enjoying widespread public support. Therefore, as the benchmark presidential popularity rises, so should the probability that a given senator will vote to confirm the nominee of that president; the relationship should be positive.

Variable: Presidential Strength

This variable is also a dummy variable. It is coded 0 when the president is in a weak position relative to the Senate and 1 when the president is in a position of strength. The president is believed to be strong when he is not in the fourth year of his term and his party holds a majority in the Senate. As discussed earlier, a senator should be more likely to vote for the nominee of a strong president; therefore, the expected relationship is positive.

Table 8.2
Regression of Senate Confirmation Vote on Individual and Institution Factors

Variable	Maximum Likelihood Coefficient	Heteroskedasticity-Consistent Standard Error	Impact
Ideological Distance	-6.207**	1.1704	-.141966
Partisanship (same as president)	.985854**	.320681	.10721
Benchmark Approval	.297509*	.141296	.000001
Presidential Strength	2.301748*	1.20011	.165049
Constant	-11.91174*	6.757727	---
Log Likelihood		-191.42487	
Number of Observations		675	
Pseudo R^2		.1723	
Percent Predicted Correctly		90.52%	
Proportional Reduction in Error		12.39%	

$*p < .05$ (one-tailed test).
$**p < .01$ (one-tailed test).

RESULTS

Since the dependent variable is dichotomous, the model was estimated using logit analysis. Because the data are cross-sectional, heteroskedasticity-consistent standard errors were calculated for the coefficients in order to avoid the common pitfalls of this type of data. The results of the logit analysis may be found in Table 8.2. Overall, the model performed rather well. All of the coefficients were significant and in the predicted direction. Over 90 percent of the votes were predicted correctly. Although maximum likelihood estimation does not allow for the calculation of an R^2, the pseudo R^2 provides an analogous goodness-of-fit measure. Our model explained slightly more than 17 percent of the variance. Although this is certainly not as high as we had hoped, it is a significant amount. Much of the remaining variance may be accounted for by factors or characteristics that we were unable to measure or control for in this model (see below).

The results demonstrate that the further a nominee is from a senator ideologically, the less likely that senator is to vote for his or her confirmation. However, since maximum likelihood coefficients may not be interpreted in the same manner as ordinary least squares regression coefficients, we know little more than the fact that ideological distance had a significant impact in the predicted direction. For this reason, we also calculated impact scores for this variable, as well as the other independent variables.

Impact scores reflect the change in the probability that a senator will vote for the confirmation of a nominee due to an increase of one standard deviation from the mean of a given independent variable, with the probabilities resulting from the other independent variables held constant at their mean. In our model, an increase of one standard deviation from the mean ideological distance produced a change in the probability that a senator would vote for confirmation of $-.141966$. Put another way, having an ideological distance from the nominee that is one standard deviation higher than the mean results in a 14.2 percent drop in the probability that a senator will vote for a given nominee.

As expected, the coefficient for partisanship is significant and in the predicted direction. Being of the same party as the nominating president increases the probability that a senator will vote for that president's nominee by almost 11 percent. However, presidential popularity seems to have very little impact on the probability that a senator will cast a yea vote for confirmation. Despite this negligible impact, the coefficient is still significant; what should we make of this variable?

It might be important to note that the standard deviation of benchmark presidential approval was rather small, meaning that it is numerically possible for popularity to vary by several standard deviations around the mean. We might extrapolate from this finding that wide movement in popularity will not derail a nomination unless the trend for a given president is *several* standard deviations above or below the mean. Only a wildly popular, or extremely despised, president will affect his nominee's odds of being confirmed. However, the fact that this variable is significant shows us that senators take presidential popularity into account when they cast their votes, but base their final decisions on other factors as long as the president is somewhere within an expected range of popularity.

Finally, the greatest influence on senatorial votes for nominees to the Board of Governors comes from presidential strength. The variable is significant and in the predicted direction. More importantly, for our purposes, being nominated by a stronger president increases the probability that a senator will vote for a given nominee by 16 percent. Obviously, the most important influences on senators' vote choices come from the president. The president influences voting behavior directly through his strength and partisanship and indirectly through his choice of nominee (liberal or conservative).

What does this mean for the role of the president in the nominating process? What does this tell us about the relationship between the Senate and the president? What does this tell us about the Federal Reserve? We address these questions, as well as the limitations of the model in the following section.

CONCLUSIONS AND IMPLICATIONS FOR PRESIDENTIAL INFLUENCE

This study clearly demonstrates the importance of the president in the nomination and confirmation of members of the Board of Governors, as suggested by two of our model's variables, benchmark approval and presidential strength.

The large number of voice votes suggests that the Senate may have been deferring to the president in the nomination process.[4] The lack of a roll-call vote may also suggest that senators are more concerned with the confirmation of members of the United States Supreme Court than with the confirmation of members of the Board of Governors. One of the conclusions that can be drawn from this finding is that the president and Senate are not equal partners, nor are their roles constant across various nominations.

One of the clearest implications for the Federal Reserve is that the nominees are being chosen with less scrutiny *by the Senate* than are nominees for other posts requiring Senate confirmation. This does not mean that there is no scrutiny, only that scrutiny by the Senate is minimal. We still do not know the level of scrutiny the nominees are subjected to before their names are sent to the Senate. It would seem however, that the Senate is deferring to the president in this area.

FUTURE STUDIES

This study has two major limitations that will need to be addressed in future studies. First, our model does not include economic variables. Second, we need to refine our ideological difference measure.

With regard to the first, the model likely is misspecified in that it neglects economic conditions. We need to develop an index of economic conditions and to think it out further. We should decide whether or not to use an index of actual economic conditions or an index of perceived economic conditions.

While much of our work departs from studies of confirmation of Supreme Court justices, we may have to include additional environmental variables that the studies of judicial nomination and confirmation do not consider. That is, we may need to add variables that reflect economic performance—both perceived and actual. The general public may not pay much attention to the totality of the Supreme Court's work but does have a sense of the overall performance of the economy.

The second limitation of our study, the ideological distance measure, needs two reforms. First, we used ADA scores to tap senators' ideology. This is problematic given that monetary and political ideology are not necessarily compatible. One can be a political conservative and still support easy money policies—a monetary liberal—in order to avoid a recession.

One possibility is to use scores from the Chamber of Commerce of the United States. While these are pro-business, they may not necessarily tap the appropriate economic issues. Many of the issues that favor business development may not necessarily be consistent with sound monetary policy. For example, low interest rates almost always tend to favor business since aggregate demand is increased. On the other hand, low interest rates may not—depending on the inflation rate and other economic indicators—be good for the economy.

The second modification we should make in the ideological distance measure is to improve the ideology scores of the nominees. We have to develop stricter criteria for monetary ideology, and we need to use a wider range of newspapers in our study. We should develop a list of criteria that would encompass specific issue areas as well as general statements of perceived ideological leanings. We need to include a wider range of newspapers in the hope of finding more material on some of the nominees who we had little reported material to work with.

Going beyond the study of the president's and Senate's role in federal judicial appointments and looking at their role in the appointment of members of the Board of Governors and other low-profile appointments are important for a number of reasons. First, the dynamics of the process are considerably different in the case of the Board of Governors, with the Senate apparently deferring to the president. Second, if members of Congress do indeed have less interest in the nomination and confirmation of members of the Board of Governors, then understanding how these people are chosen becomes critical. Finally, it is essential to understand how people are selected for agency posts that are subject to little congressional oversight since there will be no opportunity for checks after the person has been confirmed and policy has been implemented.

This is clearly a fresh area with room for future research. In an age of high-deficit (or debt) budgeting at the national level, monetary policy will become an ever more important tool of policy formation. Even if the deficit at the federal level is eventually reduced to zero, the size of the debt may render fiscal policy options irrelevant in smoothing business cycles and outlining policy preferences.

NOTES

1. It is true, however, that William Proxmire opposed the nomination of John LaWare because that would have meant that all the members of the Board of Governors would have been Reagan appointees (*Wall Street Journal*, May 25, 1988).

2. The *n* of the model, 675, is the result of missing values elsewhere; this number does not include those senators who abstained.

3. No information could be found regarding the preconfirmation ideology of John LaWare; therefore, he was dropped from the model.

4. The only reason we had as many roll-call votes as we did was due to Tom Harkin forcing a roll-call vote on Alan Greenspan's 1996 nomination to chair the Board of Governors (*New York Times*, June 9, 1996; June 8, 1996; and May 18, 1996). This also gave us roll-call votes for Alice Rivlin and Laurence Meyer. It is interesting to note that

William Proxmire's opposition to John LaWare (*Wall Street Journal*, May 25, 1988) did not result in a roll-call vote on LaWare's nomination.

REFERENCES

Beck, Nathaniel. 1990. "Congress and the Fed: Why the Dog Does Not Bark in the Night." In *The Political Economy of American Monetary Policy*, ed. Thomas Mayer. New York: Cambridge University Press.

Cameron, Charles, Albert Cover and Jeffrey Segal. 1990. "Senate Voting on Supreme Court Nominees: A Neoinstitutional Model." *American Political Science Review* 84: 525–34.

Gildea, John A. 1990. "Explaining FOMC Members' Votes." In *The Political Economy of American Monetary Policy*, ed. Thomas Mayer. New York: Cambridge University Press.

Havrilesky, Thomas. 1988. "Monetary Policy Signaling from the Administration to the Federal Reserve." *Journal of Money, Credit, and Banking* 20(1): 83–101.

—— and Robert Schweitzer. 1990. "A Theory of FOMC Dissent Voting with Evidence from the Time Series." In *The Political Economy of American Monetary Policy*, ed. Thomas Mayer. New York: Cambridge University Press.

Huffmon, Scott H. and John E. White, Jr. 1996. "A Spatial and Dynamic Model of Supreme Court Confirmations." Paper presented to the Southern Political Science Association, Atlanta.

Kernell, S. 1978. "Explaining Presidential Popularity." *American Political Science Review* 72: 506–22.

Kettl, Donald F. 1986. *Leadership at the Fed*. New Haven: Yale University Press.

Khoury, Salwa S. 1990. "The Federal Reserve Reaction Function: A Specification Search." In *The Political Economy of American Monetary Policy*, ed. Thomas Mayer. New York: Cambridge University Press.

Lombra, Raymond E. and Nicholas Karamouzis. 1990. "A Positive Analysis of the Policy-Making Process at the Federal Reserve." In *The Political Economy of American Monetary Policy*, ed. Thomas Mayer. New York: Cambridge University Press.

MacKuen, Michael. 1983. "Political Drama, Economic Conditions, and the Dynamics of Presidential Popularity." *American Journal of Political Science* 27: 165–92.

Mayer, Thomas. 1990. "Minimizing Regret: Cognitive Dissonance as an Explanation of FOMC Behavior." In *The Political Economy of American Monetary Policy*, ed. Thomas Mayer. New York: Cambridge University Press.

Moore, Carl H. 1990. *The Federal Reserve System: A History of the First 75 Years*. Jefferson, NC: McFarland.

Munger, Michael C. and Brian E. Roberts. 1990. "The Federal Reserve and Its Institutional Environment: A Review." In *The Political Economy of American Monetary Policy*, ed. Thomas Mayer. New York: Cambridge University Press.

Ostrom, Charles and Dennis Simon. 1985. "Promise and Performance: A Dynamic Model of Presidential Popularity at the Individual Level." *American Political Science Review* 79: 334–58.

——. 1988. "The President's Public." *American Journal of Political Science* 32: 1096–1119.

———— and Renee M. Smith. 1992. "Error Correction, Attitude Persistence, and Executive Rewards and Punishments: A Behavioral Theory of Presidential Approval." *Political Analysis* 4: 127–84.

Segal, Jeffrey, Charles Cameron and Albert Cover. 1992. "A Spatial Model of Roll Call Voting: Senators, Constituents, Presidents, and Interest Groups in Supreme Court Confirmations." *American Journal of Political Science* 36: 96–121.

Timberlake, Richard H. 1993. *Monetary Policy in the United States: An Intellectual and Institutional History*. Chicago: University of Chicago Press.

Weisberg, Herbert and David Kimball. 1995. "Attitudinal Correlates of the 1992 Presidential Vote: Party Identification and Beyond," In *Democracy's Feast: Elections in America*, ed. Herbert Weisberg. Chatham, NJ: Chatham House, pp. 72–111.

Part III

New Political and Cultural Frontiers

Chapter 9

The Presidency as a Cultural Pulpit

KEVAN M. YENERALL

The popular literature on the presidency has often centered on the more traditional terrain of institutional matters—such as constitutional duties, relations
with Congress, and executive leadership in foreign policy. Beginning with Richard Neustadt's seminal work on presidential persuasion and behavior, *Presidential Power* (1960), presidential research segued into several relevant areas of
interest, prompted by Neustadt's central thesis that true presidential power is the
"power to persuade" and the growth—in power, size, and expectations—of the
presidency and the "presidential branch" of the federal government (see Hart
1995). As a result of this phenomenon, many presidents have since been defined
not only by their successes in fulfilling their basic constitutional duties, but also
by the scope and style of their persuasion in implementing major economic,
foreign policy, and social policy agendas. Literature studying the evolution and
dynamics of an increasingly behavioral, extraconstitutional, modern, "personal"
(Lowi 1985), "post-modern" (Barilleaux 1988; Rose 1991), and "rhetorical"
(Medhurst 1996; Tulis 1987) presidency has expanded exponentially in recent
years.

Of these diverse forays into theories of presidential leadership and governance, the most relevant in terms of this study is the phenomenon of the *rhetorical presidency*. In an extenuation of an argument originally presented in 1981
with James Ceaser, Glen Thurow, and Joseph Bessette, Jeffrey Tulis (1987)
asserts that, since the presidencies of Theodore Roosevelt and Woodrow Wilson,
popular or mass rhetoric has become "one of the principal tools of presidential
leadership" (Barilleaux et al. 1996: 9). For Tulis, the history of the rhetorical
presidency is best understood in light of the existence of two distinct constitutional presidencies. Although the first constitutional presidency (1789–1913) was
a restrained office rooted in deliberation and rare public speeches, the second

constitutional presidency (1913–present) has been dominated by direct appeals to the public. Illustrative of this new strategy of leadership is the aggressive rhetorical presidency of Woodrow Wilson (1913–1921), which ushered in the second constitutional presidency. Consequently, in the era of the second constitutional presidency, leadership by popular and mass rhetoric has become the norm—whereas until Wilson, and to a lesser and different extent, Theodore Roosevelt, such a public presidency had been discouraged by both the Constitution and tradition.

BEYOND THE RHETORICAL PRESIDENCY

The rhetorical presidency carries with it tremendous promise for dynamic leadership, perhaps best exemplified by Theodore Roosevelt's successful public crusade for the Hepburn Act. Tulis, however, is apt to point out the immediate and long-term dangers and dilemmas presented by overreliance on public oratory as a means of leadership. Presidential routinization of crisis rhetoric in the twentieth century, for example—often in order to gain short-term advantages—has had grave consequences for effective policy, governance, and the presidency as an institution. Nonetheless, since the institutionalization of the rhetorical presidency, presidents have routinely used the "bully pulpit"—the president's strategic use of rhetoric as a "vantage point for inspiring people"—to legitimize their leadership and advance their agendas by going directly to the public for popular support (Troy 1991: 3). As Samuel Kernell (1993) points out, one prominent tactic which various twentieth-century presidents have used is that of "going public"—the process of bypassing the deliberative process with Congress and taking one's message directly to the public. In addition to and often in concert with the process of "going public" is the propensity for modern presidents to create carefully orchestrated political speeches—or "spectacles"— designed to gain popular support for themselves and specific policies (Miroff 1994). The political spectacle, cloaked in pageantry, civil religion, and patriotism and choreographed with the most effective images, lighting, backdrops, props, symbols, and rhetoric, has become commonplace in the contemporary presidency, serving as "a kind of symbolic event, one in which particular details stand for broader and deeper meanings" (274).

This study of presidential leadership and campaigning strategy in the Clinton era will examine how a distinct dimension of the rhetorical presidency—the *Cultural Pulpit*—has emerged as a significant form of popular presidential leadership. The central research agenda of this chapter, therefore, is to examine how Bill Clinton has creatively used a variety of the institutional, quasi-institutional, and rhetorical powers of the presidency to form a governing and campaigning strategy based largely on addressing and advancing a noneconomic, nonforeign policy-related "values" agenda. In short, the Clinton presidency is a case study in how the contemporary presidency can be used as a *Cultural Pulpit*. Specifically, this chapter asks: (1) What strategic role have Bill Clinton and the resources of the presidency played in addressing cultural issues? (2) How can the Cultural Pulpit illuminate and guide future scholarship on the presidency? In this endeavor, Clinton's execution of particular initiatives and speeches aimed at noneconomic cultural matters will be highlighted. Lastly, this chapter will consider the possible ramifications of the Cultural Pulpit for new frontiers of presidential research.

THE CULTURAL PULPIT: A COROLLARY TO THE RHETORICAL PRESIDENCY

The Cultural Pulpit, as a corollary to the concept of the rhetorical presidency, is the method by which presidents use the resources, constitutional powers, and image of the presidency to address and influence a wide variety of noneconomic, nonforeign policy-related cultural issues. Specifically, the Cultural Pulpit is a product of the synergy between the rhetorical and institutional dynamics and powers of the presidency. It is a typology that consists of three central elements of presidential behavior: (1) *institutional*, (2) *quasi-institutional*, and (3) *rhetorical actions*. Whereas the rhetorical presidency is, as its title suggests, an acknowledgment of the propensity for presidents to use *rhetoric* as a form of leadership, the Cultural Pulpit involves using institutional and quasi-institutional, *in addition to the rhetorical functions of the office*, as a form of presidential leadership. Given this distinct classification, two immediate questions concerning the Cultural Pulpit immediately arise: (1) What precisely is meant by institutional, quasi-institutional, and rhetorical powers and (2) what exactly are "cultural issues"?

Institutional Acts

Institutional acts refer to the execution of those powers specifically enumerated to the president in Article II of the U.S. Constitution. Such powers include executing the laws, recommending to Congress "such measures" the president "shall deem necessary and expedient" (i.e., proposing and signing legislation), periodically giving Congress information concerning the "state of the union" (what has since evolved into the annual ritualistic State of the Union address), and appointment powers (Supreme Court justices, ambassadors, bureaucracy, etc.). Similarly, State of the Union addresses, constitutionally sanctioned events that the Washington establishment has come to view as the primary method by which presidents define their agendas, are inherently institutional acts (see Light 1991: 1–12). Signing legislation and issuing executive orders are two other prominent examples of institutional acts.

Quasi-Institutional Acts

Quasi-institutional acts, the second and at times more elusive element of the Cultural Pulpit, are harder to define, for they are not specifically mentioned in

Article II. Such powers encompass presidential actions that are a reasonable extenuation of directly sanctioned constitutional powers. For example, a quasi-institutional action that presidents have increasingly relied on in recent years is the White House "summit" or conference—the executive branch's equivalent of congressional hearings. Simply put, "quasi-institutional" powers are White House-organized activities such as conferences, press conferences, summits, meetings, and other educational forums in which the president participates in some fashion, be it as host, moderator, discussant, or keynote speaker. The common characteristic binding these types of actions are that they are at once designed to assist the president in both (1) carrying out one or more of his expressed institutional powers—such as signing or proposing legislation (i.e., gathering information necessary to inform his decision) and (2) performing a political function, such as mobilizing key supporters and constituencies. Whereas Congress, as an institution, has the power to establish committees (and subcommittees) to hold hearings to aid in both the drafting of legislation and the process of executive oversight, executive quasi-institutional actions—while they may indeed have implicit political purposes—serve presidents in much the same fashion. In the Clinton era, quasi-institutional actions have included White House conferences on television violence, hate crimes, teen pregnancy, and early childhood development.

Rhetorical Acts

Rhetorical actions—whether stump speeches, acceptance speeches, weekly radio addresses, political spectacles, "going public," interviews, phone conversations, or the strategic use of individuals, props, and images for symbolic purposes—are those presidential activities *not mandated by or reasonably related to Article II of the Constitution*. Nor do such actions fall into the second category of quasi-institutional powers. The exercising of purely rhetorical powers is largely a "one-way street," in that such actions do not legitimately serve as educational forums in which the president is able to conduct necessary research and outreach to inform his careful consideration of "such measures" that he deems "necessary and expedient" for the betterment of the country. Furthermore, whereas quasi-institutional actions may indeed play a vital role in the president's ability to make key policy decisions, purely "rhetorical" speeches and events are basically creative avenues for presidents to advance their agendas and gain political support.

This does not mean, however, that rhetorical actions are not legitimate exercises of presidential power. Rather, they are distinct from institutional and quasi-institutional activity because they are fundamentally without a clear constitutional basis. Thus, rhetorical acts, while often of strategic importance in governing and campaigning (i.e., FDR's "Fireside Chats"; Ronald Reagan's pressure to pass his 1981 budget package), are categorically distinct from institutional and quasi-institutional presidential action.

Cultural Politics and Values Issues

Now that the three elements of the Cultural Pulpit have been explicated, let us turn to the matter of "values" issues that dominate cultural politics and concerns in America. What exactly is meant by "values" or "cultural" issues? Cannot any policy or speech adhere to or promote some salient value? Certainly. And it is undeniably difficult to provide a seal-proof, all-encompassing definition of values. To operationalize values as they relate to the current social and political environment is a hard task indeed. In short, while "values issues" can include a virtual smorgasbord of cultural concerns, *what unites all of the "values issues" discussed in this study is that they are essentially independent of purely economic and foreign policy concerns.* Values issues in contemporary American politics run the gamut of social policy from religious freedom, prayer in school, parental rights, and protection of children to sexual norms, gay rights, drug use, movie and television violence, and much, much more. Before examining the specific institutional, quasi-institutional, and rhetorical aspects of Bill Clinton's Cultural Pulpit, it is necessary to gain an appreciation of the sociopolitical milieu in which such presidential action has transpired. It is to this endeavor that this chapter now turns.

The Contemporary Values Environment

Discussion and debate concerning "family values," American culture, religious heritage, and values in general has dominated much of the headlines, popular literature, and, at times, political discourse in recent years. Since the election of baby-boomer, Southern Baptist, "new" Democrat Bill Clinton in 1992, however, conversations over values have seemingly grown exponentially—with sermons emanating from both his bully pulpit and a wide variety of activists, politicians, pundits, scholars, and philosophers. Moreover, this commentary on the state of American culture, virtue, and values has come from all dimensions of the ideological and political spectrum—left, right, and center. From Republican virtuecrat and former Secretary of Education and Drug Czar William Bennett to the American Enterprise Institute's Ben Wattenberg; from liberal philosopher and former activist Michael Lerner to moderate Democratic Senator Joseph Lieberman (CT); from C. DeLores Tucker of the progressive National Political Congress of Black Women to conservative Robert Bork, a pervasive values debate and discussion has been taking place. In addition, both Pat Buchanan and Bob Dole devoted major speeches during their most recent presidential campaigns to the issue of cultural decay.[1] Rap lyrics, movie and television violence, divorce, family values, gay rights and marriage, character education, tolerance, discipline, drug use, sexual mores and promiscuity, personal responsibility—all of these topics and then some have been discussed and debated over the airwaves and on the printed page during the Clinton presidency.

THE CLINTON PRESIDENCY AND THE CULTURAL PULPIT

The presidency and, in particular, the 1996 candidacy of Bill Clinton illustrate the possibility and propensity of the modern presidency to be a Cultural Pulpit— from which America's chief executive skillfully uses the institutional, quasi-institutional, and rhetorical resources at his disposal to address cultural concerns. As the following presidential words and deeds indicate, Clinton's Cultural Pulpit consists of three values: (1) raising and protecting children (2) protecting and promoting religion, and (3) racial harmony.

Value No. 1: Raising and Protecting Children

"The President, from day one, has laid out a strategy about investing in and protecting children" (Bennet 1997a). So said Rahm Emanuel, a senior adviser to Bill Clinton, early in the president's second term. While Emanuel was responding to critics of the president's appearance in new Ad Council-produced commercials, newspaper ads, and radio spots encouraging effective parenting, his comments quite aptly describe one major value that, through rhetoric, legislation, and various other institutional and quasi-institutional tools, Bill Clinton has consistently addressed (see Figure 9.1).

TV ratings, the V-chip, children's television, and the Internet. After the Democrats' disastrous showing in the 1994 midterm elections, Clinton used the 1995 State of the Union message, an institutional tool of the presidency, to emphasize a "Middle Class Bill of Rights" designed to steal some of the thunder from the new Republican congressional majority. Yet in addition to this proposal and a call for repairing the "common bonds of community which have been the great strength of our great country from its very beginning," Clinton chose to devote a significant portion of his speech to a host of noneconomic concerns—in particular, family values, citizenship, and community. Among the items included within this rubric of values was the issue of explicit violence and sex in America's films, television, and music. Clinton urged members of the entertainment industry to assume more responsibility for their art:

For people in the entertainment industry in this country, we applaud your creativity and your worldwide success and we support your freedom of expression but you do have a responsibility to assess the impact of your work and to understand the damage that comes from the incessant, repetitive, mindless violence and irresponsible conduct that permeates our media all the time. (Clinton 1995i)

Similarly, Clinton used the 1996 State of the Union to address the raising and protection of children—placing family-related issues at the front of his agenda. Of the seven explicit "challenges" that Clinton issued for the nation, the first was to "cherish our children and strengthen our families" (Clinton 1996h). Included under this seminal challenge, which received top national priority, were pleas to require the V-chip for all televisions, reduce movie and television violence, end tobacco advertising aimed at children, and dramatically reduce teen pregnancy. Again stressing the need to help protect children from inappropriate or destructive forms of entertainment, Clinton targeted the entertainment industry and urged that his initiatives—the V-chip and TV ratings— be approved by Congress and the entertainment industry:

I say you should create movies, CDs and television shows you would want your own children and grandchildren to enjoy. I call on Congress to pass the requirement for the V-chip in TV sets. . . . To make the V-chip work, I challenge the broadcast industry to do what movies have done, to identify your programming in ways that help parents protect their children. (Clinton 1996h)

Using the increasingly popular quasi-institutional presidential resource known as the "White House Conference" as a means to promote his child-friendly agenda, Clinton continued to revisit the issue of violence and sex in American television, movies, and music. At the White House Conference on Character Building for a Civil and Democratic Society on May 20, 1995, Clinton urged industry giants such as Time-Warner to curb their production of questionable entertainment and to practice more corporate responsibility in what they distribute to children. Furthermore, Clinton announced that he would also convene a special White House Conference on June 21, 1995 to further discuss violence in television and movies with top corporate executives. As in the 1995 and 1996 State of the Union addresses, the president acknowledged that there was "excessive, repetitive, mindless violence coming through entertainment," yet he also welcomed the "networks' recent efforts to reduce prime-time violence" and applauded Time-Warner for agreeing to set standards for "controversial music" and "balance creative expression with corporate responsibility" (Clinton 1995d).

On February 29, 1996, a month after the State of the Union, Clinton brought industry heads together yet again to solidify the temporary pledges made in 1995. At this White House Conference, some thirty top executives from NBC, ABC, CBS, Fox, and major Hollywood studios agreed to, possibly as early as 1997, begin carrying ratings for television shows (Clinton 1996e; Stern 1996; Zoglin 1996). Furthermore, the Children's Television Act, which was part of the Telecommunications Act signed by President Clinton in February 1996 and promoted vigorously by Clinton and Vice President Al Gore on the campaign trail, required that local stations "provide three hours of quality children's shows a week" (Janofsky 1996). The Telecommunications Act also mandated that the Federal Communications Commission (FCC) establish an advisory committee to design its own television ratings system should television executives fail to establish a ratings system "acceptable to the Commission" by February 8, 1997 (Mifflin 1996b). Moreover, the legislation also required that television manu-

Figure 9.1
Value No. 1: Raising and Protecting Children

ACTION	TYPE OF PRESIDENTIAL BEHAVIOR
TV, Music, Film, Fashion, The Internet	*TV, Music, Film, Fashion, The Internet*
1. State of the Union: January 24, 1995	1. Institutional
2. State of the Union: January 23, 1996	2. Institutional
3. Telecommunications Act of 1996:	3. Institutional
Communications Decency Act (CDA)	
Children's Television Act	
4. Supreme Court Case Challenging the Constitutionality of the	4. Institutional*
CDA: *Reno v. ACLU*, 1997*	
5. White House Conference on Character Building: May 20, 1995	5. Quasi-Institutional
6. White House Conference with Television and Movie Executives:	6. Quasi-Institutional
June 21, 1995	
7. White House Conference with Entertainment Industry Executives:	7. Quasi-Institutional
February 29, 1996	
8. U.S. Conference of Mayors: May 21, 1997	8. Rhetorical
School Uniforms & Curfews	*School Uniforms & Curfews*
1. 1996 State of the Union	1. Institutional
2. Speeches in California, New Mexico, and Louisiana: June 1996	2. Rhetorical
3. Directive to Education Department: February 24, 1996	3.Institutional
Tobacco Advertising & Teen Pregnancy	*Tobacco Advertising & Teen Pregnancy*
1. 1994 State of the Union	1. Institutional
2. Oval Office Roundtable on Teen Smoking: August 10, 1995	2. Quasi-Institutional
3. MTV Interview: August 11, 1995	3. Rhetorical
4. White House Roundtable on President's Teen Pregnancy	4. Quasi-Institutional
Campaign: January 29, 1996	

	Classification
5. 1996 State of the Union	5. Institutional
6. "Alcohol, Tobacco and Firearms Youth Crime Gun Interaction Initiative": July 8, 1996	6. Quasi-Institutional
7. FDA Administration Rule on Children and Tobacco: August 23, 1996	7. Institutional
8. Radio Address: October 4, 1996	8. Rhetorical
9. Radio Address: October 19, 1996	9. Rhetorical
10. Radio Address: November 9, 1996	10. Rhetorical
11. New Tobacco Regulations: February 28, 1997	11. Institutional
12. White House Press Conference Denouncing Liquor Ads on Televison: April 1, 1997	12. Quasi-Institutional
13. "Kick Butts Day" Speeches: May 7, 1996; April 15, 1997	13. Rhetorical
Strengthening Families	*Strengthening Families*
1. 1995 State of the Union; 1996 State of the Union	1. Institutional
2. "Family and Media Conference": Nashville, July 10, 1995	2. Quasi-Institutional
3. "Drive-By Deliveries" Legislation: September 26, 1996	3. Institutional
4. Additions to the Family & Medical Leave Act: (a) Acceptance Address, August 29, 1996; (b) 1997 State of the Union	4. (a) Rhetorical; (b) Institutional
5. Radio Address: April 12, 1997 ("White House Conference on Early Child Development and Learning")	5. Rhetorical
6. White House Conference on Early Child Development and Learning: April 17, 1997	6. Quasi-Institutional
7. Executive Memorandum to Secretary of Transportation: Increasing Seat Belt Use, January 23, 1997	7. Institutional
8. Executive Order: Increasing Seat Belt Use in the United States: April 16, 1997	8. Institutional

Reno v. ACLU was Decided on June 26, 1997

*The Supreme Court Struck Down the CDA, Finding it in Violation of the First Amendment facturers equip sets with the V-chip—the program-blocking technology touted by Clinton, parents groups, and many members of Congress.

While Clinton's bully pulpit, White House summits, and the telecommunications legislation of 1996 succeeded in bringing about voluntary television ratings, the fine details of the new ratings system, released in early 1997 by Jack Valenti—president of the Motion Picture Association of America and chairman of the industry group devising the ratings system—caused quite a stir among members of Congress and several children's advocacy groups. Designed much like the rating system for motion pictures, the plan would rate programs as appropriate for particular age groups but would "not tell parents specifically whether or not a program contains sex, violence or foul language" (Mifflin 1996a).

Clinton's initiatives aimed at protecting children did not end with television and music. The Telecommunications Act also included a controversial amendment authored by Senators Exon (D-NE) and Dan Coats (R-IN) known as the Communications Decency Act (CDA), which made it illegal to transmit pornographic or "obscene" materials to minors over the Internet. A strong proponent of the CDA, Clinton spoke on its behalf, and the Justice Department submitted *amicus curiae* in defense of the CDA when it was immediately challenged in federal district court. After being found unconstitutional by a panel of judges at the district level, the CDA came before the Supreme Court and, despite Attorney General Janet Reno's vigorous defense of the law's merits, was found to be in violation of the First Amendment (see Greenhouse 1997a; *Reno v. ACLU* June 26, 1997). Even before the Supreme Court's verdict was in, however, the Clinton administration began devising a new strategy to regulate obscenity on the Internet that would replace the invalidated CDA (Broder 1997). Regarding another issue related to the protection of children—the glamorization of drug use in fashion ads in popular magazines—Clinton used the occasion of the U.S. Conference of Mayors on May 21, 1997 to denounce the "glorification of heroin" in the fashion industry (WHPR May 21, 1997).

School uniforms and curfews. Under the second great national "challenge" listed in his 1996 State of the Union—education—Bill Clinton included the advocating of school uniforms in public schools. To emphasize the effectiveness of school uniforms in bringing about discipline and fostering a proper learning environment, Clinton, through an Executive Memorandum on February 24, 1996, instructed the Department of Education to distribute manuals to the nation's sixteen thousand public schools discussing the merits of school uniforms (Clinton 1996c; Porter 1996). A few months after the memorandum and a presidential "roundtable" discussion of school uniforms in Long Beach, California—the first public school district to mandate school uniforms—Clinton explored the rhetorical possibilities of the modern presidency by staging "spectacles," or campaign-style policy addresses. In June 1996 Clinton further touted school uniforms—as well as curfews for young adults—in speeches in Glendale,

California; Albuquerque, New Mexico; and New Orleans, Louisiana (Clinton 1996f, 1996g).

Tobacco advertising and teen pregnancy. In deeds and words designed to further advance his protecting and raising children agenda, Clinton's State of the Union address in 1996 also included pleas for tobacco companies to stop aiming advertising at children and for the nation to make a concerted effort to drastically lower the teen pregnancy level, two causes he had championed in the 1994 State of the Union (Clinton 1996h; DeParle 1994). In selected interviews, such as one with MTV's Tabitha Soren on August 11, 1995, Clinton reinforced his aversion to tobacco advertising, devoting his longest responses to this particular issue (Clinton 1995b). He also incorporated the popular quasi-institutional White House summit or "roundtable" as a tool in promoting the issue, holding an Oval Office Roundtable on Teen Smoking on August 10, 1995—the day prior to his MTV interview (Clinton 1995h). Regarding the issue of teen pregnancy, the president held a White House Roundtable on January 29, 1996, unveiling his "National Campaign Against Teenage Pregnancy," a collection of grass-roots community groups, social clubs, mentoring programs, and a national advisory board made up of representatives from the corporate, education, and health sectors. Dr. Henry Foster, the president's rejected choice to replace Joycelyn Elders as surgeon general, agreed to serve as Clinton's senior adviser on the National Campaign (WHPR January 29, 1996).

"The Great Communicator" Ronald Reagan began the tradition of the Weekly Radio Address in 1981. Bill Clinton skillfully resurrected this rhetorical technique of the modern presidency and used it to complement his institutional and quasi-institutional presidential resources. For example, Clinton's Weekly Radio Address of October 4, 1996 was devoted entirely to teen pregnancy (WHPR October 4, 1996). He then used the Weekly Radio Address of October 19, 1996 to focus on the related concerns of teen smoking, drinking, and drug use (WHPR October 19, 1996). Similarly, he used the Weekly Radio Address of November 9, 1996 to discourage smoking and to further explicate the steps his administration had taken to curtail both tobacco use and advertising aimed at children—such as the ban of tobacco advertising on billboards near schools and further restricting the availability of cigarette machines (WHPR November 9, 1996). During the same radio address, he also called on liquor companies to continue their self-imposed ban on television and radio advertising, a ban they were now seeking to end.

As for other techniques of presidential leadership in the area of tobacco use, Clinton announced his quasi-institutional "Alcohol, Tobacco and Firearms Youth Crime Gun Interaction Initiative" during a meeting at the Old Executive Office Building on July 8, 1996, and later that summer, on August 23, he unveiled sweeping new rules regarding the sale of tobacco to minors (WHPR July 8, 1996). The new FDA rules required that proper ID be presented when purchasing cigarettes; cigarette vending machines be banned from anywhere children or teenagers can go; children be free from cigarette advertising on billboards near schools and playgrounds; ads in children's and teenagers' publications be in black and white with no pictures; and companies discontinue marketing ploys aimed at children, such as gym bags and t-shirts (WHPR August 23, 1996). On February 28, 1997, one month into his second term, Bill Clinton announced new FDA regulations concerning tobacco use, including making what was already the law in every state—no sale of tobacco products to anyone under the age of eighteen—a federal regulation. Moreover, the FDA would now require that anyone under twenty-seven provide photo verification for the purchase of tobacco products (WHPR February 28, 1997). Clinton also used campaign-style rhetoric at two well-organized political spectacles known as national "Kick Butts" Days—one on May 7, 1996 at Woodbridge High School in Woodbridge, New Jersey, and another on April 15, 1997 at Andries Hudde Junior High School in New York City—to further his anti-tobacco credentials and reduce the allure of smoking (WHPR May 7, 1996; WHPR April 15, 1997). Clinton's speech during the 1997 "Kick Butts Day" ceremony was broadcast via satellite to over four thousand schools across the nation (Bennet 1997b).

Strengthening families. At the "Family and Media Conference" held in Nashville on July 10, 1995, Clinton gathered with annual hosts Al and Tipper Gore to discuss raising children in the midst of provocative films, music, and television. Clinton used this quasi-institutional presidential forum to again highlight methods by which the federal government and parents could strengthen and protect American families—especially via the V-chip, more children's television, and increased parental and corporate responsibility. Charging that the V-chip was "not censorship" but rather a way to enhance "parental responsibility," Clinton again used the resources of the presidency to promote his children and family agenda (Clinton 1995g).

With the stroke of a pen on September 26, 1996, Clinton used the institutional power of signing legislation to protect newborn children and their mothers by outlawing so-called Drive-Through Deliveries—the practice of sending mothers and their newborns home from the hospital less than forty-eight hours after delivery (Purdum 1996). Regarding other presidential acts designed to "strengthen families," Clinton used his acceptance address at the Democratic National Convention on August 29, 1996—as well as his 1997 State of the Union speech on February 4, 1997—to suggest minor additions to the 1993 Family and Medical Leave Act, which allowed citizens (in a workplace that included fifty or more employees) up to twelve weeks of unpaid leave in order to care for newborn or disabled children, as well as ailing parents. Among other things, Clinton asked that Congress extend the Family and Medical Leave Act to include an extra twenty-four hours that could be used for various parenting responsibilities—such as parent-teacher conferences (Clinton 1996a, 1997).

The strengthening families agenda continued with piecemeal presidential action aimed at health and safety measures. The president issued an Executive Memorandum on January 23, 1997, ordering the secretary of Transportation to devise a plan to "increase the use of seatbelts nationwide" and to report back to him in forty-five days. Acting on the secretary's recommendations, Clinton issued an executive order on April 16, 1997 which required, among other things, that "Federal employees use seat belts while on official business," and he also outlined policies for seat belt use in national parks and Defense installations (WHPR January 23, 1997; WHPR April 16, 1997).

Using the quasi-institutional forum of the White House Conference, Clinton and First Lady Hillary Rodham Clinton addressed issues of child-rearing and early brain development by bringing researchers, parents, and child development experts to the White House on April 17, 1997 to convene the White House Conference on Early Child Development and Learning. The conference, which was the subject of Clinton's Weekly Radio Address five days earlier on April 12, was beamed by satellite hookup to more than sixty sites across the United States (WHPR April 12, 1997; WHPR April 17, 1997).

Value No. 2: Protecting and Promoting Religion

Bill Clinton has made religion and religious liberty a central theme of his presidency. As Figure 9.2 makes clear, he and his administration have engaged in a variety of institutional, quasi-institutional, and rhetorical acts to portray himself as a leader with religious and moral roots.

Religious Freedom Restoration Act (1993). We all have a shared desire . . . to protect perhaps the most precious of all American liberties—religious freedom (*Christian Century* 1993: 1202)

I won't use the legalese—the bottom line was that if the Government is going to restrict anybody's legitimate exercise of religion they have to have an extraordinarily good reason and no other way to achieve their compelling objective. . . . You have to bend over backwards to avoid getting in the way of people's legitimate exercise of their religious convictions. That's what the law said. (Clinton 1995e)

On November 16, 1993, Clinton signed the Religious Freedom Restoration Act (RFRA), marking an end to a three-year campaign for the law. The RFRA sought to reverse a 1990 Supreme Court ruling, *Employment Division v. Smith*, that increased the state's abilities to restrict religious practices in the name of the general good (Anderson 1993b; Eastland 1994). The new law would "hold the government to stricter standards for intervening in religious practices" and would, in the words of the Center for Law and Religious Freedom, repair the "devastation the U.S. Supreme Court wreaked in its *Employment Division v. Smith* decision" (*Christian Century* 1993: 1202). Specifically, the law would make the government show a "compelling state interest" before involving itself with regulating or prohibiting religious practices. In signing the legislation, Clinton urged that all citizens "respect one another's faiths," "fight to the death to

Figure 9.2
Value No. 2: Protecting and Promoting Religion

ACTION	TYPE OF PRESIDENTIAL BEHAVIOR
Religious Freedom Restoration Act	*Religious Freedom Restoration Act*
1. Signing of the Religious Freedom Restoration Act (RFRA): November 16, 1993	1. Institutional
2. Presidential Directive to Justice Department to Drop Its Legal Support of Creditors in a Suit Against a Minnesota Church: September 1994	2. Institutional
3. Change in SBA Loan Plan Policy on Religion: June 14, 1996	3. Institutional
4. Filed *Amicus Curiae* in RFRA Test Case *City of Boerne v. Flores* (Supreme Court Case): 1997*	4. Institutional*
5. Filed *Amicus Curiae* in *Agostini v. Felton* (Supreme Court Case): 1997**	5. Institutional**
Religious Freedom in Schools	*Religious Freedom in Schools*
1. Executive Memorandum to Education and Justice Departments: July 12, 1995	1. Institutional
2. Vienna, Virginia Speech: July 12, 1995	2. Rhetorical
Outreach to Religious Leaders	*Outreach to Religious Leaders*
1. Congressional Prayer Breakfasts: 1993-1997	1. Quasi-Institutional
2. White House Interfaith Meeting: August 30, 1993	2. Quasi-Institutional
3. Interviews with Religious Journalists: February 2, 1995	3. Rhetorical
4. Regular Consultations with Religious Leaders: 1993-97	4. Rhetorical
5. Meeting with the Pope: August 12, 1993	5. Rhetorical
6. Meeting with Southern Baptist Convention President Ed Young: September 16, 1993	6. Rhetorical

	Classification
7. Speech at Full Gospel AME Zion Church, Temple Hills, Maryland: August 14, 1994	7. Rhetorical
8. Keynote Speech at National Baptist Convention, USA: September 1994	8. Rhetorical
9. "A Time of Healing" Prayer Service, Oklahoma City: April 23, 1995	9. Rhetorical
10. Progressive National Baptist Convention: Charlotte, NC: August 9, 1995	10. Rhetorical

Religious Allusion and Symbolism

1. 1992 Acceptance Address	1. Rhetorical
2. 1993 Inaugural Address	2. Institutional
3. 1997 Inaugural and State of the Union	3. Institutional
4. Radio Address from Indianapolis, Indiana Church: May 14, 1994	4. Rhetorical
5. U.S. Postal Service Madonna & Child Stamp Reinstated: November 1994	5. Institutional
6. Rev. John and Diana Cherry (Mt. Zion AME Church): Featured Guests at the 1995 State of the Union	6. Institutional
7. Billy Graham: 1993 and 1997 Inaugurals	7. Institutional
8. Robert Schuller: 1997 State of the Union	8. Institutional
9. Defense of Marriage Act: September 1996	9. Institutional

* City of Boerne v. Flores was decided on June 25, 1997

** Agostini v. Felton was decided on June 23, 1997

* The Supreme Court Struck Down the RFRA

** The Supreme Court agreed with Clinton's Amicus Curiae and overturned its 12-year-old precedent preserve the right of every American to practice whatever convictions he or she has,'' and ''bring our values back to the table to heal our troubled land'' (1202).

Responding to events that closely or directly fell under the spirit of the legislation, Clinton used the institutional resources at his disposal to encourage compliance with the RFRA. In September 1994, he instructed the Justice Department to drop its legal support of creditors in a suit against a Minnesota church that ''had been ordered to turn over $13,500 in tithes donated by a couple who later filed for bankruptcy'' (*Christianity Today* 1994: 81). In another related case, Clinton asked the Supreme Court in 1996 to overrule an eleven-year-old decision—*Agostini v. Felton*—which barred public school teachers from traveling to parochial schools to offer federally financed remedial classes and counseling (Greenhouse 1996, 1997b). The Clinton Justice Department filed *amicus curiae* urging the Court to overrrule its precedent, and on June 23, 1997, in the case of *Agostini v. Felton*, the Court abandoned its precedent and ruled that public school teachers could provide Title I-mandated remedial education at parochial schools (see *Agostini v. Felton*, No. 96–552).[2]

Similarly, Clinton used the institutional powers of the presidency to challenge another Court case that he believed was an obstacle to execution of the RFRA. In *City of Boerne v. Flores*, the Clinton Justice Department submitted *amicus curiae* on behalf of a church that wished to expand its sanctuary, even though the construction area in question was officially within a city-designated historical district in Boerne, Texas. Not believing the historical district classification to be a compelling reason to curtail the church's planned expansion, the Clinton Justice Department urged that the renovations be permitted and that the RFRA be upheld. On June 25, 1997, the Supreme Court disagreed, however, and invalidated the RFRA and its attempt, through legislation, to overrule the Court's decision in *Employment Division v. Smith* (see *City of Boerne v. Flores*, No. 95–2074).

In a similar fashion, the Clinton administration, seeking to reduce the obstacles to religious expression in the marketplace, announced on June 14, 1996 that the Small Business Administration (SBA) had changed its loan plan policy regarding religion. The new SBA regulations would make it easier for religiously oriented businesses to qualify for federal small business loan guarantees. According to Philip Lader, administrator of the SBA: ''The administration . . . is concerned about increasing secularization [of America] through unintentional obstacles to the expression of faith in the marketplace'' (*Christian Century* 1996: 711–12).

Religious freedom in the schools. Using his institutional powers, on July 12, 1995 Bill Clinton issued a ''Memorandum on Religious Expression in Public Schools'' to both the Justice and Education departments, instructing them to issue a statement to every school district in the nation informing them of what types of religious expressions are allowed under current law. Asserting that public schools are not ''religion-free zones,'' Clinton went to James Madison High School in Vienna, Virginia, to deliver a major address concerning the memorandum and the issue of religious expression in schools. In the speech, Clinton went to great lengths to explain the Constitution's protection of the free expression of religion and its prohibition of the establishment of any religion, citing his signing of the RFRA in 1993 and his commitment to making it extraordinarily hard for students to be deprived of their right to religious expression (Clinton 1995c and 1995e). The executive memorandum and corresponding political spectacle in Vienna represent Clinton's skillful coupling of institutional and rhetorical actions, an approach to presidential leadership that is nearly identical to his leadership strategy regarding execution of the RFRA.

Outreach to religious leaders and communities. Whether he was issuing a "moratorium on revenge," providing self-criticism, or asking fellow Washington politicians to rid themselves of this "toxic cynicism," Bill Clinton has routinely used the annual Congressional National Prayer Breakfasts, usually held in the first week in February, to, among other things, "condemn hateful speech, call for more humility in politics and reflect on man's flawed place in a fallen world" (Purdum 1997). The quasi-institutional National Prayer Breakfasts present the president with a forum for interaction and consultation—akin to a congressional hearing, yet from a uniquely executive perspective. Clinton's prominent role in the Prayer Breakfasts illustrates the level of importance he places on congregating and socializing with diverse religious leaders (Clinton 1995f).

Other events are indicators of Clinton's consistent outreach to clergy and other spiritual leaders. On August 30, 1993, the president convened a White House Interfaith Prayer Breakfast, calling some 250 spiritual leaders together in an ecumenical forum. Lamenting that U.S. society had become "entirely too secular," Clinton warned against the tendency of some politically liberal Americans to mistrust those who take public positions based on religious convictions (Anderson 1993a; Drinan 1993; Lauter 1993). Whether engrossed in one of his regularly scheduled telephone or face-to-face consultations with select ministers (Niebuhr 1994, 1997), or granting a lengthy interview to religious journalists— as was the case on February 2, 1995, when Clinton gave several prominent religious journalists an interview in the Oval Office (Clinton 1995a; Jones 1995)—Clinton's persistent dialogue with religious leaders and communities has served as a rhetorical tool in advancing his goal of protecting and promoting religion.

Other actions of Clinton's Cultural Pulpit in this rhetorical vein include delivering a sermon at Rev. John and Diana Cherry's Full Gospel AME Zion Church in Temple Hills, Maryland, on August 14, 1994 (Ferranti 1994); serving as "public mourner and healer" after the Oklahoma City bombing by presiding over the "Time of Healing" Prayer Service in Oklahoma City on April 23, 1995 (WHPR April 23, 1995); seeking to define the national values debate while speaking at the National Baptist Convention USA in September 1994; meeting with Pope John Paul II in Denver in August 1993 (Gavin 1993); discussing social and moral issues with Ed Young, president of the Southern Baptist Convention, on September 16, 1993 (Brunsman 1993); and delivering a fifty-minute sermon, at times touching upon his transgressions, to the Progressive National Baptist Convention in Charlotte, North Carolina on August 9, 1995 (Purdum 1995).

"Repairer of the breach"—Religious allusion and symbolism. From his acceptance speech at the 1992 Democratic Convention calling for a "New Covenant" between citizens and their government to his 1993 Inaugural Address recalling the seasonal promise of Galatians 6:9 and his 1997 Inaugural and State of the Union speeches calling leaders and Americans alike to be "repairers of the breach"—Bill Clinton has displayed a penchant for grounding his rhetoric and actions in religious symbolism and allusion (Clinton 1997; Wall 1993).

Symbolic gestures and the use of religious images have helped Clinton further accentuate his broad theme of protecting and promoting religion. In this endeavor, he has been particularly adept at using rhetoric and institutional gestures, both trivial and not so trivial, to further ensconce himself and the institution of the presidency in religious imagery. Whether delivering a Weekly Radio Address from an Indianapolis, Indiana, church on May 14, 1994, or designating January 12, 1996, as "Religious Freedom Day," or lobbying the postmaster general to reinstate the Madonna and Christ Child stamp after it had been canceled for production, Clinton uses the resources of the presidency, small and large, to accent certain values (*Christian Century* 1994).

In the 1995 State of the Union message, Clinton once again revisited the successful Ronald Reagan tactic of singling out heroes. For this speech, the heroes Clinton presented to the nation were Rev. John and Mrs. Diana Cherry of the Full Gospel AME Zion Church in Temple Hills, Maryland—individuals whom the president cited for their dedicated efforts in conducting hands-on marriage counseling for their seventeen thousand member congregation. As the well-staged presentation of the Cherrys at the 1995 State of the Union illustrates, individuals can and often do serve as the most effective symbols. The Cherrys' presence, along with Clinton's introduction of their story, evoked religiosity, family, and volunteerism all at once. Thus, scholars of the presidency must be cognizant of the various individuals who are called upon to make presentations, prayers, and appearances on the same stage as the president of the United States. It is surely no coincidence that one of the most universally renowned elder statesmen of religion in America, Rev. Billy Graham—a guest at the last eight presidential inaugurations—gave the blessings for both the 1993 and 1997 Clinton inaugurations. Similarly, the prominent presence of Rev. Robert Schuller at the 1997 State of the Union address is also very important symbolically. By presiding over the address, Schuller, without giving any prayer or speech, was granting immediate religious legitimacy to the otherwise secular presidential ritual. And while these two individuals stand as powerful symbols of religious expression, they are also examples of a president's institutional powers—as both men were called upon to attend constitutionally mandated events: the Inaugural and the State of the Union.

Finally, another highly symbolic act vis-à-vis the protection and promotion of religion was Clinton's low-key and rather awkward signing of the "Defense of Marriage Act" in September 1996. The law, designed to permit individual states to disavow same-sex marriage licenses from other states, was signed by Clinton, even as he expressed some misgivings about the measure. Nonetheless, it would appear to be an appropriate institutional measure to protect and promote religion, as so much of the debate surrounding gay marriage has been conducted under the guise of Judeo-Christian law and heritage.

Value No. 3: Racial Harmony

Along with families and religion, Bill Clinton has used his Cultural Pulpit to promote the value of racial harmony. As Figure 9.3 illustrates, this promotion has focused primarily on the subject of hate crimes and identification with the legacy of Dr. Martin Luther King, Jr.

Church burning, hate crimes, racial diversity The mysterious outbreak of fires at black churches throughout 1995–1996 caused Bill Clinton to employ a variety of presidential resources to help rebuild houses of worship, promote racial reconciliation, assist in the apprehension of the arsonists, and determine whether or not the fires were the result of any conspiracy. The Weekly Radio Addresses proved to be a particularly comfortable forum for Clinton to address the problem of the church burnings, as he devoted his June 8, 1996 and January 18, 1997 Weekly Radio Addresses to the issue (WHPR June 8, 1996; WHPR January 18, 1997). Using the institutional powers at his disposal, Clinton signed into law the Church Arson Prevention Act on July 10, 1996, which made hate crimes against churches a federal crime, doubled the maximum sentence for such crimes, and increased the statute of limitations from five to seven years (WHPR July 10, 1996). Clinton also created the National Church Arson Task Force on June 19, 1996, a special mobilization of the Departments of Justice and Treasury and the Federal Emergency Management Agency (FEMA) to assist in the investigation, provide precautionary measures, and help with rebuilding the churches. The Task Force worked in concert with state and local law enforcement agencies and provided some $6 million for law enforcement and community efforts related to the fires (WHPR July 10, 1996). Lastly, Clinton himself traveled to several of the newly rebuilt churches that had been devastated by the fires, including the Salem Missionary Baptist Church in Fruitland, Tennessee, and officially rededicated many of the new houses of worship (Clinton 1996d). By the time Clinton delivered his January 18, 1997 Weekly Radio Address detailing progress made in investigating the church burnings, some 143 suspects in connection with 107 fires had been arrested (WHPR January 18, 1997).

Clinton has frequently used public forums and the institutional powers of the presidency to address an array of the peripheral issues surrounding the legacy of racial discrimination in America. On July 19, 1995, for example, he used a

Figure 9.3
Value No. 3: Racial Harmony

ACTION	TYPE OF PRESIDENTIAL BEHAVIOR
Church Burnings, Hate Crimes, Diversity Issues	*Church Burnings, Hate Crimes, Diversity Issues*
1. Affirmative Action Memorandum for Heads of Executive Departments and Agencies: July 19, 1995	1. Institutional
2. Radio Address: June 8, 1996 (Church Burnings)	2. Rhetorical
3. National Church Arson Task Force: June 19, 1996	3. Institutional
4. Church Arson Prevention Act: July 10, 1996	4. Institutional
5. Dedication of the Salem Missionary Baptist Church, Fruitland, Tennessee: August 19, 1996	5. Rhetorical
6. Speech at St. Paul's AME Church, Tampa, Florida: November 3, 1996	6. Rhetorical
7. Radio Address: January 18, 1997 (Update on Church Burnings)	7. Rhetorical
8. Radio Address: March 29, 1997 (Racially-Motivated Beating of Leonard Clark, a 13-year-old African American Child, in Chicago)	8. Rhetorical
9. Speech at Annual Meeting of American Society of Newspaper Editors (Racial Diversity): April 10, 1997	9. Rhetorical
10. Apology for Tuskegee Syphilis Study: (a) White House Press Conference, May 16, 1997; (b) May 18, Commencement Address at Morgan State University, Baltimore.	10. (a) Quasi-Institutional; (b) Rhetorical
11. Radio Address: June 7, 1997 (White House Conference on Hate Crimes)	11. Rhetorical

12. The President's Advisory Board on Race, June 13, 1997: (a) Executive Order; (b) Oval Office Announcement/Press Conference; (c) Advisory Board	12. (a) Institutional; (b) Quasi-Institutional; (c) Quasi-Institutional
13. White House Conference on Hate Crimes: November 10, 1997	13. Quasi-Institutional

Legacy of Dr. Martin Luther King, Jr.

1. 86th Annual Holy Convocation, The Church of God in Christ, Memphis: November 13, 1993	1. Rhetorical
2. Radio Address: MLK and the "National Day of Service," January 15, 1996	2. Rhetorical
3. Speech at MLK Memorial Service: January 15, 1996	3. Rhetorical
4. Signing of HR 4236, "Omnibus Parks and Public Lands Management Act of 1996," Establishing a (1) Martin Luther King, Jr. Memorial in Washington, DC and (2) the Selma-Montgomery National Historical Trail	4. Institutional
5. Proclamation, "National Day of Hope and Renewal" January 20, 1997	5. Institutional

Racial Harmony and Reconciliation: Major Addresses

1. Affirmative Action Speech, National Archives, Washington, DC: July 19, 1995	1. Rhetorical
2. University of Texas at Austin: October 16, 1995 (Day of Million Man March)	2. Rhetorical
3. Commencement Address, University of California at San Diego: June 14, 1997	3. Rhetorical

speech at the National Archives to outline his administration's "mend it, don't end it" approach and commitment to affirmative action programs, and issued an Affirmative Action Memorandum for Heads of Executive Departments and Agencies designed to eliminate any programs that created a quota, preferences for unqualified individuals, or reverse discrimination. Simply put, while supporting affirmative action, Clinton's memorandum used the strict scrutiny guidelines established by the 1995 Supreme Court decision *Adirand v. Pena* (Clinton 1995a). At a dual sermon/campaign speech delivered from the pulpit of St. Paul's AME Church in Tampa, Florida, on November 3, 1996, Clinton donned his role of "repairer of the breach" and devoted his address to closing the divisions in American society, urging the congregation and America to "rise above the 'politics of division and gridlock' and to say 'no to racial and religious hatred' " (Mitchell 1996). And in May 1997, Clinton used two events—an official White House Press Conference on May 16 and a commencement address at Morgan State University in Baltimore on May 18—to offer a formal national apology for the Tuskegee syphilis study (WHPR May 16, 1997).

Citing recent hate crimes committed against African Americans and gays in Atlanta and Washington, DC, Clinton used his June 7, 1997 Weekly Radio Address as a vehicle to denounce the acts. The president concluded the address by announcing that he would convene a White House Conference on Hate Crimes on November 10, 1997 in order to "confront the dark forces of division that still exist" (WHPR June 7, 1997). Announcing the first White House Conference of its kind, Clinton asserted that the hate crimes conference would bring together community and religious leaders and law enforcement officials, providing a forum in which to review shared experiences and outline relevant laws as well as individual and community-based solutions to the problem of hate crimes (WHPR June 7, 1997).

Just a few days later, on June 13, 1997, Clinton announced the creation of the highly anticipated President's Advisory Board on Race, a seven-member panel of presidential appointees that would conduct a year-long investigation and discussion of racial attitudes and problems. After establishing the Advisory Board through an executive order, Clinton made the project official with an announcement ceremony in the Oval Office. Moreover, Clinton further outlined the mission of the Advisory Board during a commencement address on racial diversity at the University of California at San Diego on June 14, in which he cited the immediate negative impact that California's controversial anti-affirmative action referendum, Proposition 209, was having on minority college and law school admissions (WHPR June 13, 1997a; WHPR June 13 1997b). The speech also served as a reaffirmation of Clinton's oft-questioned commitment to affirmative action, with the president citing an integrated military as a clear example of the merits of affirmative action programs (Mitchell 1997).

The legacy of Dr. Martin Luther King, Jr., and racial reconciliation. On November 13, 1993, Clinton chose to deliver a sermon on race, youth violence, and the breakdown of the family in Memphis, Tennessee, from the same hallowed pulpit where Martin Luther King delivered his final sermon on April 3, 1968 (WHPR November 13, 1993). In addition to public speeches, a variety of small institutional gestures further cemented Clinton's homage to the late civil rights leader and the issue of racial reconciliation, including a Weekly Radio Address praising King and establishing January 14, 1995 as a National Day of Service; the signing of HR 4236, the Omnibus Parks and Public Lands Management Act of 1996, establishing a King Memorial in Washington, DC, and the Selma-Montgomery National Historic Trail; and a proclamation naming January 20, 1997 a National Day of Hope and Renewal in honor of King. In this vein, Clinton has also used well-staged and timed public addresses to revisit the legacy of race in America. On the morning of the Million Man March on October 16, 1995, Clinton gave a major address on race relations at the University of Texas at Austin and, not by coincidence, staged his most recent speech concerning race and affirmative action at the University of California at San Diego, a school system directly affected by California's Proposition 209.

PRESIDENTIAL FRONTIERS: THE CULTURAL PULPIT AND FUTURE RESEARCH

From V-chips to teen pregnancy to tobacco advertising to religious freedom in schools; from legislation to memoranda to proclamations to executive orders; from prayer breakfasts to interfaith meetings to telephone conversations and interviews; from well-orchestrated political spectacles to Weekly Radio Addresses to the annual State of the Union ritual, Bill Clinton has consistently utilized the institutional, quasi-institutional, and rhetorical powers of the presidency to address three distinct cultural values. Even if scholars separate the many rhetorical actions of this president from the rest of his activities, the sheer number of institutional acts attest to the unique level to which Bill Clinton has used the constitutional resources of the modern presidency to focus on cultural matters. And judging from his activity in the first year of his second term—such as his race, volunteerism, and education initiatives—Clinton is definitely poised to continue using the resources of the Cultural Pulpit.

How can the notion of the Cultural Pulpit illuminate and guide new frontiers of presidential scholarship? Since the presidency's implicit symbolism and explicit institutional powers have profound implications for a president's ability to influence cultural policy in America, examination of a few key questions would seem most prudent. When studying the bully pulpit and presidential leadership, there is often an implicit assumption that the president deserves credit for molding public opinion. Yet such an assumption can hinder scholarship and cloud reality. At the outset of the 1996 campaign, Bill Clinton's most trusted pollsters came to the conclusion that the race would be about "values." Pollster Mark Penn advised the president that many voters were especially drawn not to "religious values" but to "secular values like protecting their children and duty to their parents" (Stengel and Pooley 1996). This revelation leads to the consideration of an important question that presidential scholar George Edwards has asked: Are presidents *facilitators* or *directors* of change? A president who is truly a ''director of change'' establishes goals and leads the nation ''where it otherwise would not go''—while a president who is a ''facilitator of change'' merely uses the bully pulpit to reflect and intensify ''widely held views,'' exploiting political opportunities to ''help others go where they want to go anyway'' (Edwards 1997: 327). Considering Edwards' pertinent distinction and pollster Penn's remarks, the case could certainly be made that Bill Clinton was at times much more of a facilitator than a director of change. Future studies in presidential rhetoric and leadership should seek to distinguish between facilitators and leaders, and avoid making the implicit assumption that presidents are automatically leaders.

The *Public Papers of the Presidents* provide another enlightened avenue for research concerning the Cultural Pulpit. Has there been a Cultural Pulpit during the entire era of the rhetorical presidency? Is the Cultural Pulpit largely a phenomenon of the age of Clinton, or have presidents quietly been using similar strategies and execution of institutional, quasi-institutional, and rhetorical powers for some time? How have the revolutions in communication technology assisted presidents in this endeavor? Scholars can revisit the Public Papers in order to better evaluate the degree to which the diverse resources of the office have been used to address cultural issues. Moreover, in this vein, future research could also serve to identify the specific values articulated by twentieth-century presidents, and, upon further comparative studies, determine which of these values have been either universal or unique in the progression of the American presidency.

NOTES

1. Examples of the literature concerning the state of American values include William Bennett's *The Book of Virtues*, Ben Wattenberg's *Values Matter Most*, and Robert Bork's *Slouching Towards Gomorrah*. Pat Buchanan's address at the 1992 Republican National Convention in Houston—as well as his announcement speech in New Hampshire in 1995—made explicit mention of a ''religious and cultural war'' raging throughout the United States. Republican presidential nominee Bob Dole used targeted political spectacles in Los Angeles and elsewhere in 1995 and 1996 to criticize violent and sexually explicit movies and music, labeling such expressions of American popular culture ''nightmares of depravity'' and calling on corporate giant Time-Warner to divest itself of any financial involvement in distributing such controversial music and films. He later criticized magazines and the films *Pulp Fiction* and *Trainspotting* for glamorizing a ''culture of heroin.''

2. Title I of the Elementary and Secondary Education Act of 1965, signed by President Johnson, requires that all disadvantaged children receive necessary remedial education. In *Agostini v. Felton*, 1985, the Supreme Court ruled that New York City's Title I plan, which involved public teachers offering remedial services at parochial schools, constituted an unnecessary government entanglement with religion and, as such, violated the Establishment Clause of the First Amendment.

REFERENCES

Agostini v. Felton, No. 96–552 (June 23, 1997).

Anderson, David E. 1993a. "Political World 'Too Secular,' President Says." *Washington Post*, September 4.

———. 1993b. "Signing of Religious Freedom Act Culminates 3-Year Push." *Washington Post*, November 20.

Andrews, James. 1994. "Clinton Steps Up Enforcement of New Religious Freedom Act." *Christian Science Monitor*, October 27, p. 1.

Barilleaux, Ryan J. 1988. *The Post-Modern Presidency*. Westport, CT: Praeger.

——— et al. 1996. "Forward to the Past: Paradigm Shifts in Presidential Studies." Paper presented at the American Political Science Association Annual Meeting, San Francisco, California.

Bennet, James. 1997a. "Clinton in Ads, Puts Out New Image: The Good Parent." *New York Times*, March 4.

———. 1997b. "In Brooklyn, Clinton Says Seize the Moment." *New York Times*, April 16.

"Bob Dole." 1996. *New York Times*, March 8.

Broder, John M. 1997. "Clinton Readies New Approach on Internet Indecency." *New York Times*, June 27.

Brunsman, Steve. 1993. "Young's Talk with Clinton: Politics Or Religion?" *Houston Chronicle*, September 25.

Carlin, David R., Jr. 1994. "It's the Culture, Stupid: The Irony of Clinton's Success." *Commonweal*, September 23, 8–9.

Ceaser, James W., et al. 1981. "The Rise of the Rhetorical Presidency." *Presidential Studies Quarterly* (Spring): 233–351.

Christian Century. 1993. "Clinton Signs Religious Freedom Bill." December 1, p. 1202.

———. 1994. "Stamp of Approval for Madonna and Child." December 14, p. 1184.

———. 1994. "Clinton Intervenes in RFRA Test Case." October 14, p. 81.

———. 1996. "SBA Loan Plan Changes Policy on Religion." July 17–24, pp. 711–12.

City of Bourne v. Flores, No. 95–2074 (June 25, 1997).

Clinton, Bill. 1995a. "Interview with Religious Journalists." *Weekly Compilation of Presidential Documents*, February 6, pp. 173–79.

———. 1995b. "Interview with Tabitha Soren of MTV, August, 11, 1995." *Weekly Compilation of Presidential Documents*, August 14, pp. 1426–31.

———. 1995c. "Memorandum on Religious Expression in Public Schools." *Weekly Compilation of Presidential Documents*, July 17, pp. 1227–30.

———. 1995d. "Remarks at a White House Conference on Character Building for a Civil and Democratic Society, May 20, 1995." *Weekly Compilation of Presidential Documents*, May 29, pp. 872–82.

———. 1995e. "Remarks at James Madison High School in Vienna, Virginia, July 12, 1995." *Weekly Compilation of Presidential Documents*, July 17, pp. 1221–27.

———. 1995f. "Remarks at the National Prayer Breakfast." *Weekly Compilation of Presidential Documents*, February 6, pp. 172–73.

———. 1995g. "Remarks at the Opening of Session I of the Family and Media Conference in Nashville, Tennessee, July 10, 1995." *Weekly Compilation of Presidential Documents*, July 17 pp. 1210–12.

————. 1995h. "Remarks Prior to a Roundtable Discussion on Teenage Smoking, August 10, 1995." *Weekly Compilation of Presidential Documents*, August 14, pp. 14–15.

————. 1995i. "We Heard America Shouting." *Vital Speeches of the Day*, February 15, pp. 258–66.

————. 1996a. "Clinton Describes His Path to the 21st Century." *Congressional Quarterly Weekly Report*, August 31, pp. 2485–89.

————. 1996b. "In His Own Words." *New York Times*, November 4.

————. 1996c. "Memorandum on School Uniforms Manual." *Weekly Compilation of Presidential Documents*, March 4, pp. 368–69.

————. 1996d. "Remarks at the Salem Missionary Baptist Church in Fruitland, Tennessee." *Weekly Compilation of Presidential Documents* 32, August 26, pp. 1468–71.

————. 1996e. "Remarks Following a Meeting with Entertainment and Media Executives." *Weekly Compilation of Presidential Documents*, March 4, pp. 387–89.

————. 1996f. Speech at Glendale Community College Broadcast Live on CNN, June 11, 1996.

————. 1996g. Speech in Albuquerque, New Mexico. Featured on CNN's *Inside Politics*, June 11, 1996.

————. 1996h. "State of the Union 1996: The Age of Possibility." *Vital Speeches of the Day*, February 15, pp. 258–63.

————. 1996i. "We're All The Creatures of God." *U.S. News & World Report*, November 4, p. 11.

————. 1997. "Text of President Clinton's State of the Union Message to Congress." *New York Times*, February 5.

DeParle, Jason. 1994. "President to Campaign Against Teen Pregnancy." *New York Times*, June 10.

Drinan, Robert F. 1993. "Clintons' Call for Prayer Moves Religious Leaders." *National Catholic Reporter*, September 10, p. 17.

Eastland, Terry. 1994. "Religion, Politics & the Clintons." *Commentary* (January): 40–43.

Edwards, George C., III. 1997. "The Presidential Pulpit: Bully or Baloney?" In *Understanding the Presidency*, ed. James P. Pfiffner and Roger H. Davidson. New York: Longman.

Ferranti, Jennifer. 1994 "Restoring Families One Family at a Time." *Christianity Today*, April 24, pp. 46–47.

Hart, John. 1995. *The Presidential Branch*, 2nd ed. Chatham, NJ: Chatham House.

Gavin, Jennifer. 1993. "Historic Meeting Draws Large Crowd to University Campus." *Denver Post*, August 13.

Greenhouse, Linda. 1996. "High Court to Reverse Ruling in a Religion Case." *New York Times*, October 31.

————. 1997a. "High Court Voids Curb on 'Indecent' Internet Material." *New York Times*, June 27.

————. 1997b. "Justices Look Anew at a Landmark Church-State School Case." *New York Times*, April 16.

Janofsky, Michael. 1996. "Gore Boasts of TV Policy and Boosts Congressman." *New York Times*, October 4.

Jones, Arthur. 1995. "The Role of God, Prayer in Clinton's Life." *National Catholic Reporter*, February 17.

Kernell, Samuel. 1993. *Going Public*. Washington, DC: Congressional Quarterly.

Lauter, David. 1993. "Clinton Voices Concerns U.S. May Be Too Secular." *Los Angeles Times*, August 31.

Light, Paul. 1991. *The President's Agenda*. Baltimore, MD: Johns Hopkins University Press.

Lowi, Theodore. 1985. *The Personal President*. Ithaca, NY: Cornell University Press.

Medhurst, Martin J., ed. 1996. *Beyond the Rhetorical Presidency*. College Station: Texas A&M University Press.

Mifflin, Lawrie. 1996a. "Fight Looms over an Age-Based TV Ratings Plan." *New York Times*, December 11.

———. 1996b. "TV Industry Vows Fight to Protect New Ratings Plan." *New York Times*, December 13.

Miroff, Bruce. 1994. "The Presidency and the Public: Leadership as Spectacle." In *The Presidency and the Political System*, ed. Michael Nelson. Washington, DC: Congressional Quarterly.

Mitchell, Alison. 1996. "Avoid 'Politics of Division,' Says Clinton." *New York Times*, November 4.

———. 1997. "Clinton Presses a Campaign to Bridge the Racial Divide." *New York Times*, June 15.

Neustadt, Richard. 1990. *Presidential Power and the Modern Presidents*. New York: Free Press.

Niebuhr, Gustav. 1994. "Clinton Working to Strengthen Ties to Clergy." *New York Times*, September 13.

———. 1997. "Not All Presidential Advisers Talk Politics." *New York Times*, March 19.

Porter, Jessica. 1996. "Department to Issue Guidelines on School Uniforms." *Education Week*, March 6, p. 27.

Purdum, Todd S. 1995. "Sins? Clinton Confesses a Couple." *New York Times*, August 10.

———. 1996. "Clinton Buoys." *New York Times*, September 27.

———. 1997. "At Gathering, Clinton Urges Moratorium on Revenge." *New York Times*, February 7.

Reno v. ACLU, No. 96–511 (June 26, 1997).

Rose, Richard. 1991. *The Postmodern President*, 2nd ed. Chatham, NJ: Chatham House.

Stengel, Richard and Eric Pooley. 1996. "Masters of the Message." *Time*, November 18, pp. 76–96.

Stern, Christopher. 1996. "White House Hosts Kids TV Rally." *Broadcasting & Cable*, March 11, p. 17.

Troy, Gil. 1991. *See How They Ran*. New York: Free Press.

Tulis, Jeffrey. 1987. *The Rhetorical Presidency*. Princeton: Princeton University Press.

Wall, James M. 1993. "Sowing and Reaping." *Christian Century*, February 3–10, pp. 99–100.

White House Press Release (WHPR). November 13, 1993. "Remarks by William Jefferson Clinton, 86th Annual Holy Convocation, The Church of God in Christ, November 13, 1993, Memphis, Tennessee."

————. August 14, 1994. "Remarks by the President During Church Services, Full Gospel AME Zion Church, Temple Hills, Maryland."

————. April 23, 1995. "Remarks by the President During 'A Time of Healing' Prayer Service, Oklahoma State Fair Arena, Oklahoma City, Oklahoma."

————. July 19, 1995. "Memorandum for Heads of Executive Departments and Agencies—Subject: Evaluation of Affirmative Action Programs."

————. July 19, 1995. "Remarks by the President on Affirmative Action."

————. January 29, 1996. "America's Challenge in an Age of Possibility: Strengthening Our Families, Ending Teen Pregnancy."

————. May 7, 1996. "America's Challenge in an Age of Possibility: Fighting Tobacco Use by Our Children."

————. May 7, 1996. "Remarks by the President at Participation in Kick Butts Day."

————. June 8, 1996. "Radio Address by the President to the Nation."

————. July 8, 1996. "Alcohol, Tobacco and Firearms Youth Crime Gun Interaction Initiative."

————. July 10, 1996. "Remarks by the President on the Church Arson Prevention Act."

————. August 23, 1996. "Remarks by the President During the Announcement of Food and Drug Administration Rule on Children And Tobacco."

————. October 4, 1996. "Radio Address of the President to the Nation."

————. October 19, 1996. "Radio Address of the President to the Nation."

————. November 9, 1996. "Radio Address of the President to the Nation."

————. January 18, 1997. "Radio Address of the President to the Nation."

————. January 23, 1997. "Memorandum for the Secretary of Transportation—Subject: Increasing Seatbelt Use Nationwide."

————. February 28, 1997. "Remarks by the President During Tobacco Regulations Announcement."

————. April 10, 1997. "President William Jefferson Clinton, Excerpts from Remarks by the President to the Annual Meeting of the American Society of Newspaper Editors, April 10, 1997."

————. April 12, 1997. "Radio Address of the President to the Nation."

————. April 15, 1997. "Remarks by the President to Students of Andries Hudde Junior High School on the New York Area's 'Kick Butts Day.' "

————. April 16, 1997. "Executive Order: Increasing Seat Belt Use in the United States."

————. April 17, 1997. "Remarks by the President and the First Lady at White House Conference on Early Child Development and Learning."

————. May 16, 1997. "Remarks by the President in Apology for Study Done in Tuskegee."

————. May 21, 1997. "Remarks by the President at U.S. Conference of Mayors."

————. June 7, 1997. "Radio Address of the President to the Nation."

————. June 13, 1997a. "Executive Order: President's Advisory Board on Race."

————. June 13, 1997b. "Remarks by the President in Meeting with the Advisory Board to the President on Race."

Zoglin, Richard. 1996. "Prime-Time Summit." *Time*, March 11, pp. 64–65.

Chapter 10

The Other Side of Power: Who Is Left Out of Presidential Rhetoric?

MARY E. STUCKEY AND RICHARD MORRIS

... when the idea of Indian tribes as nations is voiced, many Americans
laugh at the pretention, convinced that Indians have some primitive delusion
of grandeur that has certainly been erased by history.

Deloria & Lytle, 1984

There is a long tradition of political science research that explicitly questions
the meaning of "democracy" in a nation that, despite its rhetorical commitment
to the themes of political equality and individual liberty, seems persistently to
pursue policies that contravene those same principles. As a critique of ideology,
this investigative impulse can be traced back to the writings of the anti-
Federalists, who were concerned that the proposed federal system would amass
too much power within the central government at the expense of the states and
their people (Storing 1985: 8–9). However, not until the aftermath of the Great
Depression and World War II, when threats to democracy—and its limits—
became frighteningly obvious, did this impulse fully emerge as a constant concern.

Much of the concern that developed during this period focused on the question
of how democratic a nation might become without risking its stability and moral
health (Beitzinger 1972: 516)—a question that took on added resonance and
seemed to lead to different sorts of answers with the social movements of the
1960s (Piven and Cloward 1977; Schultz and Schultz 1989; Zinn 1980). Clearly
as relevant today as in 1791, debates over how best to effect stability while
minimizing risk are as contentious as they have ever been, as is roundly evidenced in discussions of the "canon" and disputations over whom to include

in the academic life of the nation (Bloom 1987; Hirsch 1987; Schlesinger 1992; Takaki 1993).

The work of Theodore Lowi notwithstanding, what is striking about the literature on the presidency and on political leadership in general is that it remains relatively untouched by such debates, in spite of the furor they have sponsored and continue to sponsor in the academy and in our national political life. This seems all the more peculiar, given the long history of such debates within political science, as well as the degree to which those debates ostensibly inform scholarship (Gaventa 1980; McConnell 1966; Mills 1956).

Aside from some very recent attention to the question of gender and the presidency (Martin and Morelli, 1997), presidential scholars traditionally have restricted their discussions to issues such as the meaning of "presidential leadership" and the "correct" balance between the branches without ever stopping to examine the premises from which such questions emerge. The definition(s) of leadership on which we rely, and the analyses that spring from those definitions, go largely unexplored, as do the consequences of those analyses for those who are not always already included.

Our main thesis is that presidency scholars would benefit from more inclusive explorations, that a broader horizon would enrich and extend the reach of our research, that dismantling some of the explicit and implicit restrictions that limit our traditional research activities would free us from roles that all too often result in complicitous support for hegemonic structures and practices. By way of advancing this thesis, in this chapter we seek to initiate a counterdialogue by interrogating the roles that academics play in supporting/challenging the political status quo, by considering alternative views of the nature of power and how those views might apply to the study of the presidency, and by reflecting on some key political consequences that such views might have for future research.

ACADEMICIANS AS POLITICAL ACTORS

Following the work of Robert Lynd (1939), numerous scholars have examined the role(s) of social scientists in the broader political arena. Wen Shu Lee's (1993) notable recent addition to this body of thought, for example, focuses attention on the ideological, noting that "problems that receive institutional and financial support over a long period of time are usually those articulated by the powerful" (221). Such a claim finds considerable support not only theoretically (Wander 1996), but also practically—for example, in the works of scholars like Soley (1995), who have paused long enough to consider who pays the academy's bills.

Rarely the recipients of grants of the magnitude that Soley considers, presidential scholars are perhaps less likely than those in the "hard" sciences to be reasonably accused of "selling out" to corporate benefactors. Nevertheless, a troubling relationship between the "issues" we study and the "problems" of the broader political arena remains; for much of the research concerned with the presidency not only reflects and implicitly endorses the prevailing hegemony, but it also tends to disregard challenges to that hegemony. This helps to explain why the mountainous literature on presidential elections, the dynamics of vote choice, and so forth is so seldom of much use to voters or candidates. This is not to say that research must be directly and obviously relevant to the "average" person to be considered worthwhile or that what we are doing as academics is inherently "wrong." But it does strongly suggest that what we are *not* doing is equally important and worthy of our attention.

A brief review of articles published on the presidency in 1995, for example, reveals considerable interest in presidential elections, presidential decision making, presidential policy-making, presidential communication, and the evaluation of presidential performance (*PRG Report* 1996a: 10–12). This is hardly a revelation given that these topics traditionally fill our journal space and constitute the basis for the syllabi of numerous graduate and undergraduate courses (DiClerico 1990; Edwards and Wayne 1994; Pfiffner and Davidson 1997; Ragsdale 1993; Thomas, Pika and Watson 1994). Furthermore, not only are all these topics clearly relevant to developing and expanding our understanding of how the presidency works, but they also share an important implicit understanding of what constitutes power and its exercise. Such an understanding supports the distribution of power within the academy and within the broader political arena.[1]

To be sure, traditional channels allow us to broaden our understanding of what is "appropriate" to study, what methods are "appropriate" to the material at hand, what styles are "appropriate" for communicating our research to others, what counts as "appropriate" data, and what conclusions we might "appropriately" draw from those data (Wander 1996). Yet, what is missing from our publications, and too often from our pedagogy, are channels that *encourage* scholars to broaden and even challenge what we all too often take as given. We sponsor no publication on the role of women, for instance, although there is one on abortion (Abramowitz 1995). We find no mention of how the policies that provide case studies may affect different minorities, although there is an article on why political scientists should focus on the policy process and not the normative consequences of that process (Mervin 1995).[2] There is no space dedicated to discussions of alternative models of leadership, although some research argues that presidents should pay more attention to the examples of their predecessors (Hartung 1995). To put the matter bluntly, there is precious little in the journals of the field that asks us to question our fundamental assumptions about how we understand the discipline, although there is a critique of the "textbook" presidency (Alsfeld 1995), as well as a suggestion that analyses of the presidency be placed inside a broader governmental context (Shafer 1995).

Instead, we find such challenges relegated (and often self-relegated) to "other" subfields. Much of the gender-related scholarship is published or presented in "women and politics." Much of significance on nonmainstream leadership within the context of the United States emerges only as an adjunct to "African-American politics," "urban studies," or "Latino studies." Comparative studies of leadership appear in journals and on panels dedicatedly focused on comparative politics. Furthermore, presidential scholars neither overtly note nor regularly cite such work. As a consequence, while we accomplish much within the boundaries of "the presidency" and "American politics," we are at odds to contextualize our research in more broadly applicable ways. A second, equally significant consequence is that women and minorities—those always already not represented—are most likely to be left out of the convention and publication processes, while those who are always already included are not only rewarded by these very same exclusionary processes, but are also rewarded for perpetuating the styles, subjects, and methodologies that define these processes as exclusionary (e.g., Aisenberg and Harrington 1988; Blair, Brown, and Baxter 1994).[3]

And, yet, talk about power among presidential scholars overwhelmingly tends to be restricted to a context delimited by the development of the federal system, which generates equally restrictive discussions such as the variety of roles presidents are expected to play, as they were first delineated by Clinton Rossiter (1956); the power of persuasion (Neustadt 1990); the importance of political time (Skowronek 1993); or how the presidency is bounded and constrained by the federal system and the Constitution (Jones 1994).

While far from exhaustive or even extensive, this list of typical, scholarly discussions is indicative of how presidential scholars view equations of power. Again, this is not inherently wrong or wrong-headed, but it does result in two tendencies that deserve attention and that constitute the subjects of the next two sections. First, such a restricted context averts serious thinking and discussion of the president's role(s)—individually and institutionally—in reflecting, maintaining, and reinforcing hegemony. Second, such a restricted focus forestalls critical examination of the roots both of our own particular system and of alternative possibilities of political organization that may well stem from those roots.

FORMULATING PRESIDENTIAL POWER

Presidential scholars question neither the validity nor the inherent merit of the federal system, although some concern has arisen over redressing issues of balance among the branches (Jones 1994). Rarely do we find someone discussing—especially in print—the lack of women and minorities in the executive branch; rarer still do we encounter discussions that extend beyond the senior civil service or the cabinet; and it is all but unheard of to suggest that through its resistance to inclusion the presidential office itself may be flawed beyond redemption. Consider, for example, that none of the leading textbooks on the presidency includes chapters or even major sections addressing issues of representation; consider also that the recent publication of a work concerned with studying the presidency is equally silent about such matters (Edwards, Kessel, and Rockman 1993).

Although we could argue that such a restricted focus is the result of gender bias among presidential scholars, arguments about biological determinism are difficult to credit; for the presidency obviously represents a crucial nexus for the maintenance of hegemony, and presidential scholars, of whatever political orientation, gender, and personal predisposition, have persistently failed to address the issue in print. Then, again, one might argue that lack of attention to the issue of ideological bias stems from the fact that presidential scholars focus on the dynamics of a single institution and leave issues of broader concern to others. But this line of reasoning is just as hard to credit, given the fact that the most noted books in the field—winners of the Richard Neustadt Award, which is given annually for the best book on the presidency, as examples—tend to focus on precisely these broader issues, thus verifying that the discipline rewards scholarship that contextualizes the institution, albeit in ideologically approved ways (e.g., *PRG Report* 1996: 18). A more plausible argument is that academicians who are trained in the parameters of a specific discipline do not question those parameters either easily or often, and it is through just such a lack of questioning that hegemony is perpetuated—by rendering some issues, some ideas, some questions are unmentionable because unmentioned, unthinkable because unthought, unaskable because unasked.

That the discipline as a whole would benefit by earnest explorations of the unmentioned, the unthought, and the unasked—supposing such exploration were actually *encouraged* by its members—seems patently obvious. As but three among many possibilities, consider how specific works of Mills (1956), Bachrach and Baratz (1962), and Gaventa (1980) conceivably might heighten our understanding of the roles the presidency plays in American society.

C. Wright Mills's *The Power Elite*, first published in 1956, is, of course, one of the classics of American politics. Mills begins his treatise by declaring that

The powers of ordinary men are circumscribed by the everyday worlds in which they live, yet even in these rounds of job, family, and neighborhood, they often seem driven by forces they neither understand nor govern. . . . The very framework of modern society confines them to projects not their own, but from every side, such changes now press upon the men and women of the mass society, who accordingly feel that they are without purpose in an epoch in which they are without power. (3)

Mills attributes this state of affairs to the increasing centralization of information and power, to the dominance of "the power elite" in the military, the social structure, and the government.

For Mills, there is no overriding conspiracy among these people; rather, there is a mutual dependence upon a shared worldview that was propagated among the mass as well as among the elite, rendering dominance unquestionable because it was perpetually unquestioned. This "elitist" model has been subjected to a variety of criticisms (Dahl 1958)—including disputes over whether power is centralized or diffused, whether the system is so well ordered and stable over time as to merit the designation "power structure," and whether Mills's theories are verifiable. Nonetheless, the fact remains that the issues of whether or how the presidency may function to support a particular hegemony within the political system and climate in which they are embedded have gone unaddressed in presidential scholarship.

Given this starting point, presidential scholars would do well to note Bachrach and Baratz's proposed definition of power (1962): "Of course power is exercised when A participates in the making of decisions that affect B. But power is also exercised when A devotes his energies to creating or reinforcing social or political values and institutional practices that limit the scope of the political process to public consideration of only those issues which are comparatively innocuous to A" (948). While extensive work has been done on agenda setting (Ebring 1980; Gandy 1982; Kenski 1996), much of it directly relevant to the presidency (Gilberg et al., 1980; Iyengar, Kinder, and Peters, 1984; Wanta et al. 1989), such research tends to focus on the president's ability to set the agenda on an issue-by-issue basis.

Yet, Bachrach and Baratz also interrogate both the processes by which decisions about the agenda are made and the ways such decisions are *not* made (949). Nondecisions, like the latent groups of pluralist theory, are problematic not least because it is difficult to analyze what did not occur. As a theoretical matter, however, scholars of the presidency would do themselves a service by asking what we are *not* studying, as well as by focusing more earnestly on the implications of what we *do* privilege by according such issues revered places in scholarship and pedagogy.

Then, again, focusing one's attentions on nonevents could be intellectually or empirically fruitless. Given the results of one scholar's research on what did not happen in one Appalachian valley, such a fear seems clearly unfounded. John Gaventa's 1980 study of "powerlessness, of power, and of how the two could serve to maintain inaction upon injustice, even in a 'democracy' " (v), provides an interesting analysis of why, given the extraordinarily harsh conditions of the Central Appalachian Valley and the presence of perceived injustice there, no rebellion occurred. His conclusion—drawn from an absence, a nonevent—is that the answer lay in ideology, in the development and maintenance of quiescence, the internalization of powerlessness.

Too often, presidential scholars assume that the president's role as "national representative," as "head of state," means that he speaks for all of the people (see Gregg's discussion of this point in Chapter 2 of this volume). We too readily analyze the varieties of interests that coalesce in presidential elections or support policy initiatives without even considering those who are systematically excluded from both sets of processes. In examining who is *included* in these coalitions, we too easily dismiss those who are always already *excluded*. In defining presidential power in clearly delineated ways, we too frequently forget that there are multiple ways of defining power and that we might better understand the operations of presidential power by looking at what it is *not* as well as what it is.

REFORMULATING PRESIDENTIAL POWER

Presidential scholars, like students of American politics generally, tend to ground their research and pedagogy in the writings of the *Debates of the Federal Convention* and *The Federalist*, which are generally considered the proper antecedents to, and the best discussions of, the federal Constitution. Occasionally, we find it instructive to reach back still further to the European roots of American democracy—to Locke, Rousseau, Hume, Montesquieu, or even ancient Greece or Rome. A research strategy that might be equally useful is to examine the roots of the federal system as they grew in American soil.

Albeit often disregarded, it is now widely accepted that significant portions of the framers' thoughts on federal union derived from their knowledge of and, in some cases, experience with various Native nations,[4] including the Haudenosaunee (in English, "People of the Longhouse"—commonly referred to as the Iroquois League).[5] Composed of the Onondaga, Seneca, Oneida, Cayuga, Mohawk, and Tuscarora Nations, the Haudenosaunee have existed at least since the 1400s as a confederation of sovereign nations that act together whenever matters are common to all participants: "For the Five Nations, themes of reciprocity and exchange, war and peace, and alliance and spiritual power entwined to define most relationships among persons, kin groups, and villages. They also were at the heart of the most significant of all connections between one village and another, the entity called the great League of Peace and Power" (Richter 1992: 29).

Matters of significance for the Haudenosaunee are debated by delegates of the original five sachems (nations). The delegates are selected by the various clan mothers, who in turn retain removal power (Janiewski 1995). Those who have earned the right may also speak at Haudenosaunee councils. Importantly, the confederation does not operate based on majority rule, and the various delegates do not represent their clans either formally or informally (Tooker 1984: 113). Rather, the key organizational and decision-making principle is that all council members must strive to be of "one heart, one mind, one law" (O'Brien 1989: 19). In the absence of this most desirable of outcomes, each nation goes its own way. Furthermore, because the sachems have no coercive power, either over one another or over their people, they must rely on persuasion rather than on coercion or force, which means that individuals and groups are free to ignore decisions they do not endorse (Richter 1992: 45).

There is considerable evidence that the framers of the federal Constitution were aware of the political organizations of the Native nations who were, variously, friends, allies, trading partners, and military opponents. Both Benjamin Franklin and Thomas Paine, for instance, had substantial dealings with the Haudenosaunee (Weatherford 1988), and it is more than plausible that they incorporated their knowledge of this successful and long-lasting confederacy, which covered an extensive geographical territory, into the general corpus of knowledge that they took to Philadelphia. But we must be cautious here; for this was an incorporation that assumed the form of the Haudenosaunee without assuming their substance. Clearly, the framers, especially James Madison (as revealed in *Federalist* 10 and 51, especially), relied on a view of human nature taken not from American soil but from Europe and the new colonies. That view of human nature nurtures a fear of unchecked personal ambition, a greater fear of unbridled majority rule, and a faith in the necessity and ability of institutional structures to harness the dangerous passions of humanity and thus to preserve private property and social order (Barsh and Henderson 1980: 20–21).

The Haudenosaunee view, by contrast, issues from a strong religious and spiritual tradition that reinforces cultural norms of mutual respect, is grounded in a desire to promote peace (not to protect private property through the preservation of social stability), rests on the belief that merit should be rewarded, flourishes through an emphasis on persuasion (rather than on coercive power), and is sustained through networks of personal relationships, kinship, and reciprocity that privileges inclusion over exclusion (Hauptman 1986; Richter 1992; Snow 1994; Tooker 1984). The values exemplified by the Haudenosaunee are consistent with those that prevail throughout Native America.[6] A more explicit discussion of those values will help reveal what lessons alternative philosophies that undergird similar structures may contain for presidential scholars.

Consider, for example, one of the more significant differences between indigenous cultures of the Americas and the European cultures that were grafted here—viz., the roles of religion and government. Non-Indian history since the founding has stressed the importance of the separation of church and state, while for most Native cultures such a division is inconceivable. Tom Porter articulates a point of view that resonates with many Native peoples when he observes that the separation of religion and government ''was one of the big mistakes [the framers made], because when they did that, then they removed the Creator from their life—or at least from half to three-quarters of their life'' (as quoted in Hill 1994: 6). Because Native peoples generally do not make the European distinction between the state and the rest of social life, distinctions between religion and government have no frame of reference in which to make sense (Deloria 1973). In his well-known formulation of this point, Oren Lyons, traditional chief of the Onondaga, avers that ''In the absence of the sacred, nothing is sacred—everything is for sale'' (as quoted in Hill 1994: 24).

Context is of special import here. Native religions are founded in principles of mutual respect and forbearance. As an unidentified Huron said in 1635, ''You tell us fine stories, and there is nothing in what you say that may not be true; but that is good for you who come across the seas. Do you not see that, as we inhabit a world so different from yours, there must be another heaven for us, and another road to reach it?'' (as quoted in Galloway 1994: 43). Such an expression both contains and emerges from the belief that different people, with different belief systems, are entitled not simply to their beliefs but also to have others respect those beliefs (Deloria 1973). Accommodation within this frame clearly means respecting the beliefs, traditions, and rites of others.[7]

Such an abiding respect entails that, given the realities of war and the very real personal costs wars entail for all members of small communities, political and social structures must be geared toward the maintenance of peace rather than the prevention of tyranny. Consequently, social and political structures are horizontal rather than vertical, with emphasis on nurturing the common good and maintaining the community, not on the representation of interests or groups, whether defined geographically, economically, or socially. Sun Bear of the Chippewa explains a key dimension of his tribal tradition succinctly: ''A man was chief only as long as he did the will of people. If he got too chiefly, he'd go to sleep one night, and wake up the next morning to find that he was chief all to himself. The tribe would move away in the night, and they didn't wait four years to do it either'' (as quoted in Hill 1994: 42). Within such a worldview social structures are fluid, with emphasis on consensus and community, and are not static, with emphasis on stability and the protection of particular, propertied classes. Alanis Obomsawin of the Abenaki phrased the matter well in 1982:

In our language there is no word to say inferior or superiority or equality because we are equal, it's a known fact. But life has become very complicated since the newcomers came here. And how does your spirit react to it? . . . It's painful. You have to be strong to walk through the storm. I know I'm a bridge between two worlds. All I ask is for people to wash their feet before they try to walk on me. (as quoted in Hill 1994: 49)

Such horizontal structures, which support the values of equality and mutual respect, work precisely because they are embedded in contexts in which the acquisition and maintenance of private property are not particularly central— because ''worth'' is defined and achieved by contribution to the group. Believing systematically in such a culturally embedded view of character, members of Native societies generally see education, social structures, religion, and the relationships of these to one another as the creation of human personality, which is why they expect no less of their people and institutions (Deloria 1991: 20).

This helps explain the integral role of elders in Native cultures; for those who instruct the young do so not on the basis of age or economic status or knowledge of technique or connections, but on the basis of their experience and accumulated wisdom. Although the massive fragmentation wrought by four centuries of transculturation has considerably attenuated the process for some contemporary Native groups, what Vine Deloria, Jr. (1991) of the Standing Rock Sioux observes about the role and status of education among Native cultures in the past is still very much applicable in the present: ''The old ways of educating affirmed the basic principle that human personality was derived from accepting the responsibility to be a contributing member of society. Kinship and clan were built upon the idea that individuals owed each other certain kinds of behaviors and that if each individual performed his or her task properly, society as a whole would function'' (22). Standing in sharp contrast to the framers' view of character as the quality one most desired in leadership but could not hope to depend on or to create, the view that animates most Native views of eldership—and of life in general—is an abiding love of difference that serves as a counterbalance to self-interest. As Vickie Downey of the Tewa Tesuque Pueblo recently remarked: ''The Instructions during that time, at the beginning, were to love and respect one another even with all the differences, different cultures, different languages'' (as quoted in Wall 1993: 2).

Rather than fearing exploitation of the passions of the unwashed masses, Native worldviews generally include a respect for rhetoric and the arts of persuasion, placing faith in the collective wisdom of an equal people. Concomitantly, both the ends and the means of power derive from and serve collective rather than individual motives:

As Indians we will never have the efficient organization that gains great concessions from society in the marketplace. We will never have a powerful lobby or be a smashing political force. But we will have the intangible unity which has carried us through four centuries of persecution. We are a people unified by our humanity—not a pressure group unified by conquest. And from our greater strength we shall wear down the white man and finally outlast him. We shall endure. (Deloria 1969: 23)

In noting such differences, we are not in any sense suggesting that the federal system must be reshaped into a system that more clearly reflects Native values and traditions. Nor are we suggesting that scholars adopt an instumental view, that they conceive of Native America as yet another ''resource'' for their personal use, however noble their motives or aims. Far less are we suggesting that the federal system or society more generally—individually or collectively— ought to incorporate bits and pieces of Native worldviews or spirituality as a remedy for present ills. As Oglala Lakota spiritual elder Matthew King correctly points out, each part of Native worldviews and spirituality ''has its own power and it purpose. Each people has their own ways. You cannot mix these ways together, because each people's ways are balanced. Destroying balance is a disrespect and very dangerous'' (as quoted in Churchill 1996: 359). What we are suggesting is that, especially in an increasingly multicultural polity, scholars would do well to take the lead in respecting, learning about, and applying the values of nonhegemonic cultures to the institutions that are supposed to govern the cultural amalgams that comprise the United States.

How might such values be brought to bear on the study of the presidency? Rather than assuming the worldview of the framers and the current hegemony, for example, presidential scholars might profitably examine the practice and institutions of leadership as experienced and understood from the margins. By envisioning alternatives, presidential scholars might better see the institution as it has developed and thereby provide a better vision for how it might yet unfold.

As Don Coyhis, a Mohican, says, "We move forward and become like that which we think about. Isn't it time we began to think about what we're thinking about?" (as quoted in Hill 1994: 34).

FUTURE DIRECTIONS

The incentives of academia often insinuate through reward ever-increasing areas of specialization. Most of us are scholars not of the presidency but of presidential communication or administration or foreign policy or some other similarly specific area of study. Many of us increasingly are wedded to a specific administration or to a specific time period or to a particular aspect of a particular presidency. Professional success increasingly means developing a professional niche, nurturing it and defending it. One obvious and very measurable result is that we now possess a mountainous heap of knowledge.

But something has also been lost—or perhaps it was never attained: we are not, by and large, scholars who examine the functioning of the system as a whole, who see the presidency as but one dimension of a larger system. Some of us may teach it this way, but few of us devote much time to thinking about or publishing it this way. Many of our assumptions and presumptions about how power works or about how presidential or governmental power affect majorities and minorities in our system therefore remain unquestioned, unaddressed, unexamined. Because we too often contribute to nothing so much as the maintenance of a political status quo, both within the academy and within the larger, more explicitly political policy area, we too often overlook a useful site for the generation of theory—a perennial problem in presidency research. Yet, by exploring alternative approaches to leadership, we might begin to consider the relationships between culture, leadership, and governance in ways that are both more theoretically informed and more empirically grounded.

The case we have stressed here is indigenous to the continent and undoubtedly was in many respects initially influential in developing the federal system. We are convinced that presidential scholars and others would do well to begin analyses of the presidency and the political system by thinking and researching more broadly—to ask questions about how power is defined, constituted, and enacted, to ask what its consequences are not just in terms of the hegemony's values and practices, but also in terms of values and practices that challenge that hegemony. Other cases, including analyses that investigate perspectives from Latin America or Asia or Africa or immigrant experiences that have developed in the continental United States, may also provide useful insights into the functioning of that same system.

Of course, beginning to consider how such alternative perspectives might enrich and broaden our research and pedagogical activities is but one among a limitless set of starting points. Other possibilities include investigating the boundaries and mechanisms of inclusion and exclusion, how those boundaries limit or encourage certain choices, how nurturing specific kinds of individualism over and against other options constrains and disciplines choice and perspective, how privileging certain forms of communication and decision-making processes inhibits or prohibits other forms of communication and decision-making processes, how such inhibitions and prohibitions enable some kinds of solutions while disabling others, how some forms of power lead to the generation and perpetuation of specifiable elements within collective memory while negating others. This is a very short list, to be sure; but whatever starting point one might choose, moving forward with an explicit understanding that we occupy a planet that is vastly smaller and more fragile than the framers ever might have conceived demands that we look very seriously at the other side of power.

NOTES

1. We are advancing a generic criticism here rather than a critique of specific individuals.

2. Civil rights policy aside—and minorities are affected by policies that do not bear the labels "civil rights" or "welfare."

3. We think it important to note that both authors have served in numerous professional capacities. Our experiences in those capacities—all too often severely tested and almost always defined by the need to respect the parameters of our disciplines while fostering an atmosphere of inclusion—have made us painfully aware that these tensions are immense and not easily reconciled.

4. *Editor's Note*: I have left this statement as the authors have written it, although I disagree with their claim. Most scholars accept the idea that the framers were aware of the Iroquois League and other associations, but the very word "federalism" has its roots in "feudalism." It was not a completely new concept to the Euro-American mind.

5. We use the present tense throughout when referring to the Haudenosaunee because the League still functions and continues to assert and practice its sovereignty—as evidenced, for example, by their declaration of war on Germany in 1942 (Hauptman 1981).

6. We hasten to add that we offer this observation as a generalization that is not meant to apply to all Native nations.

7. We wish to make it clear that we are not suggesting that the original inhabitants of this land were universally peaceful, bucolic beings who lived in perfect peace and harmony. Such arguments are disingenuous, at best.

REFERENCES

Abramowitz, A. 1995. "It's Abortion Stupid: Policy Voting in the 1992 Presidential Election." *Journal of Politics* 57: 176–86.

Aisenberg, N. and M. Harrington. 1988. *Women of Academe: Outsiders in the Sacred Grove*. Amherst: University of Massachusetts Press.

Alsfeld, R. 1995. "The Presidency Reconfigured? The Textbook Presidency Yet Again." *Presidential Studies Quarterly* 25: 677–82.

Barsh, R. and J. Henderson. 1980. *The Road: Indian Tribes and Political Liberty*. Berkeley: University of California Press.

Beitzinger, A. 1972. *A History of American Political Thought*. New York: Harper & Row.

Blair, C., J. Brown and L. Baxter. 1994. "Disciplining the Feminine." *Quarterly Journal of Speech* 80: 383–409.

Bloom, A. 1987. *The Closing of the American Mind: How Higher Education Has Failed Democracy and Impoverished the Souls of Today's Students*. New York: Simon & Schuster.

Churchill, W. 1996. *From a Native Son: Selected Essays on Indigenism, 1985–1995*. Boston: South End Press.

Dahl, R. 1958. "A Critique of the Ruling Elite Model." *American Political Science Review* 52: 463–69.

Deloria, V., Jr. 1973. *God Is Red*. New York: Dell.

———. 1991. *Indian Education in America*. Boulder, CO: American Indian Science and Engineering Society.

——— and C. Lytle. 1984. *The Nations Within: The Past and Future of American Indian Sovereignty*. New York: Pantheon.

DiClerico, R. 1990. *The American Presidency*, 3rd ed. New York: Prentice-Hall.

Ebring, L. 1980. "Front Page News and Real World Cues: A New Look at Agenda-Setting by the Media." *American Journal of Political Science* 24(1): 16–49.

Edwards, G., J. Kessel and B. Rockman, eds. 1993. *Researching the Presidency: Vital Questions, New Approaches*. Pittsburgh: University of Pittsburgh Press.

——— and S. Wayne. 1994. *Presidential Leadership: Politics and Policy Making*, 3rd ed. New York: St. Martin's Press.

Galloway, C., ed. 1994. *The World Turned Upside Down: Indian Voices from Early America*. Boston: Bedford Books.

Gandy, O. 1982. *Beyond Agenda-Setting: Information Subsidies and Public Policy*. Norwood, NJ: Ablex.

Gaventa, J. 1980. *Power and Powerlessness: Quiescence and Rebellion in an Appalachian Valley*. Urbana: University of Illinois Press.

Gilberg, S., C. Eyal, M. McCombs and D. Nichols. 1980. "The State of the Union Address and the Press Agenda." *Journalism Quarterly* 57: 584–88.

Hartung, W. 1995. "Nixon's Children: Bill Clinton and the Permanent Arms Bazaar." *World Policy Journal* 12: 25–35.

Hauptman, L. 1981. *The Iroquois and the New Deal*. Syracuse, NY: Syracuse University Press.

———. 1986. *The Iroquois Struggle for Survival: World War II to Red Power*. Syracuse, NY: Syracuse University Press.

Hill, N. 1994. *Words of Power: Voices from Native America*. Golden, CO: Fulcrum.

Hirsch, E. D. 1987. *Cultural Literacy: What Every American Needs to Know*. New York: Vintage.

Iyengar, S., D. Kinder and M. Peters. 1984. "The Evening News and Presidential Evaluations." *Journal of Personal and Social Psychology* 46 (April): 778–87.

Janiewski, D. 1995. "Gendering, Racializing, and Classifying: Settler Colonization in the United States, 1590–1990." In *Unsettling Settler Societies: Articulation of Gender, Race, Ethnicity, and Class*, ed. D. Stasiulis and N. Yuval-Davis. London: Sage, pp. 132–60.

Jones, C. 1994. *The Presidency in a Separated System*. Washington, DC: Brookings Institution.

Kenski, H. 1996. "From Agenda Setting to Priming and Framing: Reflections on Theory and Method." In *The Theory and Practice of Political Communication Research*, ed. M. Stuckey. Albany, NY: SUNY Press, pp. 67–83.

Lee, W. S. 1993. "Social Scientists as Ideological Critics." *Western Journal of Communication* 57 (Spring): 221–32.

Lynd, R. 1939. *Knowledge for What? The Place of Social Science in American Culture.* New York: Grove Press.

Martin, J. and M. Morelli, eds. 1997. *The Other Elites: Women, Power, and Politics in the Executive Branch.* Boulder, CO: Lynne Rienner.

McConnell, G. 1996. *Private Power and American Democracy.* New York: Vintage.

Mervin, D. 1995. "Political Science and the Study of the Presidency." *Presidential Studies Quarterly* 25: 669–75.

Mills, C. W. 1956. *The Power Elite.* New York: Oxford University Press.

Neustadt, R. 1990. *Presidential Power and the Modern Presidents: The Politics of Leadership from Roosevelt to Reagan.* New York: Free Press.

O'Brien, S. 1989. *American Indian Tribal Governments.* Norman: University of Oklahoma Press.

Pfiffner, J. and R. Davidson. 1997. *Understanding the Presidency.* New York: Longman.

Piven, F. and R. Cloward. 1977. *Poor People's Movements: Why They Succeed, How They Fail.* New York: Random House.

PRG Report: Newsletter of the Presidency Research Group. 1996a. *American Political Science Association* 18(1).

PRG Report: Newsletter of the Presidency Research Group. 1996b. *American Political Science Association* 18(2).

Ragsdale, L. 1993. *Presidential Politics.* Boston: Houghton Mifflin.

Richter, D. K. 1992. *The Ordeal of the Longhouse: The People of the Iroquois League in the Age of Colonization.* Chapel Hill: University of North Carolina Press.

Roberts, M. and M. McCombs. 1994. "Agenda Setting and Political Advertising: Origins of the News Agenda." *Political Communication* 11(3): 249–62.

Rossiter, C. 1956. *The American Presidency.* New York: Harcourt Brace.

Schlesinger, A. 1992. *The Disuniting of America: Reflections on a Multicultural Society.* New York: Norton.

Schultz, B. and R. Schultz. 1989. *It Did Happen Here: Recollections of Political Repression in America.* Berkeley: University of California Press.

Shafer, M. 1995. "An Aerial Photograph of Presidential Leadership: President Clinton's National Energy Plan Revisited." *Presidential Studies Quarterly* 25: 287–99.

Skowronek, S. 1993. *The Politics Presidents Make: Leadership from John Adams to George Bush.* Cambridge, MA: Harvard University Press.

Snow, D. 1994. *The Iroquois.* Cambridge, MA: Blackwell.

Soley, L. 1995. *Leasing the Ivory Tower: The Corporate Takeover of Academia.* Boston: South End Press.

Storing, H., ed. (1985). *The Anti-Federalists: Writings of the Opponents of the Constitution.* Chicago: University of Chicago Press.

Takaki, R. 1993. *A Different Mirror: A History of Multicultural America.* Boston: Little, Brown.

Thomas, N., J. Pika and R. Watson. 1994. *The Politics of the Presidency*, 3rd ed. Washington, DC: CQ Press.

Tooker, E. 1984. "Women in Iroquois Society." In *Extending the Rafters: Interdisci-*

plinary Approaches to Iroquoian Studies, ed. M. Foster, J. Campisi, and M. Mithun. Albany, NY: SUNY Press.

Wall, S. 1993. *Wisdom's Daughters: Conversations with Women Elders of Native America*. New York: HarperPerennial.

Wander, P. 1996. "Marxism, Post-colonialism, and Rhetorical Contextualization." *Quarterly Journal of Speech* 82(4): 402–26.

Wanta, W., et al. 1989. "How Presidents' State of the Union Talk Influences Media Agendas." *Journalism Quarterly* 66 (Autumn): 537–41.

Weatherford, J. 1988. *Indian Givers: How Indians of the Americas Transformed the World*. New York: Fawcett.

Zinn, H. 1980. *A People's History of the United States*. New York: Harper & Row.

Chapter 11

First Partner: First Ladies and Their Roles

PAMELA J. VAN ZWALUWENBURG

> We don't fit easily into a lot of our preexisting categories. . . . And I think
> that, having been independent, having made decisions, it's a little difficult
> for us as a country, maybe, to make the transition of having a woman like
> many of the women in this room. . . . So I think the standards and to some
> extent the expectations and the demands have changed, and I'm trying to
> find my way through it and trying to figure out how best to be true to
> myself and how to fulfill my responsibilities to my husband and my daugh-
> ter and the country.
>
> Hillary Clinton (Duffy 1994)

These words from Hillary Clinton highlight the difficulties inherent in the role
of First Lady and in attempts to study these women in a systematic way. This
study is directed toward the intersection of the existing literature on First Ladies
(mainly historical biographies) and the theories found in scholarship on women
in politics that seek to explain the various levels of women's political participation. There are several questions that drive this study: What are the roles of
the First Lady? How and to what extent does a First Lady influence politics and
policy? Why are some First Ladies more public or political than others? What
life-space variables affect role performance? How can we draw together existing
research and theories into a more systematic study of description and explanation? Why should political scientists and, in particular, presidential scholars be
interested in First Ladies?

Although there has recently been an increase in expeditions, certain territories
of the scholarly frontier of First Ladies remain relatively unexplored. The goals
of this chapter are to explore both the charted and uncharted areas, describe the

various roles and effects of First Ladies, classify each First Lady according to these roles, and explain some of the variance among individuals performing these roles. The principal hypothesis is that the level of activity within each role (Hostess, Public, Advocate, Political) can be explained by life-space variables such as education, age, children, health, and political experience. Qualitative and quantitative methodologies, guided by empirical theories adapted from the scholarship on women in politics, will allow us to take the best of existing research and combine it into a systematic analysis of First Ladies.

THE FIRST LADIES FRAMEWORK: AN OVERVIEW

Scholars who have studied First Ladies agree that it is difficult to measure the influence that a First Lady has on her husband. O'Connor et al. explain that not only is influence hard to detect or measure, but social norms dictate that a First Lady at least appear as if she is not influencing the president, making it even more difficult to examine (O'Connor et al. 1996: 837). As hard as it may be to study the effect that the First Lady has on her husband, further examination of First Ladies may deepen our understanding of presidential performance. Whether it is the president's road to the White House, his personal power, his psychology, his role as symbolic leader, or his public image and popularity, each area of power may be affected by the president's spouse. *CQ Researcher* asserts that ''the First Lady plays a key role in setting the emotional tone of a president's administration (Clark 1996: 510). Other critics (Campbell 1996; Gould 1990) have also pointed out the inattention to the First Lady's influences on the chief executive, even by the most predominant presidential scholars.

Why should First Ladies be of scholarly concern to presidential scholars or political scientists? For one reason, the First Lady influences presidential power, perceptions, popularity, and performance. A First Lady may provide advice that influences the president's decisions or attitudes, or she may affect public perceptions of her and her husband, thereby making his job either easier or more difficult. The more we learn about these women, the more we realize the unmistakable impact that most of them had on their husbands' career. What the public thinks of the First Lady can also affect the president (Burrell 1997). *CQ Researcher* provides insight into the controversies surrounding the role of First Lady, what proponents and opponents of her activities have to say, and how this affects the president (Clark 1996). The First Ladies' influence may have gone as far back as pushing their husbands for public office or campaigning; their effect may have gone as deep as influencing important policy decisions and appointments; or their impact may have been as widespread as public opinion and the president's popularity. Another reason to study First Ladies is to further our understanding about the president and his goals and ideals. As Gould points out, ''The way in which a president uses or manages the political and cultural assets that the First Lady provides says a great deal about the styles and impact of that administration'' (Gould 1990: 678). Unfortunately, Gould does not explain how.

The Literature on First Ladies

While noting the lack of scholarly attention from presidential scholars, it is also important to turn a critical eye on the work that has been done on First Ladies. Until the 1980s, the limited exploration of First Ladies was dominated by impressionistic and anecdotal biographical tidbits that lacked serious academic rigor. There was little written that contributed more than basic description; Brooks' *First Ladies of the White House* (1969) and Logan's *Ladies of the White House* (1964) are examples of the biographical anecdotal works. Even more recent books lack serious analyses of First Ladies, such as Anderson and Baxendale's *Behind Every Successful President* (1992) whose title suggests more than its contents. Smith's *Mrs. President* (1990) also fails to move beyond biographical cameos.

As the terrain of First Ladies began to be explored further, scholars developed an understanding of the power and influence of First Ladies (Anthony 1990), the development and use of communication power (Gutin 1989), the feminist understanding of First Ladies within political culture and the women's movement (Caroli 1993; Guy 1995), and the various roles demanded of these individuals (Rosebush 1987). The development of the office of First Lady has also been more recently explored terrain (Patterson 1988; Smith and Ryan 1989). Other scholars have begun to tap into the theories in the presidential literature to make comparisons regarding the roles of First Ladies (parallels with the vice presidency in O'Connor et al. 1996) and the inherent difficulties of fulfilling these contradictory roles (rhetoric and symbolism of the presidency in Campbell 1996).

Lacking, however, are a systematic investigation of the different levels of role fulfillment and an attempt to explain why these levels vary among these individuals. In ''Wives in the White House,'' O'Connor et al. begin the process of compiling different biographical data (education, employment, marriage age, children, and political ambition). The article also discusses the ceremonial, political/representative, and policy-making roles. While the authors bring this material together in a systematic way that advances examinations of First Ladies, they stop at description and do little explanation. Under the categories of the biographical variables, the authors do not even suggest directional hypotheses of how certain factors may influence activities within the three roles. Even more disappointing is that, although they address measures of First Lady influences (e.g., influencing appointments or public policy, discussing politics privately or publicly), they only tally the number of First Ladies that fall within each category of activity. The authors do not provide a list of names or a complete data set that can be replicated or used to do further statistical analyses.[1]

Toward a Better Framework

The framework employed in this chapter has its foundations in several books and articles found in different disciplines—history, women's studies, and communications. Perhaps the most fundamental concepts in this chapter are the categories of the four roles of First Ladies—Hostess, Public, Advocate, and Political. These roles are defined in James Rosebush's *First Lady, Public Wife* (1987). Rosebush describes the responsibilities of each role and then gives examples of particular First Ladies and their activities within these roles. The Hostess role consists of the responsibilities of the First Lady as social manager of the White House, including all social events such as state dinners, teas, and luncheons. The Public role is defined by the First Lady's relationship with and use of the media—whether print or broadcast. The Advocate role deals primarily with the various social causes that a First Lady may choose to take up—whether she is merely a symbolic representative of a cause or whether she is a strong policy advocate on behalf of a cause. The Political role is the influence that a First Lady has on her husband regarding policy issues or administration matters. Both *Congressional Quarterly's Guide to the Presidency* (Nelson 1989) and *The Encyclopedia of the American Presidency* (Caroli 1994) focus on the Hostess, Public, Advocate, and Political roles of the First Ladies and present examples of how First Ladies performed each role. The definition of each role and the classification of the levels of activity within each role will be operationalized later in this chapter.

Barbara Burrell (1997) also defines four categories of First Ladies' influences on presidential politics. One type of influence is the direction and promotion of her spouse's political career. It encompasses overt activities such as campaigning but also includes her strong desire to protect the health and well-being of her spouse. Burrell distinguishes this type of activity from the desire to politically influence one's husband. The "gatekeeping," protectionist actions of Nancy Reagan and Edith Wilson have often been misinterpreted as the attempt to influence rather than the attempt to protect (Burrell 1997: 16). A second form of influence is the sway that a First Lady may have on presidential appointments, as history revealed in the input of Mary Todd Lincoln and Helen Taft, and recently, Hillary Clinton (Burrell 1997: 17). This kind of influence has occurred covertly on several occasions, and when it happens overtly (e.g., Mrs. Clinton and the travel office) there is usually a political or public backlash. A third type of influence comes as the First Lady serves as a political adviser, in the form of policy or administrative recommendations—what would be best for the president politically? Fourth, the First Lady may also affect substantive policies (Burrell 1997: 17). She may influence the president to enforce or even change his position on issues such as women's rights, the environment, or welfare policies, or countless other issues. Although Burrell offers insights that further our understanding of First Ladies' influence, she overlooks other arenas in which a First Lady can have an impact; the hostess role, the public role, and the advocate role, all have their own means and ends for a First Lady's influence. What Burrell is really explicating are different levels of influence within the political role.

Myra Gutin's book, *The President's Partner* (1989), has goals and methods similar to ours in this chapter. One goal is to classify different types of First Ladies, a classification based on not only the types of roles fulfilled but the level at which each First Lady in the twentieth century filled it. Gutin includes three categories: Hostess/Ceremonial; the Emerging Spokeswoman; and Political Surrogates/Independent Advocate. Gutin classifies each individual in one particular category. This chapter, however, will look at how each First Lady fits into all four of the Rosebush roles. Gutin also goes a step beyond description and classification as she seeks to explain the factors that affected the different levels of involvement. Gutin addresses the route to the White House, the First Lady's relationship with her husband, the First Lady's access to presidential decision making, and the president's and First Lady's perception of women as the major factors of influence. Her basis of classification (or her "dependent variable") is the major communication activities of the First Lady—Did she give speeches? Did she campaign? What was her relationship to the press? Did she advocate a cause? Did she express policy/political opinions in private or in public? Gutin's framework becomes a useful tool for further exploration because of the systematic way she describes and explains the activities (although primarily communication) of the First Ladies in the twentieth century. Her conclusions are that a First Lady's level of communication activity is determined largely by her husband's support for her public role. The social/ceremonial First Ladies received no support from their husbands to be public speakers, and the emerging spokeswomen had only mediocre support. The political surrogate received "unqualified support" from their husbands to fully utilize the opportunities presented in the media (Gutin 1989: 175). Gutin also concludes that "age, state of health, family obligations, the president's attitude toward the degree of his wife's participation in his administration, and the social and historical attitudes of the time are all determinants of how active a woman will be as a public communicator in the White House" (Gutin 1989: 176). Gutin's study is limited to the First Ladies of the twentieth century and focuses on use of the media. Her study can be built upon to include all First Ladies in a different classification scheme that further develops the First Ladies' roles and assists in the quantitative testing of these hypotheses.

Bringing in the Issue of Women's Political Participation

Beyond understanding First Ladies in and of themselves, further exploration of this unique or, perhaps in some respects, typical group of women can also advance our understanding of women's political activities. It is perhaps more accurate, however, to argue that our understanding about women's political participation can deepen our understanding of the First Ladies' activities. Why are some women more politically active than others? What relationship or influences do life-space variables such as age, education, and children have on woman's political interest and involvement?

In *The Making of Political Women* (1978), Kelly and Boutilier incorporate First Ladies into a study of other political women and seek to explain different levels of activity. Kelly and Boutilier's work, like that of other political/women's studies, shows that determinants of women's political behavior are a combination of (1) effects of childhood socialization; (2) immediate constraints of their individual situation (e.g., education, number of children, age); and (3) structural explanations (also in Randall 1982: 62). Using qualitative methodology, the authors focus on the relationships these political women had with their parents, how they viewed men, children, and family life, and how these relationships affected their political behavior. They then go on to classify these women into three categories—private woman, public woman, and achieving political woman—with the goal of trying to find what they had in common, how they were socialized, and what effect this had on them. The "private woman" is tradition-bound and has little interest in transforming her private position into public power (Bess Truman and Pat Nixon fall into this category) (Kelly and Boutilier 1978: 93–102). The "public woman" has a "moderately activist sex-role ideology" and although she remains traditional in her relationship with her husband and family, she has some public activities of her own (Jacqueline Kennedy, Lady Bird Johnson, and Eleanor Roosevelt are examples of this type of woman) (Kelly and Boutilier 1978: 103–17). The "achieving woman" entered politics independently of her husband and displays a strong sense of political efficacy that was present in her whole life (Kelly and Boutilier 1978: 118–57). Up to now, there have been no First Ladies in this category. There are also categories of women that fall under "achieving women" but are not related to any First Lady.

The theoretical underpinnings of Kelly and Boutilier's work may be found in Maslow as well as in Stanley Renshon, who linked Maslow's theory of psychological needs to political efficacy. Stage one in an individual's political development is the formation of a sex-role ideology that defines the parameters of social female roles. Stage two is the sense of personal control over "life-space" and day-to-day existence. Stage three is the incorporation of the saliency of politics into the sense of control over life-space. Stage four is the development and success of political participation. It is important to understand that a stage must be fulfilled successfully before moving on to the next stage. Thus, Kelly and Boutilier explain, socialization, values, and sex-role perception "determine whether or not one will vote or become politically active. The beliefs and predispositions learned about the more basic orientations will weigh how the individual will perceive the cost of action" (Kelly and Boutilier 1978: 11). Life-space variables such as childhood socialization and parental relationship are most strongly related to the first stage of developing sex-role ideology. Variables such as children and employment have a stronger negative effect on the

political involvement of women who remain in the first stages of psychological/
political development. Variables such as health, age, and children are most
strongly related to the transition between stage two and stage three. To illustrate
their theory:

An activist woman for whom politics has become salient will not find that lack of a
babysitter, uncooperative husband, or young children are sufficient to keep her from
voting or possibly even from running for an office. The cost of her **not** engaging in the
behavior may be too high. *The relative importance of these adult commitments may
mediate the type of participation she may undertake; but they are not likely to negate
completely an activist orientation.* Conversely, for a women with a very traditional female
sex-role perception for whom politics has not become particularly important, the mere
threat of rain might be sufficient to keep her away from the ballot box. (1978: 11,
emphasis added)

Kelly and Boutilier provide the theoretical foundations for understanding how
life-space variables affect the level of political participation of First Ladies and
for explaining the different types of First Ladies.[2]

OPERATIONALIZING AND HYPOTHESIZING LEVELS OF INVOLVEMENT

Extensive work has been done to tell the life stories of First Ladies, but much
less has been done to analyze their activities in the White House. However, very
few scholars have used biography to explain these activities. In this chapter, the
primary research question is, What is the relationship between various life-space
variables and a First Lady's level of activity within each role? Do different
background and biographical variables explain why one First Lady is more active in the Hostess, Public, Advocate, or Political role than others? How does
age, education, health, children, or political experience correlate with role fulfillment? The null hypothesis is that the categorization within each role is independent from any of the life-space variables.

The unit of analysis for this study is the individual. Wives of presidents who
served in office for more than one year were included in the sample ($n = 34$).
Excluded are First Ladies who died within the first year (Letitia Tyler) or whose
husbands died within the first year (Anna Harrison, Margaret Taylor, and Lu-
cretia Garfield) and those who were surrogate First Ladies (women who served
as hostesses but were not married to the president, for example, Martha Jefferson, Sarah Jackson, and Angelica Van Buren).

Dependent Variables

One special problem encountered in formulating and testing hypotheses was
how to identify and measure impact. A new classification scheme was developed

to measure both attitudes and behavior. The independent variables will be tested to predict/explain where the First Ladies fall within the classifications of each role. The variables used to construct a role classification scheme are based primarily on O'Connor et al. (1996), Rosebush (1987), Gutin (1989), and Kelly and Boutilier (1978). An active/passive, implicit/explicit classification scheme will be used.[3] What the classification is attempting to capture are three different points of focus—characteristics, orientations (attitudes and beliefs), and actions (Babbie 1989: 87). The active/passive dichotomy compartmentalizes actions, whereas implicit/explicit applies to beliefs and attitudes. Having four categories with such a small n (only thirty-four cases) may pose some methodological problems when we are attempting to do statistical analyses. Substantively, however, the implicit/explicit dichotomy is crucial to understanding the different attitudes and actions of First Ladies. Although some First Ladies were active in a particular role, they may have done only the minimum and did so out of a sense of duty to their husbands. Others used the opportunities presented in certain roles to the fullest extent and with their own interests in mind, not just obligation to the president. The basis for categorizing into implicit or explicit is found in the historical evidence (primary and secondary sources) that indicates what a particular First Lady's attitude was in regard to certain roles. Many of the First Ladies were candid about what they thought about the various roles, and it is on this basis (as reported in secondary sources) that the implicit/explicit distinction is made.

Hostess Role

From the earliest days of the Republic, the job of the president's wife was primarily social. The hostess function, usually assisted by family members, consists of teas, banquets, receptions, and state dinners and requires selecting menu, choosing entertainment, and supervising decorations. As trivial as some of these tasks seem with regard to impact, these social events have often been opportunities for political influence. Throughout the First Ladies literature, scholars have shown how some First Ladies used the hostess role more politically than others, such as Dolley Madison, trying to win over enemies of the president or push a certain issue in a more neutral setting. Although the role of First Lady as Hostess is neglected in presidential literature (distinct from First Ladies literature), further examination may reveal that the better the First Lady fulfills the hostess role, the less demand there is on the president to be the symbolic chief of state. First Ladies help fulfill head of state functions and, like the vice presidents, can act as surrogate, especially on ceremonial occasions or in certain types of travel (Rosebush 1987: 48–83). The hostess function and its effect on presidential performance have been overlooked by presidential scholars, even those who focus on the symbolic nature of the presidency (such as Denton 1982 and Buchanan 1978).

Congressional Quarterly (Nelson 1989) and Gutin distinguish three levels of hostess role activity. Dolley Madison is the most renowned hostess, throwing extravagant parties and using such events for political ends (to soften or win over her husband's opponents). Julia Tyler also made full use of this role. The second category of hostesses are those who accepted the role as an important duty. Eleanor Roosevelt and Hillary Clinton carried out the ceremonial/symbolic duties successfully but did not relish being hostess or manager of the White House. These First Ladies usually devoted most of their efforts to other roles that competed with entertainment efforts. The third level that this study adds to Gutin's and *CQ's* classifications consists of First Ladies who did not enjoy the role of hostess but tried to fulfill the minimum requirements. Elizabeth Monroe, Sarah Polk, and Nellie Taft seem to fit this category. The fourth category includes those who avoided the role of hostess altogether. These women were usually ill (or used illness as an excuse) and often employed relatives to fulfill the job (Abigail Fillmore and Jane Pierce are examples). Abigail Adams, however, rejected the role of hostess in pursuit of her political role.

Some of the main questions raised in order to classify were: Was the hostess role the one in which the First Lady put forth all her efforts? Did she express enjoyment in carrying out her obligations in this role? Did she use the opportunities in this role to advance some political goal (even minor issues)? Did she seem to begrudge having to play the role of symbolic head of state?

Active Explicit—embraces the role; uses it to the fullest extent; may use it to advance political goals.

Active Implicit—accepts the role but does not use it to its fullest extent; other roles may take precedence.

Passive Implicit—does not enjoy being hostess but performs a minimum number of duties out of obligation to her husband.

Passive Explicit—rejects all ceremonial duties; may have had a replacement hostess (e.g., daughter). Historical evidence may reveal that she openly rejected or even spoke out against this role for a number of reasons.

	ACTIVE			PASSIVE
EXPLICIT	Madison J. Tyler Grant Hayes	Cleveland Ellen Wilson LB Johnson Clinton		L. Adams Fillmore Pierce E. Johnson
IMPLICIT	Washington Adams Lincoln McKinley Edith Roosevelt Edith Wilson	Harding Coolidge Hoover Eleanor Roosevelt Truman Eisenhower	Kennedy Nixon Ford Reagan Bush	Monroe Polk C. Harrison Taft Carter

Public Role

Some observers have argued that "the First Lady contributes to the nation as the most nationally visible woman in politics, even though she holds no elected position . . . particularly in the latter 20th century, her role has also been to extend the visibility and legitimacy of public roles for women" (cited in Clark 1996: 510). The emergence of First Lady as public figure, mostly in the second half of the Nineteenth century, came about primarily because of two developments: growing literacy and the advancement of mass communications (Nelson 1989).

This role can be seen as a means to the ends pursued in the other roles—ceremonial, advocacy, and political goals. Some First Ladies abdicated the public role, due either to ill health, to a devastating personal tragedy, or simply to a distaste for the limelight. Louisa Adams, Jane Pierce, Abigail Fillmore, and Eliza Johnson belong to this category. Gutin describes a second category of First Ladies that had "extremely limited contact with the public and devoted little if any thought to communicating their ideas to the country" (1989: 3). They were passive in this role but not as explicitly as the first group. Martha Washington, Edith Roosevelt, Helen Taft, Bess Truman, and Mamie Eisenhower exemplify this group. The third group (Gutin's "emerging spokeswoman") did engage in more communication activities and "were more aware of a need to share their ideas and projects with national audiences" (Gutin 1989: 3). Conversely, these women may have enjoyed the spotlight somewhat but did not actively pursue it or necessarily use it to promote a cause. In other words, they were active in their public role but not as candidly as others. Abigail Adams, Ida McKinley, Lou Hoover, Jacqueline Kennedy, and Pat Nixon fit in this category. The most active in the public role (Gutin's "political surrogates and independent advocates") "used all available communication outlets to support projects or positions forcefully" (1989: 4). These outlets may have included press conferences, writing for publication during their tenure, or speeches. Some earlier First Ladies, including Dolley Madison, Julia Tyler, and Julia Grant, did not have as many outlets for public communication as exist today, but made full use of the means they did have to communicate to the public about a number of matters, both trivial and substantive, from preserving and redecorating the White House to the annexation of Texas.

Questions that help guide classification include the following: Did she make herself available to the press? to what degree? Did she allow interviews? Did she hold press conferences? Did she use the media to support projects or positions?

Active Explicit—relished publicity; utilized all available outlets; sought interviews.

Active Implicit—in the public eye to a lesser degree; more controlled exposure, though not opposed to it; may have used it to publicize a personal project.

Passive Implicit—tight control over exposure; used occasionally not by desire but out of necessity for ceremonial/symbolic duties.

Passive Explicit—despised publicity; rarely seen.

	ACTIVE		**PASSIVE**	
EXPLICIT	Madison	Cleveland	L. Adams	
	Johnson	Harding	Polk	
	J. Tyler	Eleanor Roosevelt	Pierce	
	Grant	Carter	Lincoln	
	Hayes	Clinton	E. Johnson	
IMPLICIT	Adams	Kennedy	Washington	Taft
	McKinley	Ford	Monroe	Wilson
	Ellen Wilson	Reagan	Eisenhower	Coolidge
	Hoover	Bush	Fillmore	Truman
			C. Harrison	Nixon
			Edith Roosevelt	

Advocate Role

The First Lady has a tremendous opportunity to advance a social cause. Rosebush points out two reasons for the emergence of the advocate role. First, Americans tend to join groups and promote causes for the public good. Second, since our earliest history, women have been at the forefront of social work (Rosebush 1987: 84). Advocacy work by First Ladies has not gone unnoticed by scholars. A great deal of discussion about advocacy activities is found in *Presidential Studies Quarterly*'s special First Ladies edition—for example, Lou Hoover's causes which included Girl Scouts and Women's Amateur Athletics (NAAF). Lady Bird Johnson's campaign for highway beautification became the first official, funded cause of a First Lady. Even the earliest First Ladies were somewhat public about certain causes—Abigail Adams and women's rights; Lucy Hayes and prison and asylum conditions; Nellie Taft and suffrage (Guy 1995: 247). There are different levels of involvement in advocating a cause. Some First Ladies devote a great deal of time, energy, and even presidential/congressional resources to pursue some particular ends. Other First Ladies become spokeswomen for a particular cause without many policy demands. Most causes advanced by First Ladies are politically neutral. One of the most common "causes" or projects among First Ladies is the restoration of the White House (Dolley Madison, Elizabeth Monroe, Julia Tyler, Sara Polk, Mary Lincoln, Julia Grant, Edith Roosevelt, Bess Truman, Jacqueline Kennedy, Pat Nixon, and Nancy Reagan) (Rosebush 1987: 29).

Criteria used to classify First Ladies into categories are whether or not she had a cause or project, and the extent to which she was involved in promoting the cause. In other words, was she simply a spokeswoman, or did she devote a great deal of time and resources and even political power to advance that cause?

Active Explicit—chooses a social cause, organizes and promotes it; may seek the assistance of the president or Congress.

Active Implicit—mostly philanthropic or symbolic representation of a cause.

Passive Implicit—does not focus attention on this realm.

Passive Explicit—openly rejects any advocacy work.

	ACTIVE		**PASSIVE**	
EXPLICIT	Taft	LB Johnson	Washington	E. Johnson
	Ellen Wilson	Ford	L. Adams	McKinley
	Harding	Carter	Pierce	Edith Roosevelt
	Eleanor Roosevelt	Clinton	Lincoln	Edith Wilson
IMPLICIT	Adams	C. Harrison	Monroe	Coolidge
	Madison	Hoover	Polk	Truman
	J. Tyler	Eisenhower	Fillmore	Kennedy
	Grant	Reagan	Cleveland	Nixon
	Hayes	Bush		

Political Role

The role of surrogate or informal adviser is different from the other roles because it is usually carried out more covertly and because it better serves to reveal the relationship between the First Lady and the president. The other roles are functions the First Ladies are said to have "in their own right." The political role also brings with it the harshest public criticism. Edith Wilson was attacked for running a "petticoat government"; Florence Harding was accused of running her husband's career; Eleanor Roosevelt was criticized for speaking for (i.e., putting words into the mouth of) her husband; and both Nancy Reagan and Hillary Rodham Clinton have been attacked for using their clout to get people fired (Hay 1988: intro.). Terms such as "Presidentress," "Mrs. President," and even "Billary" are strikes fired at First Ladies. Political or policy influence is not unique to Eleanor Roosevelt or Hillary Rodham Clinton. As far back as Abigail Adams and Sarah Polk, First Ladies were criticized for their political views.

Why is this the most harshly criticized activity of any First Lady? Rosebush asks,

How much power does a First Lady really have? In any political situation, the perception of power may be as important as the actual ability to effect change. A president's wife attains her position through marriage. Public trust has not been placed in her through the process of election or appointment. No accountability process, except perhaps consensus reached through public debate, covers the presidential spouse. (1987: 112)

Rosebush adds that Americans are also terribly protective of their vote and somehow feel a certain "ownership" of those they elect. This does not seem a sufficient answer, however. Although there are many unelected advisers who have a great deal of influence on the president, it is still the First Lady's influence that draws the most criticism. Hillary Clinton observed that part of the criticism is "deflected criticism of her husband and part is a feeling of unaccountable power" (Clark 1996: 512). Some attribute the harsh criticism to sexism; in society, a great deal of conflict still arises over the proper role of women, and in reflecting women in society, the First Lady reflects the tensions. Another explanation is that her private role is used as a basis for her political participation. Some say it's merely a matter of personality (Clark 1996: 512–13).

The classification scheme enables us to categorize the First Ladies based on their interest in politics, their expression of political ideas to the president (as much as we can ever truly know that), and their openness about it to the public. O'Connor et al. define the political role as (1) acting as informal policy adviser; (2) discussing politics with the husband; (3) "screening correspondence, highlighting news articles, and editing speeches;" and (4) making one's policy preferences clear (O'Connor et al. 1996: 846).

Questions that were asked to define political role activity include: Did she assist in his gaining political office? Did she try to keep up with the issues? Was she a political confidante? Was she an adviser (more than a confidante)? Did she state policy preferences privately? or publicly? Did she influence appointments/nominations/firing? Did she attend policy meetings? Did she influence public policy from the inside or by using her public influence? Did she visit heads of state for hostess role, advocate role, or political role? Burrell assists in the operationalization of political impact by elaborating on four types of influence that First Ladies have had on presidential politics: (1) "directing and promoting a spouse's career, including climbing the political ladder . . . [and] protection of health and well-being"; (2) "control over the social hierarchy of life in the capital"; (3) political adviser in the way of what is good for the president politically; and (4) public policy concerns (1997: 16–17). These four types of influence illustrate the different levels of political impact or activity that a First Lady may have and relate to the following classification scheme:

Active Explicit—political partner and adviser as primary role; works within the political realm to influence president and other government officials. Includes all four areas of influence discussed by Burrell.

Active Implicit—covertly influences and advises president to a lesser degree.

Passive Implicit—political observer; some interest but no involvement; more protectionist of health and well-being (as Burrell points out); may campaign as a symbolic figure.

Passive Explicit—avoids politics completely; may think politics inappropriate for self or for women in general.

	ACTIVE		PASSIVE	
EXPLICIT	Polk Grant Harding	Eleanor Roosevelt Carter Clinton	Monroe L. Adams Pierce Lincoln Cleveland	Edith Roosevelt Coolidge Eisenhower Kennedy Nixon
IMPLICIT	A. Adams Madison J. Tyler Fillmore E. Johnson	Taft Ellen Wilson Hoover LB Johnson	Washington Hayes C. Harrison McKinley Edith Wilson	Truman Ford Reagan Bush

INDEPENDENT VARIABLES—LIFE-SPACE INDICATORS AND HYPOTHESES

Now that the levels of role involvement have been operationalized, the next step is to formulate the independent variables that may affect these individuals within their roles. In almost every independent variable, the original data that were collected at the highest level possible, or the variables began with more classifications. However, in order to cross-tabulate with an *n* of thirty-four, the categories had to be collapsed even further to be of any use in finding relationships.

Effects of Childhood Socialization

Kelly and Boutilier's theory suggests that childhood socialization is a fundamental component in understanding the level of an individual's political activity. Three factors are relevant here: birth order, absence of either or both parents, and vocation of primary provider.

Birth order. Theorists disagree about the effect of birth order on the development of political identity and activity. Renshon argues that the lower a child is on the birth order, the more successful she will be in gaining control over her life-space (1974: 127).[4] Kelly and Boutilier assert, however, that the first born is pushed to be an achiever and is therefore more likely to become the "achieving woman" (1978: 281). Our hypothesis is that First Ladies who are the oldest child will more likely fall into the active categories in all four roles, particularly in the public and political roles. This variable was classified as follows: (0) other; (1) oldest child.

Absence of either or both parents. The absence of either parent is likely to affect the development of one's sex-role ideology. The hypothesis is that the absence of the father may have provided the individual woman with a strong role model in her mother, broadening a child's sex-role parameters. This would indicate that First Ladies who were missing a parent will likely fall into the active categories of all roles, particularly the hostess role (if she had more responsibility at home). This variable was categorized as (0) one or both parents absent; (1) both parents present.

Vocation of primary provider. This variable was included primarily to test whether or not the father's vocation, particularly if it is in the legal or political arena, significantly influences an individual level of political involvement later on. There are several categories (small business or farm owner, large business or plantation owner, or professional—minister, teacher, lawyer, politician) which were collapsed into a dichotomous variable of (1) professional and (0) nonprofessional.

Life Experiences

Employment before marriage. Employment outside of the home has been shown to have a strong correlation with political involvement. Jacquette states that women in the labor force vote more than women not employed outside the home (1974: 9). Beckwith (1986) examines all levels of political involvement (vote, electoral activism, conventional activism, involvement, and efficacy) and different types of occupation (housewife, blue-collar, clerical, and professional). She reports that at all different levels of involvement women who work outside the home are generally more active and that professional women are substantially more active than women who work inside the home. This conclusion is consistent with Kelly and Boutilier's theory of saliency and control over life-space, primarily women who have moved to the third and fourth stages. With regard to First Ladies, it can be hypothesized that if the individual worked before marriage (and sometimes during), she has moved into the third stage and has developed a sense of efficacy and the relevance of politics to her life. Therefore, we can predict that she will be more active in all four roles, standing out particularly in the advocate and political roles. The number of First Ladies who were employed before and even during marriage is not large enough to categorize into what type of employment, only if the individual was employed. The classification is as follows: (0) not employed; (1) employed.

Education level. One of the most important factors (if not *the* most important) in explaining and predicting women's political participation is education (Jacquette 1974: 8). The literature on women in politics also suggests that education cancels out any other life-space restrictions (such as the number of children). Kelly and Boutilier explain that education deepens a woman's sense of political efficacy and enables her to feel more control over her life-space. Jacquette asserts that education makes a greater difference for women than for men as to whether or not they vote (1974: 8). Applying this statement to First Ladies, the hypothesis is that the higher the education level of a First Lady, the greater her level of activity will be in each role because she will have a stronger sense of political efficacy.

Collecting the data and operationalizing education were difficult, particularly to reach an interval-level of precision. This difficulty stemmed from the lack of historical records on education (not precisely reported for the biographies), and it is also due to changes in the formality of education over the course of U.S. history. Therefore, the data were collapsed into categories whose rankings corresponded with level of education. The divisions are as follows: (1) none or very little education; (2) tutored at home; (3) grade school equivalent (may have had some tutoring at home with some formal school); (4) high school equivalent; (5) some college or post–high school studies; (6) college degree; (7) post–college training; (8) advanced degree (master's, J.D., M.D., or Ph.D.). The average (mean) years of schooling of the First Ladies is eleven years, so the categories were collapsed into the categories of (1) high school or below; (2) college or beyond. In order to control for the effects of time, an initial effort was made to compare each First Lady's level of education with the mean level of women's education in her era. However, this type of statistic was not collected until the mid-1900s or so, and therefore it is impossible to do such a comparison.

Age when first married. O'Connor et al. observe that many First Ladies married later than the norm, in an era when most women married in their teens. The average age at marriage of First Ladies is twenty-four, with Eliza Johnson and Elizabeth Monroe being the youngest (at age seventeen) (O'Connor et al. 1996: 840).[5] The hypothesis is that the younger a woman is when she gets married, the less independence she has developed and the less control she feels over her life-space. An early marrying age may also interrupt or end a woman's education or employment. Based on the average age, the categories are: (1) married before the age of twenty-four and (2) married after the age of twenty-four.

Immediate Constraints on Her Situation

Age when becoming First Lady. The average age when becoming First Lady is forty-eight. Previous studies reveal that the highest proportion of nonvoting women is found in the oldest age category (over fifty), followed by the second lowest group of twenty to twenty-nine year olds. The strongest participation comes from the thirty to thirty-nine year olds, with forty to forty-nine year olds coming in second (Jacquette 1974: 10). More recent statistics from women's voter turnout in the 1992 election shows that this trend has changed only slightly, with the percentage of participation increasing with age[6] (Jennings 1993: 11). However, the age of a First Lady is likely to correlate strongly with the number of children in the White House during her tenure (i.e., the younger she is, the younger her children will be). The number of children may affect participation more strongly than age. Based on the average, the categories are:

(1) entered White House younger than forty-eight years old and (2) entered White House equal to or older than forty-eight years old.

Number of children under the age of eighteen in White House. Only two First Ladies were childless (Sara Polk and Florence Harding), while a few others had children only from previous marriages (Martha Washington, Dolley Madison, and Edith Wilson). The number of children is not as relevant to our study as is the age of the children during tenure in the White House. Numerous scholars have observed the dampening effect that young children have on the political participation of mothers (Campbell et al. 1960; Pomper 1975). The hypothesis, therefore, is that if a First Lady has a child or children under the age of eighteen during her tenure, she will be less active in her roles. The data are coded as follows: (0) no children under eighteen in White House; (1) one or more children.

Health status while First Lady. With advancements in medicine and technology, healthy First Ladies are more the norm now than in earlier years. Many First Ladies had ailments that incapacitated them (e.g., Jane Pierce) or limited their ability to fully perform their role (e.g., Mamie Eisenhower). They were also more frequently affected by the deaths of their children than recent First Ladies, leaving them psychologically incapable of performing their roles (e.g., Mary Todd Lincoln). One difficulty in this variable is that while some First Ladies could not perform their duties because of their illness, others used illness as an excuse to shirk their duties, according to historians' records. Fortunately, the role classification scheme allows for differentiation between attitudes, not just actions. The health status of each First Lady is consistently reported in the secondary sources that were used. This variable is coded "0" = "healthy" and "1" = "sick."

Political Experience

Serving as governor's wife and/or vice president's wife. The following variables help quantify different levels of political experiences that a First Lady may have had prior to serving as First Lady. The hypothesis is that the greater her political experience before serving, the more likely she is to be active in all four roles as First Ladies. A secondary hypothesis is that serving as vice president's wife ("Second Lady") provides the experience that best prepares for serving as First Lady, including the publicity, some level of responsibility and scrutiny, and a close view of what the First Lady must endure. Serving as governor's wife also provides similar opportunities and responsibilities as that of First Lady, with the same roles but without as much publicity. The hypothesis is that both the governorship and vice presidency experiences positively influence the level of activity in all four roles but particularly the hostess role. Each variable is coded as 0 = did not serve under these positions and 1 = did serve under these positions.

METHODOLOGY

Data Collection

In order to make systematic use of the biographical statistics and make informed decisions about classifying First Ladies into their respective role categories, a questionnaire (much like the one used by Kelly and Boutilier—see Appendix) was developed to guide the research. The questionnaire helped ensure consistency among the facts and between different authors' assessment of First Ladies. The chief sources were secondary sources: Gould (1996), Gutin (1989), Anthony (1990–1991), Caroli (1987), and CQ's biographical cameos (Nelson 1989).

Because history is open to interpretation and because it is difficult to measure impact, not all scholars attribute the same impact or attitude to a particular First Lady. Furthermore, collecting even basic data such as number of children in the White House, age at marriage, or years of education was not a simple task. This chapter is one of the first attempts to produce a systematic classification scheme, and as such it is open to dispute. O'Connor et al. (1996) attempted similar data collection and admitted that their "appraisals of many First Ladies, although gleaned from many secondary sources, may not reflect their true influence" (p. 837).

Data Analysis

The issue of a small population has plagued researchers of the presidency in their attempts to do quantitative analyses—and there are even fewer First Ladies. In this study, initially several attempts were made to do correlations and non-parametric statistics appropriate to the nominal and ordinal levels of the data set. Due to the small n of 34, very few results were statistically significant. However, furtherance of the research on First Ladies may be served just as well by providing some insightful cross-tabulations and reporting cell frequencies. This technique provides a descriptive, and perhaps initially explanatory look at how First Ladies with different life-space variables differ in each role category. The cross-tabs will be presented (as percentages of totals), and some observations will be made about the more revealing outputs.

HOSTESS	Passive Explicit	Passive Implicit	Active Implicit	Active Explicit
Birth Order:				
Other	3	3	8	4
Oldest	0	2	7	3
Both Parents:				
No	3	3	6	3
Yes	1	2	11	5

HOSTESS (continued)	Passive Explicit	Passive Implicit	Active Implicit	Active Explicit
Parent Job:				
Non-Professional	2	1	1	3
Professional	2	4	16	5
Employed before marriage:				
No	3	2	9	6
Yes	1	3	8	2
Education:				
≤ High school	4	1	5	2
College +	0	3	11	6
Married:				
24 yrs old	2	4	6	5
≥ 24 yrs old	2	1	11	3
Age in WH:				
< 48 yrs	1	1	6	6
≥ 48 yrs	3	4	11	2
Children in WH:				
No	2	2	10	2
Yes	2	3	7	5
Healthy:				
No	4	3	7	1
Yes	0	2	10	7
Governor's Wife:				
No	3	1	12	4
Yes	1	4	5	4
VP's Wife:				
No	3	4	10	7
Yes	1	1	7	1
PUBLIC				
Birth Order:				
Other	5	5	4	4
Oldest	0	4	3	5
Both Parents:				
No	4	4	2	5
Yes	1	7	6	5
Parent Job:				
Non-Professional	1	2	0	4
Professional	4	9	8	6

PUBLIC (continued)	Passive Explicit	Passive Implicit	Active Implicit	Active Explicit
Employed before marriage:				
No	5	5	4	6
Yes	0	6	4	4
Education:				
≤ High school	4	4	4	3
College +	1	6	7	6
Married:				
< 24 yrs old	4	3	3	7
≥ 24 yrs old	1	8	5	3
Age in WH:				
< 48 yrs	3	4	1	6
≥ 48 yrs	2	7	7	4
Children in WH:				
No	2	5	6	3
Yes	3	6	2	6
Healthy:				
No	4	6	4	1
Yes	1	5	4	9
Governor's Wife:				
No	3	7	5	5
Yes	2	4	3	5
VP's Wife:				
No	4	6	5	9
Yes	1	5	3	1
ADVOCATE				
Birth Order:				
Other	6	3	7	2
Oldest	2	2	2	6
Both Parents:				
No	3	6	2	4
Yes	5	2	8	4
Parent Job:				
Non-Professional	1	3	1	2
Professional	7	5	9	6
Employed before marriage:				
No	5	5	6	4
Yes	3	3	4	4

ADVOCATE (continued)	Passive Explicit	Passive Implicit	Active Implicit	Active Explicit
Education:				
≤ High school	6	2	3	1
College +	2	5	7	6
Married:				
<24 yrs old	4	3	7	0
≥ 24 yrs old	4	5	3	5
Age in WH:				
< 48 yrs	4	5	4	1
≥ 48 yrs	4	3	6	7
Children in WH:				
No	4	2	8	2
Yes	4	6	1	6
Healthy:				
No	3	5	7	4
Yes	5	3	3	4
Governor's Wife:				
No	5	4	8	3
Yes	3	4	2	5
VP's Wife:				
No	6	5	8	5
Yes	2	3	2	3
POLITICAL				
Birth Order:				
Other	6	7	4	1
Oldest	2	2	3	5
Both Parents:				
No	5	4	3	3
Yes	5	5	6	3
Parent Job:				
Non-Professional	2	1	3	1
Professional	8	8	6	5
Employed before marriage:				
No	8	3	7	2
Yes	2	6	2	4
Education:				
≤ High school	3	2	5	2
College +	6	7	4	3
Married:				
< 24 yrs old	5	4	4	4
≥ 24 yrs old	5	5	5	2

POLITICAL (continued)	Passive Explicit	Passive Implicit	Active Implicit	Active Explicit
Age in WH:				
< 48 yrs	6	3	2	3
≥ 48 yrs	4	6	7	3
Children in WH:				
No	2	7	5	2
Yes	8	1	4	4
Healthy:				
No	6	4	4	1
Yes	4	5	5	5
Governor's Wife:				
No	6	6	6	2
Yes	4	4	4	4
VP's Wife:				
No	7	6	5	6
Yes	3	3	4	0

Observations

Birth order. Kelly and Boutilier maintain that women who are the oldest are pushed to be achievers and therefore are more likely to become "achieving women" (1978: 281). A higher number of active First ladies are expected to be in the "oldest child" category and fewer in the "passive" or in the "other" categories. The table output is consistent with this hypothesis in the public and particularly in the political roles, whereas it is not the case in the hostess or advocate role. The strong pattern in the political role between the oldest child and more activity is consistent with Kelly and Boutilier's assertion that childhood socialization, of which birth order is a part, affects political saliency. Further examination of the other independent variables also reveals a difference in how life-space and socialization variables affect the four First Lady roles differently.

Presence of both parents. One might expect that growing up without one or both parents would lead one to be a more independent individual. Kelly and Boutilier assert that the absence of either parent is likely to affect the development of one's sex-role ideology (1978: 212). The projection is that a larger number of active First Ladies did not have both parents. However, the table reveals that there are more active and fewer passive First Ladies who had both parents. This pattern holds strongly in the hostess and advocate roles, and to a lesser degree in the public and political roles. This is the opposite of the hypothesis or expected outcome. The outcome may be explained by the effect of class and socioeconomic-status on political participation. Those First Ladies who did not have both parents likely suffered more hardship and had fewer opportunities, or even lacked the time to be socially or politically concerned.

Parent's occupation. Parent's occupation, which may also serve as an indicator of class and socioeconomic status, affects childhood socialization, sex-role ideology, and levels of political saliency. The hypothesis is that First Ladies who grew up with a parent who was a professional are more likely to fall into the active categories. The table reinforces this hypothesis in the hostess category but not in any other category. In fact, the converse is true in the political role category. The problem of historical trends, particularly the political significance of certain occupations in one era versus another, may be the reason for the weak relationship between these two variables.

Employment before marriage. The scholarship on women in politics suggests that women who are employed outside of the home are more politically active and have a stronger sense of political saliency than women who work in the home. The expectation is that employed First Ladies will more frequently fall into the active categories. The table reveals, however, that employment before marriage makes no difference in levels of activity within any of the four roles. One explanation may be that women work outside the home for different reasons. From our twentieth-century perspective, a woman's ability to work outside the home is often viewed as a privilege and as a sign of progress in women's liberation. In the past, however, many women (particularly upper class) looked down on working outside the home and were privileged enough to not be forced to work. Poorer, lower class women, however, had to work out of necessity. The different attitudes about work within various historical periods may explain why no generalizations about work and political participation can be made across such a long span of time as is covered by the First Ladies study.

Education. The more education an individual receives, the more politically active he or she is likely to be. We expect that this will also be the case with First Ladies: a greater number of passive First Ladies will be in the lower education category, and the more highly educated First Ladies will be in the active categories. Consistent with this hypothesis, the table shows that in the hostess category, a substantially larger number of active First Ladies are in the higher education category than there are passives. In public and advocate roles, we also see the outcome we would expect. In the lower education category there are more passives than actives, and in the higher education categories there are more actives than passives. Curiously, the opposite of this is true in the political category which has the same number of actives in both the low and high education categories. This classification downplays the various levels of education and the differences among historical periods. Socialization variables also affect political saliency.

Marrying age. Theories of women's political participation suggest that women who marry younger are less politically active than women who marry later in life. This is due to various factors such as feelings of independence and the fact that marrying at an early age often interrupts a woman's career plans.

The postulate is that there will be a greater number of passive First Ladies in the under twenty-four category than there will be active or there will be in the over twenty-four category. The table shows no differences in the hostess, public, or political roles. However, the First Ladies who married younger are more active in the advocacy role than those who married later in life. One explanation for lack of relationship is that First Ladies, on the whole, married later in life than the norm (age twenty-four) in eras when most women married in their teens (O'Connor et al. 1996: 840). Because they married later than average (on the whole), any effect that their marrying ages may have on their participation is canceled out. Use of interval-level data in future analyses may further confirm the hypothesis.

Children. For many women, children are a strong inhibitor of political participation (Campbell, et al. 1960; Pomper 1975). This may also be the pattern in First Ladies, and it may be projected that those with children are less active than those without children in the White House. The table reveals that the presence of children does not make a difference in the hostess role or political role and only a slight difference in the public role. The hypothesis holds true within the advocate role, however. It may be argued that advocacy work and causes can be more time consuming than the other roles, requiring a great deal of traveling, speaking, and the like, and that this is why the presence of children inhibits activity of this role more so than in any other. Some First Ladies, such as Jacqueline Kennedy, explicitly stated that their children were their "cause." The age of the children, which is not captured in the data, may also make a difference.

Health. Health is a very important life-space variable that enables a woman to be political and socially active. The expected pattern is that First Ladies who suffered from illness were likely to be more passive than those who were healthy. This is clearly the case in the hostess and public roles where fewer sick First Ladies were active and a larger number of active First Ladies were healthy. Not surprisingly, health affected pre–twentieth-century First Ladies more. In the political and advocate roles, however, a greater number of unhealthy First Ladies were active than healthy ones were. Perhaps this is because the hostess and public roles require more physical exertion than the political (which can be private) and advocate roles. That health status does not seem to be related to the two more political of the four roles suggests that women who are politically active and who are determined to participate will not let life-space obstacles stand in their way. To recapitulate the literature review, Kelly and Boutilier suggest this in their work and assert that the stronger influences of childhood socialization determine the level of the "achieving woman" more so than immediate life-space variables. They argue that obstacles will affect women who feel less saliency to begin with (because of socialization). The cross-tabulation outcomes suggest the same.

Prior experience. We expect that the experiences of serving as governor's wife and or vice president's wife will lead to greater activity within the First

Lady's roles. First Ladies who had this experience are expected to fall in the active categories. The outcome of the table reveals that prior experience has little relationship to level of activity. Even in the case of the hostess role and experience in the governorship, there is a negative relationship. (The First Ladies who had no experience were more active than those who had the experience.) The lack of relationship in the tables may illustrate the need for more exact measurement of prior political experience. One such measurement may be the number of years that her spouse was active in politics or may also need to include other political positions that a spouse may have held (diplomat, secretary of state, representative, etc.).

CONCLUSIONS

> I don't think there should be a pattern. I really think that each individual ought to be free to do what she thinks is best for herself and her husband and her country. I have a lot of respect for all the women who have been in this position and I think every one of them made a significant contribution. But they may have done it in a different way. . . . Everybody should be permitted to be who they are.[7]
>
> Hillary Clinton (Jamieson 1995: 44–45)

Although our cross-tabulations could lead to several interesting observations with some being consistent with our previous understanding of women's political participation and Kelly and Boutilier's exposition of these theories, the results are mixed. Many of the cross-tabulations reinforce existing theories and the proposed hypotheses, but it is evident that much more work needs to be done in these areas. Obviously, the problem of a small n will be resolved only with the passage of time and the positioning of more presidential spouses. The problems of measurement, however, demand more rigorous work in the examination of archives and the collection of empirical evidence of impact and influence. A need also exists to further study the socialization of each of these individuals and how they were raised. There may be a strong influence of childhood socialization that has not been explored empirically or quantitatively (can it even be measured?) that make up the foundations of a First Lady's sex-role identity and political ideology.

In addition, certain external factors dictate the level to which a First Lady can be truly active. Social norms of sex roles and, more specifically, the public's concerns with the power of the nonelected position have been explored by many scholars (Burell 1997; Campbell 1996; Caroli 1993; Guy 1995) but have yet to be measured in terms of impact on the First Lady and her subsequential influence on politics and policy.

This study concludes with enough significant results to offer hope for future analyses and yet also leaves enough questions unanswered to warrant continued exploration in this frontier. Both expansion of the data set and further analyses of the complex relationship among the independent variables will be the next step in exploration.

FUTURE QUESTIONS

Future researchers may take three main paths to explore the unscouted territories and frontiers of First Ladies research. The first path is to continue examining First Ladies as a subject all their own, as most of the literature already does. However, many gaps remain in our understanding of their relationship with their husbands, their political ideologies, and their socialization as children, each of which directly affects their level of political activity and role fulfillment. As more and more archival data are made available for public and scholarly consumption, the gaps in our understanding will continue to be filled. Continued reevaluation of the levels of activities within each role must be carried on. As more information is gathered from archival material, we will likely continue to redefine the types of influence First Ladies have had. Future statistical analyses may also examine more background/socialization variables. The hope is that new information will not only be unearthed but will also be presented in a systematic way that strives for more than description but includes explanation. Another goal is to continue the development of the data set begun in this chapter in order to perform more complete and accurate quantitative analyses.

A second path is to continue to study First Ladies within the frameworks and theories presented by scholars of women in politics. A continuation or modification of Kelly and Boutilier's work would broaden our scope of understanding contemporary First Ladies. Much of the results obtained in this chapter support their theories and other theories proposed by scholars studying women's political participation. The unique nature of the First Lady's role (obtained by marriage, not election or appointment) complicates but also enriches our understanding of women's place in the political world. The *CQ Researcher* provides a rich dialogue about the pros and cons of an active First Lady and questions what her role should be. Feminist theorists have also uncovered the inherent contradictions in the role (Burrell 1997; Campbell 1996; Guy 1995; O'Connor et al. 1996; Scobie 1995). Some feminist scholars embrace the role of First Lady as the opportunity for a woman to play a very public, political, and powerful role in social and political changes. Others argue that presidential spouses should strive to become independent actors, pursuing their own careers (Burrell 1997). Some conjecture that if the president's spouse were a man, there would be completely different standards for his behavior. Some feminists are even harsher critics and contend that "the duties expected of politicians' wives are demeaning and dishonorable. . . . It can no longer be acceptable that a person should achieve high visibility, influence, and even a degree of executive power simply because she shares a bed . . . with a head of state" (Clark 1996: 521). Studies that expand the role of political spouse would be an important step.

The third path, and the goal of this book as a whole, is to explore the frontier of First Ladies as it links to the presidency. One example is to more fully develop the parallels between vice presidents and First Ladies—staff size, campaign influence, popularity, own agenda, representative of self versus the president, internal influences, public concern with too much power, differences between presidents' uses of First Ladies and vice presidents, and so on. These two areas are ripe for systematic comparison and contrast. Most studies of the First Lady address how each individual used her position to achieve certain goals. What we lack are studies starting from the position of the president and examining how the president uses his wife, for example, Mrs. Clinton and health care. What goals does a president seek to achieve through his wife? What mistakes has he made in using or failing to utilize his spouse? What does he think of her role?

Another interesting, yet unexplored, policy territory involves the legal parameters of the First Lady's role. Legal issues are mentioned in a few articles, particularly citation of the limitations issuing from the so-called Bobby Kennedy law or the Executive Accountability Act (Public Law 95–570). Passed by Congress in 1978, this law forbids presidents to appoint family members to government positions. This portion of the law states that "a public official may not appoint, employ, promote, [or] advance a relative in an agency in which he is serving or over which he exercises jurisdiction or control." This provision prevents First Ladies from receiving a salary, although the law does permit allocation of funds to the First Lady in her functions of assisting the president (O'Connor et al. 1996: 839). With regard to this legal dilemma, Burrell suggests that the First Lady should become an official, though unpaid, White House staff member and as such would be subject to the same accountability standards as other staff members (Burrell 1997: 141). Further legal and ethical arguments may be formulated to support the repeal of this law, so that the First Lady is subject to rules of ethics both while she is in office and once she is out of office (lobbying, etc.).

As women gain more equality in all facets of public life and the political realm, including advances in education, health, child care, and the workforce, we may expect our First Ladies to become increasingly active in all areas of her office. Unfortunately, the scholarship on First Ladies has not grown as quickly as have the responsibilities of the role. This frontier needs to be explored further.

APPENDIX: QUESTIONNAIRE

1. Date of birth _____
2. Date in office _____
3. Years in office _____
4. Up to age 18 were both parents living? _____ Which parent was absent, F or M? Why? _____ What age when parent left/died? _____

5. How many siblings? ___ Was she youngest, oldest, or middle? ___
6. Vocation of mother ___
7. Vocation of father ___
8. Was mother politically active or informed about politics? ___ Was father? ___
9. Highest level of education achieved by subject:
   a. no education
   b. no formal education but was privately tutored
   c. grade school or equivalent
   d. high school or equivalent
   e. additional training of a skill type (non-professional), e.g., clerk, typist, secretary
   f. college training but not professional training
   g. professional training and advanced degree (law, M.D., Ph.D.)
10. Main subject of study
    a. business, economics, law, political economy, or politics
    b. education, teaching, or nursing
    c. general liberal arts
    d. mainly finished school, social-type graces
    e. N/A = no schooling
11. What age did she marry? ___
12. Did she have a career before marriage? ___
13. Did she engage in political activity before marriage? ___
14. Religious affiliation ___ Active or inactive?
15. Number of children ___
16. Age entering office of First Lady ___
17. Number of children (under 18) while in WH ___
18. Healthy?   Yes   No   Yes, but not debilitating
19. Served with husband while diplomat/ambassador overseas? ___
20. Served as governor's wife? ___
21. Served as VP's wife? ___
22. Number of staff ___
23. Number of the president's White House staff ___
24. Ratio of #24 to #25 ___

Hostess
25. Did she embrace this role? To what ends? Or did she delegate the job to someone else?

Media/Public
26. Did she have press conferences? For herself? For her husband?
27. Did she have a press secretary? Did she have a speech writer?
28. Did she publish during her tenure as First Lady?

Political
29. Relationship with her husband ___
30. Did she assist in his gaining office? Pushing his career? Campaigning?
31. Did she discuss politics? Publicly or privately?
32. Was she a confidant/advisor?
33. Did she state policy preferences privately?
34. Did she state policy preferences publicly?

35. Did she influence appointments/nominations?
36. Did she attend policy meetings?
37. Did she influence public policy?
38. Did she visit heads of state? (hostess role or for political role or for advocate role)

Advocate
39. Did she have an identifiable issue?
40. Did she lobby the president?
41. Did she lobby congress?

Other Interesting Activities

NOTES

1. An effort was made to obtain the data collected by O'Connor et al. (1996) in an effort to corroborate the data collected for this chapter. One author stated that the data were not put into a comprehensive data set but rather were collected on individual worksheets for each First Lady. The authors were not able to pass along what they had compiled.

2. Other scholars have statistically examined the variables that affect the type and level of political participation of women in general. Reece et al. (1983) use statistical analyses to build a predictive model of female political participation in campaign activities using variables such as mother's occupation, age, education, age of youngest child, and employment. Vicky Randall (1982) provides a summary of the hypotheses that have been tested by scholars over the years. The key variables that correlate with levels of activity are age (Jacquette 1974), education (Tedin et al. 1977), number of children (Campbell et al. 1960; Lipset 1963; Pomper 1975), and employment outside the home (Andersen 1975; Beckwith 1986).

3. The terminology that will be used (active/passive, explicit/implicit) is not based on, or related to, James Barber's active/passive, positive/negative classification (Barber 1992). I am seeking a different type of analysis that is rooted in the existing literature on First Ladies' role activity and am basing the classification on actions, not psychoanalysis.

4. Psychology has given us a plethora of literature on birth order which discusses the effect of birth order on developing leaders and so on.

5. The ages reported and used for analysis are the ages at which these women were first married (not necessarily to the president).

6. Ages 25 to 34 = 55.7%; ages 35 to 44 = 65.7%; ages 45 to 54 = 69.2%; ages 55 to 64 = 71.4%; ages 65 to 74 = 71.8%; and 75–84 = 64.3%.

7. When Larry King asked Hillary Clinton if she had changed the pattern for First Ladies, this was her response.

REFERENCES

Andersen, Karen 1975. "Working Women and Political Participation, 1952–1972." *American Journal of Political Science* 19(3): 439–54.

Anderson, Alice and Hadley Baxendale. 1992. *Behind Every Successful President.* New York: Shapol Sky Publishers.

Anthony, Carl Sferrazza. 1990–1991. *First Ladies: The Saga of the Presidents' Wives and Their Power*. 2 vols. New York: Morrow.

Babbie, Earl. 1989. *The Practice of Social Science Research*, 5th ed. San Diego, CA: Wadsworth Publishing.

Barber, James D. 1992. *The Presidential Character: Predicting Performance in the White House*, 4th ed. Englewood Cliffs, NJ: Prentice-Hall.

Beckwith, 1986. *American Women and Political Participation: The Impacts of Work, Generation, and Feminism*. Westport, CT: Greenwood Press.

Brooks, Gertrude Zeth. 1969. *First Ladies of the White House*. Chicago: Chas, Hallberg, & Co.

Buchanan, Bruce. 1978. *The Presidential Experience*. Englewood Cliffs, NJ: Prentice-Hall.

Burrell, Barbara. 1997. *Public Opinion, the First Ladyship, and Hillary Rodham Clinton*. New York: Garland Publishing.

Campbell, A., P. Converse, D. Miller and D. Stokes. 1960. *The American Voter*. New York: John Wiley.

Campbell, Karlyn Kohrs. 1996. "The Rhetorical Presidency; A Two-Person Career." In *Beyond the Rhetorical Presidency*, ed. Martin J. Medhurst. College Station: Texas A&M University Press.

Caroli, Betty Boyd. 1993. *First Ladies*. New York: Oxford University Press.

———. 1994. "First Ladies." *Encyclopedia of the American Presidency*. Vol. 2. New York: Simon & Schuster.

Clark, Charles. 1996. "First Ladies." *The CQ Researcher* 6(22) (June 14): 505–28.

Denton, Robert E. 1982. *The Symbolic Dimensions of the American Presidency: Description and Analysis*. Prospect Heights, IL: Waveland Press.

Duffy, Michael. 1994. "Open and Unflappable." *Time* 143 (May 2), p. 65.

Gould, Lewis E., ed. 1990. "Modern First Ladies and the Presidency." *Presidential Studies Quarterly* 20(4) (Fall): 677–83.

———. 1996. *American First Ladies: Their Lives and Legacy*. New York: Garland Publishing.

Gutin, Myra G. 1989. *The President's Partner: The First Lady in the Twentieth Century*. Westport, CT: Greenwood Press.

Guy, Mary Ellen. 1995. "Hillary, Health Care, and Gender Power." In *Gender Power, Leadership, and Governance*, ed. Georgia Duerst-Lahti and Rita May Kelly. Ann Arbor: University of Michigan Press, pp. 239ff.

Hay, Peter. 1988. *All the Presidents' Ladies*. New York: Penguine Books.

Jacquette, Jane, ed. 1974. *Women in Politics*. New York: John Wiley & Sons.

Jamieson, Kathleen Hall. 1995. *Beyond the Double Bind*. New York: Oxford University Press.

Jennings, Jerry T. 1993. "Voting and Registration in the Election of November, 1992." Washington, DC: Bureau of Census Population Characteristics.

Kelly, Rita Mae, and Mary Boutilier. 1978. *The Making of Political Women*. Chicago: Nelson-Hall.

Light, Paul. 1984. *Vice-Presidential Power*. Baltimore, MD: Johns Hopkins University Press.

Lipset, Seymore. 1963. *Political Man*. New York: Anchor Books.

Logan, Logna. 1962. *Ladies of the White House*. New York: Vantage Press.

Nelson, Michael, ed. 1989. *Congressional Quarterly's Guide to the Presidency.* Washington, DC: Congressional Quarterly.

O'Connor, Karen, Bernadette Nye and Laura Van Assendelft. 1996. "Wives in the White House: The Political Influence of First Ladies." *Presidential Studies Quarterly* 26(3) (Summer): 835–53.

Patterson, Bradley. 1988. *The Ring of Power.* New York: Basic Books.

Pomper, Gerald. 1975. *Voter's Choice.* New York: Dodd, Mead.

Ragsdale, Lyn. 1996. *Vital Statistics on the Presidency: Washington to Clinton.* Washington, DC: Congressional Quarterly.

Randall, Vicky. 1982. *Women and Politics.* New York: St. Martin's Press.

Renshon, Stanley Allen. 1974. *Psychological Needs and Political Behavior: A Theory of Personality and Political Efficacy.* New York: Free Press.

Rosebush, James. 1987. *First Lady, Public Wife.* Lantham, MD: Madison Books.

Smith, Nancy Kegan and Mary Ryan, eds. 1989. *Modern First Ladies: Their Documentary Legacy.* Washington, DC: National Archives and Records Administration.

Smith, Richard Norton. 1990. *Mrs. President: Biographical Sketches from Martha to Barbara.* West Branch, IA: Herbert Hoover Presidential Library.

Tedin, Kent, David Brady and Arnold Vedlitz. 1977. "Sex Differences in Political Attitudes and Behavior: The Case for Situational Factors." *Journal of Politics* 39(2): 448–56.

Afterword

One of the most interesting aspects of the American presidency is the way time continues to bring up new questions, new problems, and new issues, or revives old ones that we thought had been settled or had become dormant. While much remains the same in our politics, things do change, and anyone who has studied the nation's highest office—whether as a scholar or as a citizen-observer—knows that it does matter who is president and how that person approaches the job. Just as we can continually make recourse to the founding of our Republic for insights into the workings of our political system, so we can read today's paper to see what new developments might color our judgments. In some periods, presidents such as Franklin Roosevelt, Lyndon Johnson, and Ronald Reagan have dominated the politics of their times; in other times, chief executives such as Herbert Hoover, Jimmy Carter and even Bill Clinton have appeared to be overwhelmed by circumstances. On occasion, the office seems so powerful that the White House is the center of the world; at other times, scholars ask themselves and each other what is wrong with an institution in trouble.

Scholarship, like politics, is not static. Presidential scholars have often been affected by the events of their times, moving them to undertake research in areas they had previously overlooked or ignored. This volume is an attempt to prod us once again: to look at new issues or to look afresh at old issues. Its chapters show that some things that we have long studied—such as presidential power—are still relevant, while new questions and topics also warrant attention.

THE LONG-STANDING ISSUE OF PRESIDENTIAL POWER

Power has been a perennial issue in presidential studies. Even before Richard Neustadt published *Presidential Power*, students of the office were concerned about the formal and informal capabilities of chief executives for influencing national policy. In the years after Neustadt's book appeared, a slew of book-length and article-length studies focused on the "power of the modern presidency," the "power to persuade," the "power to command," "presidential power in the modern context," and other themes and concepts along the same lines. Unfortunately, evaluations of presidential power have often ebbed and flowed with the actions of the current occupant of the White House.

When I began Professor Bruce Buchanan's graduate seminar on the presidency at the University of Texas in 1980, the United States was in the final months of the period of the "imperiled presidency." The nation had seen a succession of chief executives who had not completed two full terms: Kennedy, Johnson, Nixon, Ford, and Carter. The conventional wisdom of the time held that the office was in a permanent downward spiral and that it would not recover. Unless Congress could muster the internal self-discipline necessary to allow it to provide national leadership (which most of the same scholars regarded as about as likely as inventing a perpetual motion machine), these same observers confidently and sorrowfully predicted a long period of national stagnation. Yet only a few months later, Ronald Reagan achieved a stunning success in winning passage of his first budget—thus reordering national priorities—and achieving other victories as well. By the middle of Reagan's first term, the conventional wisdom had changed. The presidency was still an office that could provide national leadership; now the focus shifted to the question of whether Mr. Reagan's vision for America was the right one. By the time Reagan was reelected in 1984, with an overwhelming majority, scholars were trying to explain the techniques that the president and his "handlers" were using to make it all look so easy.

In the time of Bill Clinton, scholars have continued to focus on presidential power, although Congress is treated somewhat differently than it had been before. In his recent scholarship, Charles Jones has called on American political scientists to cast off the "responsible party model" of government that has dominated our interpretations of politics both implicitly and explicitly for longer than the average assistant professor has been alive. Today, scholars are increasingly adopting what Charles Jones (1994) calls a "separationist" perspective on political power: trying to understand how presidential power really works in the context of the American system, not just holding the United States up to an unrealistic standard of responsible party government or some idealized vision of parliamentary government.

The chapters in this book all speak to the issue of power in one way or another. But as our contributors have shown, we ought to be looking down new paths to explore the nature and exercise of presidential power. The individual chapters suggest future directions for research relevant to their subjects. Overall, the cumulative lesson of this volume is that much uncharted territory remains to be covered as we try to improve our understanding of presidential power.

RECONSIDERING THE NATURE OF THE PRESIDENCY

Just as Charles Jones has challenged scholars who adhere to the responsible party model to reconsider their assumptions about American politics, so the chapters in Part I of this volume challenge us to rethink our ideas of the presidency. Yenor, Cook, and Tatalovich have shown how normative assumptions have long influenced presidential scholarship. They suggest a new line of research in which students of the presidency begin to make explicit—and subject to scrutiny—assumptions about policy, the operations of the political system, and even the ends of political power. Gary Gregg and Dan Franklin have each cast light on aspects of the fundamental nature of the presidency that have long remained shrouded from view. Their works suggest that we may not understand the institution as well as we thought we did, and they raise questions about whether other aspects of the office ought to be examined as well. Jody Baumgartner's work on the changing nature of electoral politics in both the American and foreign presidential systems suggests that we ought to move beyond the usual presidential-versus-parliamentary comparisons that often pass for comparative executive scholarship.

The presidency is our most important political office. Even if it is not the center of the world and we do not expect the president to be all things to everyone, we still need to understand the office itself. If we fail to do so, as scholars we will have little to contribute to our fellow citizens when they ask us to explain what is going on in Washington.

POLITICS AND CULTURE

Even a casual observer of the American political scene knows that our culture has undergone significant changes since the end of World War II. Our politics has certainly changed as well, and the chapters in Part III have examined the political-cultural nexus in interesting ways.

Mary Stuckey and Richard Morris have engaged in an analysis designed to prod us even further, introducing a different perspective from which to examine our politics. Their work suggests that we may gain additional insights into our political culture if we introduce alternative perspectives. We can immediately see that, in addition to the kind of perspective they employ, the work of Stuckey and Morris also raises questions about whether we might not look back in our own history (i.e., the history of Western civilization) to find other cultural perspectives that might help us find new modes of political leadership. For example, research into classical civilizations, medieval civilization, and so on might prove useful. One might profitably look at how religious leaders have exercised leadership and, extracting the special authority these leaders have been given by their divine connections, examine the ways in which they have built up communities of faithful followers and directed them.

The work of Kevan Yenerall on the "Cultural Pulpit" not only provides fascinating insights into the politics of the Clinton era, but also increases our understanding of the blurring of lines between the public and private spheres in an era of instantaneous mass communication. Yenerall's research suggests that the president may be seen as much as a cultural figure as a political one. This insight reinforces the suggestion that we look at nonpolitical leaders to help us learn more about political leadership. Pamela Van Zwaluwenburg's work on the First Ladies is relevant here, in that the president's spouse is less a political figure than a cultural one.

WHERE DO WE GO FROM HERE?

The chapters in this volume have probably raised more questions for readers than they have answered. But there is nothing wrong with asking good questions. After all, that is the essence of the Socratic method (of course, it had its drawbacks for Socrates). The contributors to this book have done what good scholars ought to do: they have identified important issues or topics that have received insufficient attention, demonstrated the relevance of their topics, and proceeded to tell us something we ought to know about these underexplored issues.

Certainly, there are more issues to be explored. As I said at the outset, I welcome any other contributions to the literature that others may care to make by pointing to new areas for scholarly concern. A single volume such as this one cannot be exhaustive, and I invite others to explore other frontiers. There is plenty of work to go around.

REFERENCE

Jones, Charles. 1994. *The Presidency in a Separated System*. Washington, DC: Brookings Institution.

Index

Adams, Abigail, 203, 204, 205, 206, 208
Ad Council, the, 156
Adirand v. Pena (1995), 172
Agostini v. Felton (1997), 166
American Commonwealth, The. See
    Bryce, James

Bas v. Tingy (1800), 122
Bennett, William, 155, 174
Bessette, Joseph, 151
Biddle v. Perovich (1927), 86
"Bobby Kennedy Law," 221
Bork, Robert, 155, 174
Bryce, James, xi, 26
Buchanan, Bruce, 228
Buchanan, Pat, 155, 174
Bully pulpit, 152
Burdick v. United States (1915), 86
Bush, George, 59, 79, 90, 93, 101, 104,
    108–9, 113, 125, 128
Butler, Pierce, 121

Cabinet, president's. *See* Presidency,
    American
Camp David Accords (1978), 119
Carter, Jimmy, 88, 90, 99, 100, 101, 106,
    113, 119, 126
Carter Doctrine, 125

Ceaser, James, 151
Cherry, Rev. John and Diana, 167
Children's television, 156–60
Children's Television Act, 157
Church Arson Prevention Act, 169
City of Boerne v. Flores (1997), 166
Clinton, Bill, 32–33, 40, 44, 45, 48, 79,
    87, 90, 92, 93, 94, 95, 100, 101, 102,
    103, 105–6, 109, 110, 228; children's
    television, 156–60; church burnings
    and hate crimes, 169–72; contemporary
    values environment, 155; "drive-
    through deliveries," 162; Internet, 160;
    President's Advisory Board on Race,
    172; protecting and promoting religion,
    163–69; racial harmony, 169–73; rais-
    ing and protecting children, 156–63;
    school uniforms and curfews, 160–61;
    State of the Union addresses: 1994,
    161; 1995, 156, 168; 1996, 156–57,
    160; 1997, 168; teen pregnancy initia-
    tives, 161; television ratings, 156–57;
    tobacco advertising guidelines, 161–62;
    use of the cultural pulpit, 153–55; V-
    chip, 159–60
Clinton, Hillary, 195, 198, 203, 205, 206,
    207, 208, 219

Commercial Trust v. Miller (1923), 124
Communications Decency Act (CDA),
    160
Conflict avoidance, 126–27
Congress, United States, 9, 12, 13, 16,
    17, 49, 102, 103–5, 106, 121–24, 125,
    126, 127, 128, 129, 130, 131, 132, 135–
    45, 228
Constitution, United States, 3–11, 14, 15,
    16, 17, 24, 25, 26, 48, 82–84, 120–22
Corwin, Edward S., 26, 127–28

Dayton Peace Accords, 129
Declarations, presidential. *See* Presidency,
    American
Defense of Marriage Act, 169
Doctrines, foreign policy, 125
Dole, Bob, 79, 155, 174

Edwards, George C., III, 174
Eisenhower, Dwight D., 14, 119, 125,
    127, 129
Elders, Joycelyn, 161
Elementary and Secondary Education
    Act, 174
Emanuel, Rahm, 156
Employment Division v. Smith, 163
Executive Office of the President (EOP),
    38, 49–50

Federal Communications Commission
    (FCC), 157
Federal Emergency Management Agency
    (FEMA), 169
Federalist, The (Federalist Papers), 4–8,
    83
Fillmore, Millard, 85, 130
First Ladies, 45; Advocate role, 205–6;
    effect on president, 195, 196–99; clas-
    sification scheme, 201–2; communica-
    tions activity, 199; Hostess role, 202–
    3, 212–13, 222; levels of role partici-
    pation, 201–2; literature on, 197; Polit-
    ical role, 206–8, 215–16, 222–23;
    Public role, 204–5, 213–14, 222; roles,
    198–99

Food and Drug Administration (FDA),
    161–62
Ford, Gerald, 79, 83
Foster, Henry, 161

Garland, Ex parte (1867), 85
Going public, 102–3
Graham, Billy, 168
Greenspan, Alan, 139, 141, 145
Grossman, Ex parte (1924), 80

Hamilton, Alexander, 4–5, 7, 83, 121–22,
    123; writing as "Pacificus," 121–22
Harding, Warren, 125
Harkin, Tom, 145
"Helvidius." *See* Madison, James
Hepburn Act, 152

Ideological distance, 140
Ideology, 138–39
Iroquois League, 185–86

Jackson, Andrew, 25
Jefferson, Thomas, 121, 123
John Paul II, Pope, 167
Johnson, Lyndon, 15, 45, 90, 101, 102,
    103, 105, 106, 107
Jones, Charles, 17, 228

Kennedy, John F., 41, 103, 125, 127
Kernell, Samuel, 152
Kissinger, Henry, 42, 44, 120

LaWare, John, 145
Lerner, Michael, 155
Lieberman, Joseph, 155
Life-space variables, 201, 208–19; child-
    hood socialization, 208–10, 216–19;
    immediate constraints, 210–11; life ex-
    periences, 209–19; political experience,
    211, 215–16
Little v. Barreme (1804), 122
Louis XIV (King of France), 38–39, 41,
    42, 43, 46, 48, 49

Madison, Dolley, 202, 203, 204, 205,
    206, 208, 211

Madison, James, 4, 5–8, 14, 121–22;
  writing as "Helvidius," 122
Marshall, John, 122–23, 124
McDougal, Susan, 79, 84
McKinley, William, 182, 187
Meyer, Laurence, 139, 141
Monroe, James, 125
Monroe Doctrine, 125

Neustadt, Richard, xi, 12–14, 39, 137,
  151, 183, 227–28
Neutrality Act of 1794, 121
Neutrality Proclamation of 1793, 121,
  126–27
Nixon, Richard, 15, 23, 40, 41, 42, 44,
  48, 79, 80, 83, 87, 102, 103–4, 107–8,
  112, 119, 128, 228
Nixon Doctrine, 125

Office of the Pardon Attorney, 80, 88–90,
  93–94, 95

"Pacificus." *See* Hamilton, Alexander
Parallel unilateral policy declarations
  (PUPDs), 126
Pardon power: amnesties, 92; constitutional provision, 82–84; King's pardon,
  80–82; pardons per year, 89–90; reasons for granting, 89–90; types of pardons, 87–88
partisanship, 138
Penn, Mark, 173
Political spectacles, 154
Presidency, American: Cabinet, 13, 107;
  Congress and, 103–5; constitutional
  provisions, 3–6, 7, 8, 30, 82–84; declarations, 125; democracy and, 23–24;
  interpretations, 3–17, 26–29; leadership
  and, 14, 23; Middle East conflict and,
  128; political partisanship and, 101,
  103, 140–41, 143; public opinion and,
  12, 31–32, 137–38, 102–3, 141; symbolic politics and, 29–30; veto power,
  7, 104–5; women and, 45, 195–197
Presidential Power. See Neustadt, Richard
Proxmire, William, 145
Pulp Fiction, 174

Reagan, Ronald, 41, 44, 47, 48, 100, 102,
  104, 105–6, 107, 108, 109, 111, 125,
  126, 130, 137, 154, 161, 168, 228
Reagan Doctrine, 125
Religious Freedom Restoration Restora-
  tion Act (RFRA), 163–66
Reno, Janet, 160
Reno v. ACLU, 160
Rhetorical presidency, 151–52
Rivlin, Alice, 139
Roosevelt, Eleanor, 203, 205, 206
Roosevelt, Franklin D., 12, 13, 16, 90,
  109–10, 129
Roosevelt, Theodore, 12, 25, 119, 128,
  151
Rossiter, Clinton, xi, 11, 13, 30

Saint-Simon, duc de (Louis de Rouvroy),
  39–40, 41–43, 46
Schuller, Robert, 168
Small Business Association (SBA), 166
Soren, Tabitha, 161
Spanish-American War, 127, 128
Story, Joseph, 123
Supreme Court, United States, 26, 34, 84–
  87

Taft, William Howard, xi, 30, 80, 86
Thurow, Glen, 151
Trainspotting, 174
Truman, Harry S, 42, 45, 47, 110, 125,
  129
Truman Doctrine, 125
Tucker, C. DeLores, 155
Tulis, Jeffrey, 151–52

*U.S. v. Curtiss-Wright Export Corpora-
  tion* (1936), 26
U.S. v. Wilson (1833), 84–85

Valenti, Jack, 160
V-chip, 159–60
Veto, presidential. *See* Presidency, Amer-
  ican
Volcker, Paul, 139

War termination, 127–28
Washington, George, 25, 121, 125, 126–
  27

Wattenberg, Ben, 155, 174
Wells, Ex parte (1855), 85
Wilson, Woodrow, xi, 3, 8–11, 25–26,
   86, 151, 152

Women in politics, 199–201. *See also*
   Presidency, American

Yellen, Janet, 139

About the Contributors

RYAN J. BARILLEAUX is professor and assistant department chairman in political science at Miami University, Oxford, Ohio. He is the author or editor of five other books and a variety of articles on politics, the American presidency, and Catholic social thought. He currently serves on the Executive Board of the Presidency Research Group and as book review editor for *Catholic Social Science Review*. In 1997 he was named Outstanding Teacher at Miami University.

JODY BAUMGARTNER is a doctoral student in political science at Miami University, Oxford, Ohio. His current research focuses on comparative presidential politics.

TRAVIS S. COOK is a doctoral student in political science at Loyola University of Chicago.

BYRON W. DAYNES is a professor of political science at Brigham Young University. He has published widely on the American presidency, public policy, and the Supreme Court. His most recent book is *Social Regulatory Policy*. His current research focuses on the presidency and the social agenda.

DANIEL P. FRANKLIN is an associate professor of political science at Georgia State University. A former American Political Science Association congressional fellow, he is the author of *Extraordinary Measures: The Exercise of Prerogative Power in the United States* and *Making Ends Meet: Congressional Budgeting in the Age of Deficits*, as well as several articles on the presidency, Congress, and budgetary politics.

GARY L. GREGG II is director of academic development at the Intercollegiate Studies Institute. He also holds the position of assistant professor of political science at Clarion University, Pennsylvania, from which he is currently on leave. He is the author of *The Presidential Republic* and other studies of politics. He was a Salvatori Fellow at the Intercollegiate Studies Institute.

SCOTT HUFFMON is a doctoral student in political science at the University of Mississippi.

CHRISTOPHER KELLEY is a doctoral student in political science at Miami University, Oxford, Ohio. His research interests include the American presidency and constitutional politics.

RUSSELL LIGHTFOOT is a doctoral student in political science at Miami University, Oxford, Ohio. His current research focuses on the politics of presidential influence in the Federal Reserve.

MARK MORRIS is a doctoral student in political science at Miami University, Oxford, Ohio. His current research interests include presidential politics and public management, as well as the influence of the Internet on political action.

RICHARD MORRIS is an assistant professor of communication at Northern Illinois University. His research has appeared in *Quarterly Journal of Speech* and other professional journals.

MARY E. STUCKEY is an associate professor of political science at the University of Mississippi. She is the author of several books, including *The President as Interpreter-in-Chief*. She serves on the Executive Board of the Presidency Research Group and was section chair for presidency research for the 1996 conference of the American Political Science Association.

GLEN SUSSMAN is an assistant professor of political science at Old Dominion University. His scholarship has appeared in such journals as *Western Political Quarterly, Congress and the Presidency, American Review of Politics, Political Communication,* and *Mass Communication Quarterly*.

RAYMOND TATALOVICH is a professor of political science at Loyola University of Chicago. A widely published scholar, he is the author of several books on American politics and policy, including *The Modern Presidency and Economic Policy* (with John Frendreis). He also serves on the Executive Board of the Presidency Research Group.

PAMELA J. VAN ZWALUWENBURG is a doctoral candidate in political science at Miami University, Oxford, Ohio. She is writing a dissertation on constitutional politics in the United States.

KEVAN M. YENERALL is a doctoral student in political science at Miami University. His current research interests include presidential rhetoric and American political culture.

SCOTT E. YENOR is a doctoral student in political science at Loyola University of Chicago.

ISBN 0-275-96107-9

EAN

9 780275 961077

90000>

HARDCOVER BAR CODE